Mops, Muffins, & Motherhood

Compiled By Nancy Martin

Practical Survival Tips for M.O.M.s {Mothers of Many}

First Printing, November 2012   3m
Second Printing, November 2013   3m

© Copyright 2012 Lilac Hill Publishing
Permission is granted to copy recipes, charts, and lists for your own use. For the remainder of this publication all rights are reserved. No part may be reproduced, stored in a retrieval system or transmitted, in any form, or by any means, electronic, mechanical, photocopying, recording, or otherwise, without the prior permission of the publishers.
ISBN 9780985582203

For additional copies contact—
Lilac Hill Publishing
Nancy Martin
Route 2, Box 62
Lancaster, Missouri 63548
Email: nancym@lilachillpublishing.com
Phone: 660.457.2139

Illustrations | Mabel Zimmerman
Layout & Design | Grace Troyer

Dedication

I dedicate this book to my mother, Ida Stauffer, who taught me by example. Five girls born to you in six years' time created a lot of opportunities for managing your household! I love you and appreciate all you taught me about being a wife and a mother. Love of cooking and the art of entertaining are two things in particular I learned so well from you.

To my sisters, who definitely deserve some credit for the housekeeper I am. (Sorry if you don't want the blame!) My three older sisters, Anna Mary, Susan, and Vera, (otherwise known as "the big girls" in our family), tried their best to get me to do my share of the work and do it right! My younger sister, Janet, and I stuck together and tried to use being called "the little girls" to our advantage in shirking our duties.

To my mother-in-law, Irene Martin, who blended in so well with what I had been taught. You were such a good example in submission and serving others selflessly. I loved you as you were, and love you as you are now, with your mind ravaged by the effects of Alzheimer's disease.

To all the women who have touched my life and helped to form my ideas on successfully coping with motherhood in such a way that children are not considered a burden, as society in general presents them to be. This includes women whom I have never seen, who lived before my time, for truly "I have a goodly heritage", passed down for generations through Godly women (and men). Let us repel the way of the world and pass on the faith!

A special thanks to my husband and nine children on whom I have "practiced the trade" sometimes well, and sometimes, well… We've proven that being a happy family doesn't depend on how neat the house is, but on what our attitudes are. I appreciate your support in this project.

For my friends and family that took the time to fill out and return the questionnaires: here is the book at last. Without your help it wouldn't be what it is. Thanks!

But most of all I dedicate this book to God! May everything you mothers read in this book point you back to the most important Source for help in raising your children for Him.

– Nancy Martin

IV —— Mops, Muffins, & Motherhood

Contents

A Note to the Reader VII

The Foolishness of Comparisons IX

Who Am I? XI

   As a Christian? XIII

   As a Wife? XV

   As a Mother? XIX

A Note from Nancy XXIII

Part 1

   1. Spiritual Refreshment - Devotions & Prayer Life 3

   2. And Then There Were Two - Honoring Our Husbands. 11

   3. Added Blessings - Children 19

   4. Time to Learn - School/Homeschool 33

   5. Ready for Company - Housework/ Housecleaning 41

   6. Flapping in the Breeze - Laundry 55

   7. Feeding the Hungry - Food Preparation/Serving. 63

   8. Preserving the Bounty - Freezing/Canning 69

   9. The Great Outdoors - Garden/Yardwork/Flowerbeds/Chores. 77

   10. What Shall We Wear? - Clothing/Sewing/Crafts 85

   11. Paying the Bills - Bookwork. 93

   12. Let's Go on a Trip - Traveling/Packing 97

   13. A New Home - Moving. 103

   14. Leftovers - Miscellaneous. 107

Part 2

   Our Meal Ideas 112

   The Recipes 117

Part 3

   Charts & Lists 154

   Contributors. 179

A Note to the Reader
What this book is not

This book is not a do-as-we-say-and-your-life-will-be-perfect sort of book. It is not a step-by-step manual to a perfect life.

If you are one of those moms who:

• plans 30 day menus…and sticks to them

• goes shopping once a month and doesn't forget things

• knows exactly what is in every box in your attic

• knows to the penny what is in the checking account

…this book was not written with you in mind. You do not need our help. I admire you and sometimes envy you.

However, if you are a mom who:

• has 50 socks (or more) with no partners

• waits until 5:00 to plan 5:30 supper

• can't seem to get out the door until it's almost time to be there

• has no good idea what all really is in your attic

• is a bit reluctant to look at the mail, because you're afraid it might include an overdraft notice. (What exactly is the checkbook balance anyway?)

…this book was written for you, by others like you! Motherhood brings duties for which there is no job description and must be accomplished with no formal training. Many of us have a rich heritage of "on the job" training provided by mothers, grandmothers, aunts, cousins, and friends. In this way, the Bible teachings of Titus 2: 4 & 5 are fulfilled. *That they* (the aged women) *may teach the young women to be sober, to love their husbands, to love their children, to be discreet, chaste, keepers at home, good, obedient to their own husbands, that the word of God be not blasphemed.* How opposite of what the world teaches! It says submission is not necessary, children are a burden, and stay-at-home moms are an unfulfilled, trodden-down part of society who is greatly to be pitied. If any of you reading this book have not had a Godly heritage; here is some help. You have the opportunity to start in your generation something that can be passed down to the next and the next, if God chooses to allow time to continue.

This book is meant to be used by real humans with real problems. We cannot solve your problems; that is up to you and God. Be assured though, as you solve one problem another one will pop up. Because that is real life. Your husband will not always be the light of your life, and sometimes you might not appreciate your children's behavior (especially if you suspect they learned it from you!), your house will be a mess, and unexpected company at the door might hear you yell at your children (something you'd really rather no one knows you do sometimes). Maybe you have read in books or gathered from hearing others talk that a real Christian mother should never have a messy house, and is always loving, kind, and considerate, perfectly controlled and would simply be shocked to hear that you actually lose control of your tongue sometimes. Maybe there really are mothers with many children who at all times possess these vital Christian virtues, but I must confess that I don't believe I have ever met any. In conversations with mothers, usually the truth comes out; funny incidences and mistakes made, that mothers everywhere can relate to.

Over the years I have read organizational books and tried to use the system that each particular book proclaimed to almost magically take a complete mess and turn it into a wonderful, orderly house. I always ended up frustrated and feeling like a failure (again). Gradually I came to accept the fact that I never will have a perfectly clean house (at least not for more than 2 minutes at a time) as long as I have young children in my home. I still get very frustrated when (once again) I'm hunting for something that isn't where it belongs. Or I'm tripping (once again) over my children's shoes in the middle of the living room floor (yes, I know that's a training issue). Or maybe I realize that (once again) I haven't spent time in prayer and meditation as I ought to. Out of this came the inspiration to ask other mothers how they handle these mini-crises and other tips to keep from being completely buried in the demands of motherhood, and then compile these ideas in a book to share with others in the same stage of life. So I sent out questionnaires to my friends and family. Most of these mothers have 6 or more children, and still have preschoolers at home. They are in the heat of the battle. (Look for a list of contributors on page 179.)

It is my prayer that this book can help mothers come to grips with the awesome job God has given us. What we do today does matter in the future. If we are drowning in the Sea of Motherhood, how can we help our children learn about God in the Ocean of Life? This book is meant to be the life preserver to help you float (through the storm of household tasks) until you get back to land and get your feet under you again.

God bless your efforts to serve Him in the career to which you have been called - Motherhood.

– Nancy Martin

The Foolishness of Comparisons

You arrive at church a little late, like usual. You really did mean to get there on time, but the minutes sped by as you tried to hurry sleepy and reluctant children through morning chores and breakfast. You couldn't find enough pairs of matching barrettes for the girls' hair, David couldn't find his shoes even though he "knew" he put them away, and then the baby needed a complete change of clothes just as you were finally ready to leave the house. It was hard to find another set of clothes for him that was good enough to wear to church, because by the time boy #4 comes along, finding clothes in the drawer that have neither stain nor tear is pretty difficult. Finally you've made it to church. As you sit there waiting for church to start, baby starts to fuss so you reach for the pacifier. After digging through the diaper bag twice, you are forced to admit that it must have been left behind. You sigh inwardly, realizing you are in for a long morning. While you are coping the best you can, various other things come into your consciousness. You forgot to give haircuts this week, Lisa's hair looks as if it hasn't been combed (she has such wiry hair), Tina's socks are sagging around her ankles (no matter how many times she's told to pull them up, she just isn't the type to care what it looks like to others), Matthew's shoe laces aren't tied right (the one tore), and a few other things that are beyond your ability to do anything about at that point. You end up spending a lot of time outside and in the baby room because of the missing pacifier. You wonder dismally why you even bothered to come to church; you are hearing very little of the sermon anyway.

You happen to notice Rachel, another mother with small children, sitting there with her sleeping baby on her lap. His pacifier is in his mouth where it belongs. Her children are neatly combed and dressed to a "T". To you it seems she is always calm and in control. You know her well enough to be pretty sure her house is in good order and her lunch will be ready when they come home from church. Oh, why, can't you be more like her? You have tried more than once to follow her example. Maybe you could keep up to what you imagine her standards are for a little while, but sooner or later you failed. What can you do?

First and most important, you must realize that God made us all unique. And He makes no mistakes! We must learn to accept ourselves for who we are and stop measuring ourselves against another's yardstick. Every one of us has room for improvement, but we must look to God and the Bible for direction on areas of growth for us. God speaks to us in His Word and during meditation. He also speaks through good reading materials and through other people. A heart-to-heart talk with this "perfect" mother just might reveal that she has many of the same struggles you have. Or if you dare to tell her how she appears to you, she might drop her jaw in shock, or snicker in amusement! We often perceive people to be completely different than what they perceive themselves to be. However, she may just be more organized than you, but likely has struggles in areas you know nothing about. Those who compare themselves among themselves are not wise!

Here are some things to consider:

#1 Discouragement is from Satan. He wants us to feel like a total failure. Lack of sufficient sleep, standards that are too high, pressure from family or friends, too much work, and worrying what others think of us are some of the things that can contribute to the problem. We need a calm faith that God is in control and will not give us more than He will help us bear.

#2 Her life has as many problems as yours, they are just different. We must each deal with what we are given. You may never know how many tears she cries into her pillow at night!

#3 Change what you can, accept the rest. It takes careful examination and prayer to discern what can be changed and what must be accepted. Many times we have to come back and start over with the acceptance when we finally realize we are trying to change something that must be accepted.

#4 You cannot be her, and you shouldn't even try. It never works! However, you may look at her example and see if you can use some of the methods of organization she uses. But it may not work for you because you are not her!

#5 Attitude is everything! It's been said that life is 10% what you make it and 90% how you take it. It is impossible to be happy all the time, but we need to focus on the positive things, not the negative.

...Whatsoever things are true, whatsoever things are honest, whatsoever things are just, whatsoever things are pure, whatsoever things are lovely, and whatsoever things are of good report, if there be any virtue, if there be any praise, think on these things. Philippians 4:8. There you have it.

#6 This, too, shall pass. In the Bible we read, "And it came to pass…" It doesn't say "it came to stay". Everything in life passes on sooner or later. We only need to deal with our problems while they are in the present. Don't try to ignore your problems, but don't let them get you down either. God asks us to live one day at a time; sometimes one minute at a time.

#7 One of our most prevalent problems is pride! When we dig out our discontent and embarrassment we will most often find pride as the root. Forget about what other people might think, and do what is right because it is right; not because someone else might be looking and see you are human and make mistakes. When we correct our children because others might think what they are doing is weird or odd, it is bound to backfire and cause our children to act even more oddly because we made them uncomfortable. If things are not going well, look for that ugly weed—pride!

Who Am I?

Before we can begin to improve our housekeeping skills, we need to understand who we are and why we are here on this earth. God has a plan for each one of us and the most important thing in life is to live for Him. We spend so much time either struggling just to stay alive from day to day without being buried in the daily duties of caring for our families, or else we tend to worry excessively about how we'll ever get our children raised right in this sinful world. Either way can lead to depression, which is one of Satan's favorite tools to lead God's children away from Him.

One important thing to remember about life is that it can be likened to "seasons". Each year we know that spring will follow winter and summer will follow spring. We just don't know exactly when. Some years, spring is slow in coming, and then summer heat starts early, making spring seem short. Just so is life. Not all is sunshine, and indeed, we know what would happen if it was. The hard times in life are when we grow closer to God, unless we choose to grow bitter, then we fall away, and things get worse and worse. We sing "Nearer my God to Thee" but forget what we're asking for when we sing the next line - "Even though it be a cross that raises me"! When things seem extremely hard and you can't see the end of the "season" it is important to remember that God knows just how much we can bear. If the burden is too heavy, it may be because we are trying to handle it alone. Not only is God right there to help if we just ask, sometimes we need others to help us. This is where our pride can get in the way. Of course we would rather do everything alone and prove to others we can. But God's plan is a brotherhood that helps each other. It seems many of us are more than willing to help others, but then when we need help, we would rather struggle alone than ask for help. If we help others with only a desire to support them and are clear of any condescension, it makes it easier to receive help when we need it. Sometimes help is not available and another solution must be found. As women, sometimes all we need to lighten the load is a good talk with a close friend. But be sure to stay away from gossip, it will tear you down just as surely as the people you gossip about. It is important for women to cultivate friendships with other Christian women who have a positive outlook in life. Two kinds of women who can be very helpful are those who are also in the middle of raising a large family, and those who have successfully come through it.

Be assured whatever "season" of life you are in, it will eventually flow into the next. If things are difficult, you can be assured that God will eventually draw you into a more restful place. If you are in a peaceful time of life, you will be drawn into a time of strengthening through testing. However, you shall not spoil your time of rest with worry about what's coming next. It is all in God's control and we can rest in that knowledge. Besides, if we're honest with ourselves, we know full well that there is absolutely nothing that we can do about it anyway.

There are many ways we can be tested. Friction in the family or between our family and the church or members in the church, are some of the most difficult problems to deal with. When people who we think are supposed to love us, hurt us instead, it can be devastating. Although Satan is the culprit in these situations, God does allow these temptations and trials, and we can choose whether they will work for the ultimate good or bad in our lives. We choose by either clinging to God for help and guidance, or try to go our own way and let Satan get us to respond with our human nature. Although this feels better at first and we may feel justified in our reactions, what follows are more severed relationships and isolation or even in extreme cases church divisions and turmoil from people taking sides. It takes self-discipline to react in a Godly manner, and sometimes it takes time to come around to controlling our feelings when they have been hurt. Since women are so emotional, we need time to work through our feelings. Sometimes when our first and instant response isn't very Christ-like, we need to bite our tongues and get out of the situation, and work through our feelings. Then we either dismiss the whole thing with love and forgiveness, or talk things out if it can be done without more strife.

A local woman who became a good friend of mine suffered through a divorce initiated by her husband. Because they had children, they had to take counseling on interacting with each other. They were told by a secular counselor that they should never say anything negative about their ex-spouse in front of or to their children. "Bite your tongue until it bleeds!" was their blunt advice. This is also good advice for any kind of interpersonal relationship problems. However, beware of burying hard feelings for they will arise again at the slightest provocation and will most certainly add fuel to the fire the next time something comes up. Many times our husbands can give us a better perspective on the problem if we're willing to listen to their advice. Many problems have been made much worse by women agitating their husbands instead of listening to them and putting things to rest.

Other tests and trials include sick or special needs children, financial struggles, mental illness, domineering wives, and husbands who don't fill their role, unbelieving spouses and children, and on and on… For any of these situations, we need God to help us find the right way through the struggle. How many times have we wished God would just tell us outright what we must do right now in this particular situation? We think it would be so easy to do the right thing then, don't we? We tend to look at the whole mountain instead of the next step and then we are overwhelmed. Sometimes we do need to step back and look at the whole picture to be sure we are headed the right direction, but then follow through by bringing our focus back on this step, then the next, and the next. Do right now what you know is right, stay close to God and He will make a way; the right way for you.

Sometimes we get happiness and joy mixed up in our minds. A Christian is not always happy, but we can always have that deep joy of knowing our sins are forgiven and that God will make a way for us even if it won't be easy or fun. Feelings can be a problem for women in particular, since we are so well known to be easily affected by them. There are many books that have been written on the different aspects of Christian living, which can help in rounding out our lives. Care must be taken that we do not let authors with wrong interpretations of Scripture sway us from the truth. Every book and every author should be examined against the pure Word of God and His principles before allowing them into your heart. Be skeptical. Hear what other Christian women have to say, and ask your husband's opinion. Look for a list of books that can be helpful on page 169.

Who Am I...
As a Christian?

The most important thing in life is to accept Christ as your Savior and the Lord of your life. It seems sometimes we hear more about needing a Savior and not as much about allowing Him to be Lord of our lives. It is very true that we can never be good enough without the help of Jesus. We must realize that the very best we can do by ourselves is as filthy rags to Him. We can appear good for a period of time, but it will eventually be revealed if we are only polishing the outside of the vessel, but are unclean inside. Many times it really starts to show up when children grow into adults and have relationship problems because of what they learned at home. The solution for this problem is a close relationship with Jesus Christ, an understanding that we will fail and need forgiveness on a daily basis, and the realization that the way to Heaven is a battle that we cannot win alone.

How can I know that I am a Christian? Satan will try his best to convince you that you're not a Christian because obviously you wouldn't sin so easily if you would be. The truth is that if you wouldn't sin, you wouldn't need a Savior, since you would be perfect. We know that is impossible! Some people feel you must be able to tell the exact time and place you accepted Christ in your life. For some people it is so, and this is good. But for some, especially those reared in Christian homes, the realization comes gradually over a period of time. The tiny seed that has been planted starts to sprout and pushes up a little stem. Then two leaves unfold and the stem continues to grow until the first "true leaves" unfold. The sprouting is the beginning of understanding and the new Christian continues to mature and develop as long as someone or something doesn't rip it out of the ground or stomp it to death. That early seedling needs nurture and tender care, food, sunshine, and water (Bible reading, prayer, and sermons) to continue to grow. As the plant develops, the Gardener will prune and shape the plant to help it produce to its full potential. If the plant would have feelings, it might protest when the Master cuts it back because it thought it was growing so well. Sometimes the storms experienced seem like they will overwhelm us, but again, God is fully aware of what is happening, and, more importantly, why! So be assured he knows when enough is enough and allow him to prune you for production of more Godly fruit. Find tips on maintaining a healthy relationship with God amidst the demands on your time as a busy wife and mother in the section "Spiritual Refreshment" on page 3.

XIV —— Mops, Muffins, & Motherhood

Who Am I...
As a Wife?

First a wife, then a mother. This is a good rule to remember as we go through life. Obviously sometimes a child must come first, but when you need to decide between the children and the desires of your husband, he needs to come first for a healthy relationship. It seems as children bless a marriage, some women tend to take all the focus off the man who was so special that she forsook all others to marry. This can happen gradually, but eventually it will dawn on the father of your children that he feels like he isn't much more than an accessory, handy to have around. After all, someone has to make money to pay the bills and do all the maintenance jobs around the house! By the time baby number four or five comes along, romance seems to be a vague memory of some long-ago days. What happened to the days when your whole week was structured around when you will get to see him again? Thoughts of him made your heart beat a little faster and you spent hours trying to decide what would be the gift that is "just right" to give him for his birthday! Of course back then we didn't usually see him in his dirty work clothes or smell his "morning breath". Generally he didn't come see us directly from the barn or place of employment, and of course he never got grouchy as far as we knew. But then, we probably hid our imperfections pretty well, too! As the marriage continues, we become more comfortable with each other and the real "me" starts to pop out. For many of us, before we have fully resolved the issues of being married, we start with morning sickness. As a youth we tend to satisfy our own desires and suddenly we have a husband that we are bound to care for. At first it is fun and fairly easy. Then the pressures start to build with each child added to the family. Lack of sleep causes weakened emotions and more easily hurt feelings. Many times men are blamed for being poor communicators, but in truth many woman are good at being martyrs. Our thoughts run on this line, "He never helps around here. He never gets up at night. I have to do everything around here. He doesn't understand me. Boohoo!"

In the first place did you ask him to help and then did you accept the way he did it? If he was too busy or tired, could you accept that and let it go, or did you roll it over and over in your mind until it became a huge problem? If this happens- go to bed and take a nap! Almost always things look better after some sleep. Most important of all, remember that housework and baby care are primarily your job, with maybe some help from him. Getting up at night usually falls on the mother, although there are cases where it works better for Daddy to get up.

"Doing everything around here" is a part of the job description when we get married (the lighter matters of life, you know). Sometimes we must lower our standards for a while. Stop looking at women who appear to "get it all done".

What about "He doesn't understand me."? You might as well adjust to the idea that men will always have a hard time understanding women. Really, that isn't surprising at all if you think about it. Because do you really understand yourself?? Women can change their thoughts to match their moods faster than most men can even think. One reason a women should never be President is because today it will be, "Peace at all costs," and tomorrow, "Let's go to war!" And just because you told him once doesn't mean he "got it". Telling him again how you feel is okay in a kind tone of voice, but avoid nagging, ("I told you so often!") The golden words "I'm sorry" and "I forgive you" should be exercised often in a healthy marriage. However, saying them with an icy tone or an upward tilt of the nose or some other such expression is not helpful and would be better left unsaid until they can be uttered in spirit and in truth.

Keep the lines of communication open. Don't allow Satan to tell you he's thinking this or that rather than talking it out. Most times he doesn't even think what you imagined he does. Approach him about his faults like you want to be approached about yours. Keeping quiet about things that bother you is not a virtue, unless you really can forget it. If it resurfaces over and over or you are squashing down bitter thoughts, it is time to face the issue squarely. Be sure to take time to pray and look for the facts and don't just go by feelings. It is hard to change feelings, but they are fickle. One time something your husband says may hurt you and the next time you might hardly notice. Sometimes it just takes a good night's sleep, or some time and space to think and pray. Many men would say they have to be extra careful at a certain time of the month (or any time our hormones are on a rampage)! However this should not be used as an excuse to be grouchy.

Opposites attract. This means that not only are we different because we're male and female (which makes a huge difference to start with); likely one is quiet and the other talks a lot. Maybe one is a morning person and the other is a late-nighter. One never gets lost and the other gets lost in the "back forty". My husband says he could take me out in one of our back fields and I wouldn't be able to find my way home. To be honest, it might take me a while! He, on the other hand, never gets lost, although every now and then he'll say he's not lost, he just doesn't know where he is. He will find his way, though, whereas I would become hopelessly lost. It is because of people like me that the GPS units were invented!

We should never assume that our husbands should know how we feel! Women and men do not think alike. Communication between husband and wife cannot be stressed too much. But it must be a right kind of communication. There is under-communication to be sure, but there is also such a thing as over-communication. Then there is also a totally wrong communication like yelling. Communication is so much more than just talking. It includes the expression on your face and body language, such as the way you hold your shoulders or the tilt of your head. For example, if I say "Wow, she's a good cook!" with a smile on my face and showing admiration by my body language, it means something altogether different than if I have a sneer on my face and roll my eyes while I'm saying it. There is a saying that "what you do talks so loud, I can't hear what you're saying" that is so true. A wife who grudgingly slaps food on the table, or sighs in an exasperated way when doing things for others speaks quite loudly about how she feels about what she "has" to do for everyone else. Incidentally, her children won't

XVI — Mops, Muffins, & Motherhood

be very likely to enjoy their lot in life either when they grow up. A mother who quietly serves others with an expression of peace tells her husband and children (without saying a word) that she loves them and wouldn't want to be anywhere else in the world. And when grown, these children have seen before them an example of what the rewards are of serving others.

Let's go back to the romance mentioned at the beginning of this section. Most important is; what really matters? If the shallow thing called romance has been replaced with real love that is deepening with time, you are moving toward the goal. Things like flowers, cards and gifts are still appreciated, but feelings no longer depend on these things. They are many times replaced with a smile over the head of a little one who has done or said some cute thing, the unity in a decision made; a job done that has been waiting for a while. Practical gifts have taken the place of trivial things. If money is tight, and schedules are tense, just a little extra such as making a favorite food, mending that favorite pair of jeans (a job you detest), or just doing one of his jobs for him is all it takes to keep love alive and growing. Look for more ideas in the section "And Then There Were Two" on page 11.

XVIII —— Mops, Muffins, & Motherhood

Who Am I...
As a Mother?

First: a Christian

Second: a wife

Then, a mother

These need to be our priorities; in this order. After this we can consider our own hobbies and projects. Many of us enter this field of motherhood with only a vague idea of what is about to come upon us. If experience with babies has been limited, we may have this idea of a smiling, cute, little infant. If we have had more exposure, we may know that not all is so pleasant about babies. For instance, their diapers have to be changed on a regular basis and they might spit up on you. Although we might know these squirmy bundles usually don't sleep all night, it isn't until you have your own that reality strikes and you find out what the words "responsible parenting" really mean. If the labor and delivery were extra hard and exhausting, you might not even have wanted to hold your newborn. This is normal and usually resolves itself pretty quickly with a little rest.

It is really hard, if not impossible, to be a good mother and selfish at the same time. God takes us one step at a time, one child at a time (or every now and then two [or more!]) from focusing on ourselves so much, to learning to serve others. Infants take a lot of giving up. Before they are even born they take over your body, giving you pains you probably never experienced before. Whoever knew it could be as hard to get out of a chair as it is when you are only a few weeks from the birth of the baby? Besides, where did your energy go? You used to go to bed and sleep all night, not toss and turn from indigestion or get up every hour or two to use the bathroom. We get to the place where we welcome labor even if we know from previous babies it's no fun, just to get ourselves back to normal. Whatever normal is?! After they are born, most of them still keep us from sleeping all night, some are very demanding and if there is a toddler in the family, they make us tired just watching them go from one thing to the next. On the other hand, babies are so sweet, such a miracle! Take time to cuddle your baby, the toddler if you have one, and certainly don't forget their daddy! Do your best to get help for the housework, so you can take the time to enjoy the newest member of your family. Babies grow up so fast! You may feel like that is not true, but I have never heard a mother with grown children say it took her children so-o-o long to grow up, have you?

As your family grows, so do your responsibilities. As more children are born, the oldest ones need more guidance, they start school, they move away from you to become their own little person. Challenges increase and seem to multiply by the day sometimes. There is no time for selfishness in your life now, either. Each child has a different nature and takes a different approach for effective parenting. It always amazes me to observe how two children born to the same two parents and raised in the same home can have such totally different personalities. It's a time for renewed attention to your children, even as other duties increase. You now have to do more managing and less of the work yourself. Training and disciplining the children to do their jobs right, getting along with each other, and interacting appropriately with non-family members are just some of the things that must have your attention. Sometimes it feels impossible to do all that is required of you.

One fine summer day, I was sitting on the porch swing enjoying a Sunday rest. We have a lot of cats and there are often kittens around. This particular day there was an old Mama cat nursing her half-grown kittens—and a few that weren't hers as well. They were pushing and shoving each other in an attempt to get the best position and it looked like they were about tearing her apart. I thought to myself, "I sure feel that way sometimes, pulled in many directions at one time, by the needs of my husband, children, household, the family business, and all the other duties that are mine." I observed how this old mother calmly lay there and even licked one or two of the kittens affectionately. My thoughts rambled on, "What a good object lesson for me to calmly go on and do the best I can and remember to bestow love and affection as I go through life even when I'm under pressure." My musing turned into a burst of laughter, when all of a sudden the Mama cat had had enough! She got up and swatted a few of the kittens and stalked off. When a few of them followed her, she growled and bared her teeth, then added a swat or two for good measure. I must say that I felt better after seeing that I'm not the only one with a breaking point. How many times do we snap at those we love the best!

Then come the teen years! It is an interesting time and frustrating time all in one. They are now old enough to be a lot of help with the work. They are also old enough to have their own opinions and most likely will tell you what they think. Control changes from physical to emotional. If you can interact with them properly, they will respect you even if they don't agree with you. It is vital to have an open and honest relationship with them or they will not confide in you. Even if you have a good relationship with them, it is unlikely they will tell you everything. Many parents have been quite surprised to find out what their child knew and experienced that they didn't tell them until they were older. This is the time to lean on God for support and wisdom as never before!

Finally they become young adults and you are no longer primarily responsible for the choices they make. It is time to let go. Sure, you've made mistakes and would like to correct them, but you must face the fact that from here on out you can teach mostly by example. Now they are your friends, no longer your children to be taught and corrected. When they get married, the relationship must change to one of being there to give advice when asked. If you feel they are making bad choices, they need to be approached just like you would any other Christian adult. Think back to your early days of marriage. Could your parents have criticized the mistakes you made? Acceptance of your child's partner goes a long way toward making a smooth transition from your house to one of their own. Never support your child in complaining about their partner. You may listen with understanding, but never undermine the respect that is vital in any marriage. I so well remember my mother listening without comment when I told her what I thought my new husband could do differently. Then she just kindly reminded me this was the man I chose. And that was that! To this day I don't know if she agreed with me or not, and I have no memory about what I was complaining. It can be a difficult thing for parents to let go of their children when they get married, but the process should have started a long time before this. As young children grow older and more mature,

XX — Mops, Muffins, & Motherhood

it is very important that they learn to do the right thing because it is right, not just because they fear their parents will find out about it. Developing the conscience is one of the most important works of child-rearing.

As you get older and more and more details are stored in your mind, you are bound to forget some. After a while you may start to wonder if you're getting Alzheimer's already or just what is wrong with you anyway?! After a chat with some friends in the same age bracket and stage in life you might feel better. Someone coined the phrase "foggy forties" and I have to add that you don't have to be 40 to feel that way. One person said they heard that you lose 10% of your brain function with each baby you bear. I found this highly amusing and suddenly I knew what my problem was! I had 9 babies, so I'm functioning with only 10% of my brain! Pity you mothers who have more than 10 children! Of course, if you lose 10% of the remaining brain, each time you lose less. Any way you look at it, it comes back to more responsibilities, more details, aging brain, and so on. Once I heard someone say it really isn't our age, it's just like the recording you might get when you dial a phone number, "All circuits are now busy. Try your call again later." Much later I might add. Meanwhile, read on for some tips to help you "keep it all together" (or at least keep everything from falling apart).

XXII —— Mops, Muffins, & Motherhood

A Note from Nancy

You will read many conflicting ideas in the following pages. This is because it has been compiled from many different mothers with different situations and in different seasons of life. Pick and choose those hints which may help you in your particular area of need. If an idea works, great! If it doesn't, just discard it and try something else or you may be able to tweak an idea to fit into your life.

It is with a bit of trepidation that I offer this book. None of the mothers, including myself, feel that we have everything figured out and under control. It is because I am disorganized and am quite familiar with the feeling that life is spinning out of control that I see the need for help for M.O.M.s. We all have to find our comfort level in life and not let other people bother us too much.

Even though the words I, me, and we are used throughout, these ideas are not just from one person. You will soon see that one family could not possibly do all the things suggested. So even if you know any of the contributors, don't even try to figure out who submitted which suggestions, or which ones came from me. Some ideas were put together and words changed so that even the contributor might not recognize her own contribution. One woman asked whether I will be putting the names of the people behind the ideas they contributed. When I told her I'm not planning to, she sighed with relief, "I'm afraid people would say, 'That sounds just like something they would do!,'" she said. You will find some ideas repeated more than once, since some things were suggested by multiple women, sometimes with a bit of a different twist to the idea. The more often you see a hint, the more women there were who suggested it.

My sister-in-law submitted several pages of hints that were compiled from a group of mothers for a ladies meeting at their church. I don't know who these ladies are, but found the tips fit right in with what I already had. Some of these had the ages of the women printed behind them and I found it interesting, so I am including that also. Thanks to you unknown mothers for your input, even if you didn't know your tips were going to be published in a book!

I hope you will glean much help and encouragement from these pages. I have been blessed by the suggestions from the other mothers and hope you will find joy in the journey of motherhood.

XXIV —— Mops, Muffins, & Motherhood

Part 1

·PRACTICAL TIPS·

Spiritual Refreshment

Exalt ye the Lord our God, and worship at His footstool; for He is Holy. Psalm 99:5

1. Spiritual Refreshment
Devotions & Prayer Life

Much prayer…much power

Little prayer…little power

No prayer…no power.

Devotions…A time devoted to communicating with God.

In Muslim countries the first prayer call is at 5:00 AM. The call lasts 15 minutes. The Muslims are so devoted to their god Allah, who does nothing for them, they observe this prayer call 5 times every day out of fear of losing his favor. As Christians, we have the blessing of praying to the one true God; how does our devotion compare to the Muslims?

Our God always hears our fervent prayers. Satan also sees and knows the results of prayer and devotions. It is the most effective weapon against the vicious cycle of rush and hurry, rush and worry, never done, by set of sun. At least fifteen minutes of quiet time in the early morning or as soon as you can fit it into your schedule, gives you a different perspective on life's problems and priorities.

Getting up just a little earlier than the rest of the family gives you a bit of quiet quality time to really think about what you are reading. When Daddy is up and reading his Bible first thing in the morning, it is easier to establish a daily habit for the children to each read their own Bibles before eating breakfast.

She riseth while it is yet night….Proverb 31:15. Early in the morning is the best time to focus on spiritual things, before other things fill your mind. As a mother spends time with God and His Word she has spiritual food to give to her children. Her candle goeth not out by night…Our influence leaves a mark. We are on call 24/7.

Having said all this, the reality of a busy mother's life is that sometimes it is not practical to be up early, such as when you have a small baby. As we find out very quickly, babies sometimes have their own schedules which might include being awake much of the night. Sick children can also cause sleepless nights. Then it might be better to sleep while the baby or children sleep and find time later to read and meditate. Some people are not morning people and are more focused in the evening. If you find it easier to get more out of a time of devotions after everyone else is in bed, by all means do it then. We are all different and need to find what works for us and our families.

Although it is important to read God's word, many mothers struggle with finding enough time to set aside all at once to have a deep devotional and prayer time. God put you in this position of motherhood and He's not asking you to put aside your children an hour at a time. Learn to be in a "prayer mode" all day. While hanging out, folding, or ironing clothes, pray for each child as you handle their clothes. While you are on your knees washing the floor, pray for the ministry. When you must be up with the baby or a sick child, pray for your siblings and their families and your parents. Anytime someone comes into your thoughts, pray for them. You never know what kind of a struggle they may be having. Praying for people who are in troubled situations helps to curb our inclination to gossip, too. And don't forget to pray for yourself!

Most mothers get their devotions in small doses. Here are many suggestions shared by other M.O.M.s to help you stay on track and keep your focus on God while still performing the necessary tasks to keep your family clean, fed, and happy.

✼ Copy Bible verses that are special to you and stick them at different spots throughout the house. Then as you work in that room you can meditate on that verse. Also having an open songbook lying in each room encourages singing.

✼ This is an ongoing, growing experience! As you are sewing or washing the dishes and people come into your mind, pray for them. As you fold your family's laundry, pray for each one as you fold their clothes.

✼ Sing! Singing is a form of worship and helps keep the mind on nobler things. It is awfully hard to sing and continue to be grumpy! Either the grumpies have to go, or you will have to stop singing. If the burden is so great you can't sing out loud, sing in your heart. There is a song for every occasion. God hears the groanings that cannot be uttered.

✼ Pray anytime! Bathe your children in prayer. Pray for Sunday services while on your knees washing up the floor on Saturday. Pray for each family member as you fold or iron their clothes.

✼ Breathe a word of prayer anytime as you go about your duties.

✼ I keep a devotional book and a Bible in the bathroom. It's the only place I can sneak away from the commotion sometimes.

✼ It is so much easier to memorize Scripture when you are young! It stays in the mind better and can more easily be relearned as we focus on passages we learned when school age. We have our Bibles now; let's hide God's word in our hearts where no one can take it away from us.

✼ Prayers morning and evening, at each mealtime, and with family devotions daily are ideal. One cannot pray too often. Children must see the reverence and fear of God in their parents.

✼ The children learn chapters and parts of chapters more easily if you add one verse at a time with a little sweet treat at the end. Older children can be challenged with whole chapters or even whole books. The reward can be adjusted according to the difficulty of the portion and the ability of the child. Even if your children have Bible memory at school, a chapter repeated together as a family every day can increase the total Bible verses stored away. It is amazing what very young children can learn if it is repeated over and over. These verses are so precious when they pop up later in life as needed.

✼ I am working with my toddler, who is an early riser, to sit quietly and look at books while I am reading my Bible. I usually try to "finish" my quiet time when she is taking her nap.

✼ Instead of trying to remember what a whole chapter spoke to me, I try to ponder one verse or thought that impressed me. Then I keep pondering it throughout the day.

✼ I have the Bible on cassettes and use a small tape player with a pillow speaker (a flat one that slides under your pillow). I listen to these either before I fall asleep or I use it to help me wake up in the morning. I have been doing this for many years and highly recommend it.

✼ Some of my times of closest communion with God have been at night when I can't sleep.

✼ Have "prayer triggers" such as when washing up the floor on your knees pray for the ministry, when ironing children's clothes pray for each one, when cleaning mirrors pray to let your life reflect God's love, etc.

✽ Don't be too hard on yourself if you feel like you aren't spending a lot of time in personal devotions. A verse on the bathroom mirror may be all you get some days, and that's okay! On less busy days, you'll get more renewal time. Don't take on guilt because you aren't doing a lot of Bible Study right now. God knows your heart and He accepts your praises as you sing while you shower, while you work, or whenever. I found praying as I did dishes was good, too. If you are reading in the morning and the pitter patter of feet is heard before you are done, it's great for them to learn that, "Mommy is reading the Bible. Do you want your Bible storybook and we can both have devotions?" I try to teach the child that this is Mommy's quiet time, and in a few minutes we'll get breakfast. They can be taught to wait. All these ideas were passed on to me by other mothers at some point in my toddler mothering, and I found them all helpful. (Age 42)

✽ Singing throughout the day, as to the Lord, is an acceptable meditation for busy mothers. Even when you are not thinking about the words, your children and others around you can also be inspired.

✽ I have an open songbook on my kitchen sink windowsill. Singing while washing dishes is a form of worship.

✽ Take time for yourself, but not in a selfish, "me first" kind of way. Take a nap when the children are sleeping, ask your husband to allow you to take a walk while he watches the children (so you can be refreshed physically and spiritually as you talk to God), and try to be consistent in having devotions with God daily. Devotions will certainly take on different forms in the different stages of life, but communicate daily with God. (Age 33)

✽ Keeping oneself healthy spiritually during mothering is especially important. Your day will not go right unless you've started out with God first, which may begin while you are still under the covers. Breathe a prayer for guidance as you stretch and wake up, before your feet even hit the floor. God's been awake and He's waiting to hear your concerns and the day's plans. Devotions for the busy mother are so important, yet how many things need to be done first? Can you find a few minutes to read while nursing your baby? Prayers for your family can be specialized while folding their clothing, as you fold each piece, thinking of each child in turn (and hubby too). (Age 67)

✽ I prefer to make devotions a way of life, rather than a certain time or length of time each day. I struggle to find time alone for Bible reading and prayer. Many times I must rest in the confidence that every hour of my life is spent with God—just not alone with Him.

✽ I love to sing. No one else needs to know that the words I sing may be my deepest longing, my heartfelt prayer, and my personal communion with God. If you have committed Scripture to memory, God's word can inspire you when you peel peaches or wash up the floor. And when the opportunity comes for time alone, count it a treasure and redeem it.

✽ Prayer can, and does, become as habitual as breathing, for "closer is He than breathing and nearer than hands and feet".   –Alfred Lord Tennyson

✽ Ideally, I like to get up before the children (although I don't always get it done), and spend some time sitting in front of the fire with devotions.

✽ A song can be sung while washing the dishes or a prayer breathed while rocking the baby.

✽ My advice would be that "God is enough". The challenge is to allow God to be all that we need in the midst of our busy days of caring for our families. He is and He has everything we need to do the job He has given us to do. (Age 37)

✽ Write meaningful verses on paper and put them

on the refrigerator or keep a notebook handy for that purpose. They will stick in your mind better if you write them down.

✳ I have a check storage box with index cards that I write meaningful verses on that I hope to someday put on rings and use as an inspirational calendar. I used different colored cards for different subjects (i.e. child training, promises, instruction, etc.)

✳ Pray as you go through your day. While washing- thank God for a washer that works, hanging up wash - pray for the child/husband whose clothes you are hanging up. In essence, as you are serving your family, you are living out your devotion to God. Do not get caught up with guilt on a day you are not able to have scheduled devotional time (one of the children gets up early, or a rough night, etc.) (Age 29)

✳ I was reminded that the Bible says, "And it came to pass…" We must remember this when things seem out of control or a bit hectic. My husband used to remind me that tomorrow would be a new day. I was often surprised at how things and feelings can change in a short time or maybe overnight. We often expect more of ourselves than we should. Maybe we need to chalk things off our list that we really do not need to do; some things can wait. It is worth a lot if we let some things undone and have peace of mind. (Great-grandmother)

✳ With a fine tip marker, write Bible verses or the names of people you want to pray for, on the side of your clothespins. This can also be done and given as a unique gift for a new bride or a new mother.

✳ A chain reference Bible has been a big help in studying various subjects. Whenever I get started into a subject, an hour is gone before I know it.

✳ I find it so strengthening to get my day started before my children get up. Yes, there are certainly times when you are up with sick children or a nursing baby that it is necessary to sleep as long as possible.

If I can be dressed, combed, and have my time with God before they get up, I am so much more ready to meet the challenges of the day. If the children do get up while I am still having my devotions, it has been a blessing for them to learn to be quiet while I finish, and for them to observe how important that part of my day is. (Age 33)

✳ When I can't sleep, I like to take that opportunity to spend time in prayer or writing notes or letters to those who God brings to mind. Writing letters of encouragement has often brought as much or more inspiration to me as the one receiving the letter.

✳ We use the *Beside the Still Waters* booklets for family devotions after we have gathered around the breakfast table. They are sent out every two months and a free subscription can be started by sending your name and address to Still Waters Ministries, 285 Antioch Rd., Clarkson, KY 42726-8663. The publishers and contributors are of the conservative Amish and/or Mennonite faith.

✳ Memorize poems. As we get older and more things crowd our minds, it becomes harder to learn and retain poems, songs and scriptures. Use papers or index cards taped up where you see them often, such as at the kitchen sink, a wall close to the rocking chair, by the bathroom mirror, or anywhere you pass by often. Make a conscious effort to at least read it each time you see it, and you will find you have "absorbed" it more than memorized it. The little black songbooks we use in our church services, *Mennonite Hymns*, offer a wealth of meaningful poems. One of my favorites is #222. Here are the first 3 verses:

And must I be to judgment brought,
And answer in that day,
For every vain and idle thought,
And every word I say.

Spiritual Refreshment —— 7

Yes, every secret of my heart
Shall shortly be made known,
And I receive my just dessert
For all that I have done.

How careful then I ought to live;
With what religious fear,
Who such a strict account must give
For my behavior here!

Church preparation

✸ If getting to church on time is so stressful that it takes you until halfway through the sermon to get into a worshipping frame of mind, it is time to change something! We were at the point that it was easier to just stay home than go through the wild rush and snapping at each other to get there on time. One Sunday morning a minister preached that our children should not ask *if* we are going to church today, they should just take it for granted that, of course we will go, unless there are sick children or other circumstances beyond our control. This was a turning point for us. I had to make some changes to make it easier to get off in time. I got the diaper bag ready and laid out the clothing for the children on Saturdays. It took some time, but eventually it was harder to miss church than it was to get there on time. The biggest change was in our attitudes.

✸ Sunday morning breakfast is a quick one, buttered toast <u>with no jelly!</u>

✸ If we have lots of things that need to go along on Sunday, I start sending children to the van with those things an hour or two before time to leave. Or even take some things out the day before.

✸ Try having an older sibling responsible for each one of the "little people", strap them in, make sure they are combed, shoes and coat on, etc.

✸ A Sunday meal we always liked that is not hard to prepare is roast beef (thawed), potatoes (you don't even have to peel them), carrots, and green beans all in a roast pan, in the oven all morning at about 275°. It is ready to eat when you come home. (Age 67)

✸ One thing we have found to eliminate the "Sunday morning rush" is starting Saturday night. We hardly ever plan to go away Saturday evening. We try to go to bed early, have a casserole prepared for Sunday lunch, and baked oatmeal (see recipe in Section 2) mixed up to pop in the oven first thing on Sunday morning.

✸ I have set times by which certain things must be done, or I know we will be rushing. For example, girls must be combed by 8:00. This helps keep a feeling of what all needs to be done yet.

✸ With small children, I like to decide on Saturday which clothing they will be wearing and lay it all out so it is ready to grab and dress them. Also have the diaper bag as ready to go as possible by Saturday evening.

✸ Have certain items specifically for the diaper bag such as toys or baby wipe containers that stay there all week. This will help avoid the scramble of finding those items at the bottom of the toy box, or wherever else they might have disappeared in the course of the week.

✸ Our Sunday morning breakfast is usually baked oatmeal or egg casserole (check Section 2) mixed the evening before and baked in the morning.

✸ One child is in charge of packing the baby's bag, and each has a part in clearing the table. Breakfast dishes are stacked and washed with dinner dishes. Our boys, ages 10 and 11, take turns doing Sunday dinner dishes.

✸ It's nice to have a casserole that can be popped into the oven on Sunday morning so lunch is ready when we arrive home from church. Sometimes I make a double batch of casserole earlier in the week and put it in the freezer, ready to be stuck in the oven on Sunday morning.

❋ It works well to pack the diaper bag and lay out coats, sweaters, shoes, etc. the day before. We make sure the Sunday clothes are in the closet so there should be no needing what is not there. It makes a huge difference to start with baths early enough. When a child is dressed and combed, he should sit quietly somewhere until it is time to leave.

❋ Have simple breakfasts on Sunday mornings.

❋ I made a fabric shoe hanger for our Sunday shoes. It is a large rectangular piece of denim with strips sewed across it to form pockets, very much like a bought shoe holder but lasts much longer. It is hanging on the inside of our shoe closet door. If we return our Sunday shoes to it every time, guess where they are on Sunday mornings when we need them again?! Belts can also be coiled up and stuffed into the one shoe for each boy. This handy item can also be used to keep gloves, bandanas, beanies and such little winter items where they can be found.

❋ Avoid smudges and stains in Sunday clothes before church by wearing bibs and aprons - yes, even the boys that aren't careful enough. This way you still have clean clothes after eating and brushing teeth.

❋ Sunday clothes should have a special place, immediately cleaned up, and put back on Monday.

❋ Have breakfast early enough that clothing can be changed after chores, eating, and brushing teeth.

• • • • • • • • •

We cannot teach what we have not learned.

At Church

❋ Church time with a restless baby and/or toddler can be pretty challenging! We want our children to learn to sit quietly, but it certainly is easier to teach some than others. For babies, have certain toys that are only used on Sunday mornings. A few toys are better than too many. Most little ones learn very quickly to throw things on the floor just for the fun of having you pick them up. While this might be good stretching exercises for you, it is not conducive to getting anything out of the sermon. It is also a distraction to those around you.

❋ Teaching a toddler to sit still can and should be started at home. Make them sit while you have devotions and during meals. If you have an extra difficult child, it may be helpful to take time every day to just sit quietly together, starting with just a few minutes and adding to it every day until they become used to it. Don't ask me when you will find time to do this, but you will find time if it becomes important enough. If you have an extra difficult time some Sunday morning, remember that it does wonders for our humility to have our pride stepped on by our unruly child. And don't give up! This child may turn out to be your best behaved child when he/she is older. Some Sunday mornings you may feel like you heard hardly anything the minister said, but try to focus on one or two nuggets you did hear, and consider that this is apparently what God felt you needed the most. Singing is also a part of the worship service and later in the week you might catch yourself singing one of the songs that was sung during the services. Also important is the fellowship with other Christians, especially other mothers who are in the same stage of life as you are.

❋ There are times it may be appropriate to stay sitting briefly during a sermon with a screaming

Spiritual Refreshment — 9

child for training purposes, but when no one around you can hear what is being said for too long, it is time to take the training outside. As a new mother I was afraid my little girl wouldn't understand why I was spanking her after we made it to the restroom. After all, by that time she was usually smiling again, happy to be out of church. What a shock she got from a smack to her backside! I confided my uncertainty to a seasoned mother and she told me it won't take a normal child long to put the misbehavior and the discipline together. Quite a few children later, I have found her to be right.

❋ Have an older child string Cheerios on a sturdy string and tie it in a circle. Babies love to chew on them. Be sure to use strong string and a good knot or you might end up with Cheerios scattering all over the floor and a red face.

❋ If you take snacks for your toddler, try to avoid sugary ones as that might make it even harder for them to sit still.

❋ Years ago when my children were small, a friend gave me this advice about preparing for church on Sunday mornings: get yourself ready first, then start with the oldest and work your way down the line. The older the child is, the more likely he will stay clean until time to leave. It also gives you a clear mental picture of who needs attention next.

❋ If there are items that can't be packed in the diaper bag yet, or put in the car ahead of time, make a "last minute list" so you can clear your brain to think other things. Cross off the items as they are packed or go out the door.

❋ Drinking a cup of coffee before church can aid you in staying alert. I find No Doze or an equivalent brand of caffeine tablet helps me to stay focused on the message. Some people have a problem with feeling on edge or jittery from caffeine, so it would be wise to start with only a little. It isn't pleasant to be sitting there, fighting drowsiness all morning, and feeling like you are missing half the sermon.

❋ Avoid gossip. It seems in our desire to relate to each other, we may be prone to stray over the line into gossiping about others. Of course, this doesn't pertain only to Sunday mornings!

❋ Be aware of where your children are and what they are doing after church. This can also be a problem whenever families are together at any sort of gathering. Mockery and all sorts of other behavioral issues come up when children are unsupervised.

❋ Take the time to fellowship together. Make an effort to fit in with others, but don't get caught up with following others in areas against your convictions or over church rules. Having friends is an important part of a Christian life and helps us stay balanced. However, there are always those who seem to be more negative about everyone and everything. Be friends with them also, but spend more time with those who are positive and display more Christian character.

❋ Do you have problems getting to church on time? How about starting on Monday or Tuesday? Wash, iron, and put Sunday clothes away. Clean Sunday shoes and put them in the closet where they belong. This gives you a head start on Sunday morning.

❋ Sunday morning is the one morning we don't eat breakfast together. We just have cereal and each one eats as they are ready.

❋ I like to take a look at each child as they go out the door. Are suit and shirt collars lying down? Shoes tied? Shirt tails tucked in? Socks pulled up?

Our 6-year-old daughter wanted to show us the handicap parking space at church. "That's the hypocrite parking space," she declared.

And Then There Were Two

> WIVES, SUBMIT YOURSELVES TO YOUR OWN HUSBANDS, AS UNTO THE LORD. ...AND THE WIFE SEE THAT SHE REVERENCE HER HUSBAND. EPHESIANS 5:22,33B

2. And Then There Were Two
Honoring Our Husbands

What an exciting time of our lives it is to get married! We look forward to starting our own home together and sharing our lives. Like most things in life, we soon realize that it isn't as easy as it may have appeared to be. But if two people love each other and God, things will be worked out in such a manner that "this is now the way we do it in our new home". Marriage has been likened to where two rivers merge to form one larger river. At the point where they start to merge, there is often turbulent water. But as it continues to flow and mingle, it calms down and flows more smoothly. Even at the point of conjunction, it is already impossible to take these two rivers apart with exactly the same water in each one. The farther downstream you go, the more they are mingled together and become one river. They flow together over some rough, shallow spots and some smooth, deep areas. So is marriage. It is impossible for one to leave the other untouched and unchanged. Together you learn to face the rough and the smooth. You don't know what is yet ahead, but as long as you have God, you know you can face it together.

One thing that has been observed is that before marriage, Satan tries very hard to push a couple together physically but as soon as they are married, he works right the opposite, trying to cause friction. Being aware of how Satan works is a start in resisting his temptations. It takes a lot of communication to work through these touchy issues, and there is no place for selfishness on the part of either one, but we need to acknowledge as humans we are all selfish by nature. Men and women think and feel so differently from each other that sometimes it almost seems like they are talking two different languages! It cannot be stressed enough how important it is to listen with your heart and try to understand what he is telling you. Many men will not tell their wives their innermost feelings until they are very sure you care and will not tell anyone else what they are sharing with you. This takes time and patience, since many women in general tend to spout off their feelings with each other pretty quickly. Be very, very careful what you share about your husband with others. Make it a rule never to say anything negative about him to others, or anything you wouldn't want him to tell others about you. If you are having struggles and need to talk it over with someone, be very careful to choose someone you can trust to keep things confidential.

It seems in our culture that snaring the "right" man and getting married is just about the most important thing in life for any young girl. So much emphasis is put on this accomplishment that many people forget that the wedding is for one day, but the marriage is for life! If as much effort was put into the marriage as is put into some weddings, there would be very few failed marriages.

Statistics for staying married in the United States are shocking. About half of first marriages end in failure, and almost three-fourths of second marriages fail. Like someone said one time, "If it didn't work

12 — Mops, Muffins, & Motherhood

the first time, and it didn't work the second time, why would you even think it would work the third time?" The statistics for successful marriages get better when you include only the people claiming Christianity. But they get better yet when you look at the conservative Christian circles. Does this mean we can sit back and give ourselves a pat on the back? Absolutely not! What about all the troubled marriages we have among us? Is God pleased just because we don't go to the courts and obtain a divorce? Doesn't divorce start in the heart? Most of us would be aghast at the thought of a divorce, but Satan starts small. He is delighted if he can just get us to think unkind thoughts about our husbands, and then he works from there. What about wives that are modestly dressed and wear a head covering to symbolize submission to their husbands, yet in private and even in public at times it becomes quite obvious that their hearts don't match what they are trying to portray outwardly. We need to watch our thoughts and actions constantly to guard against Satan's deception.

What can you do if your courtship was less than ideal? First, don't decide that it is hopeless to ever have a good marriage. God is able to help you if you are willing to work hard and let Him work in your heart. One of the ways Satan tries to wreck a marriage is by convincing one or the other (or both) that they married the wrong person. You may have been out of God's will when you married that person, but once you are married, it is His will that you stay married. God can make good come out of your mistake. You can learn to love each other even if it isn't easy. Divorce is never the solution, only adding more sin. The Bible gives direction in I Corinthians 7 for a Christian with an unbelieving spouse that wants to leave. This chapter has helpful advice for marriages in general.

Courtship is to marriage somewhat like the foundation is to a house. If you neglect to dig footers and are careless how and with what materials you build the foundation, you can build a good sturdy house on it, but you will still have a weak and crumbling foundation. But it doesn't have to stay that way. You can put supports under that house and lift it up and redo the foundation. Is it easy? No! Is it as good as if you had done it right in the first place? Probably not, but it is better than giving up in despair and letting it continue to crumble and cause more and more problems as time goes on. So with God's help and a lot of hard work and pain, a marriage can also be repaired and stand as a shelter for the children that are added to the family and a witness to the world. But here is the challenge. Do we as Christians continue on and have the attitude that immoral courtships have always been a problem and we can do nothing to change it? Or do we admit our own fault and try to teach our children there is a better way to have a courtship? It is a scourge in too many of the conservative churches that courtship and dating practices continue as they have been for decades, just because that is how we always did it. Many churches have taken a stand and are teaching a better way, and this is good.

It is true that many marriage problems would never occur if the courtship would have been better, but no matter how well a couple followed proper standards, they will still have things to work out in marriage. This is because we are people and that is how people are. Giving up to others comes more easily for some than others, but it doesn't come naturally to any of us.

Talking to our husbands is an art in itself, a skill we do well to cultivate. Considering that our husbands are human beings like we ourselves are, it is wise to approach them at the right time. The children are fighting, the baby is screaming, and we are trying to get the last of the food on the table as everyone is coming together for supper. Husband sits calmly at the table, checking out what's for supper—he's hungry, after all. This is a bad time to heatedly point out that he never sees anything going on around him. First of all, he really didn't realize anything was amiss, because he's a man! Secondly you are being a poor example to your children who certainly are learning that the way to deal with frustration is to yell. In the end it profits you nothing.

When your husband is buried in the newspaper or a good book is not a good time to express your fondest wishes, unless he has had sufficient time to shift gears. If his eyes drift back again and again to whatever he was reading, it would be better to ask him when he would like to talk, rather than babbling on and getting nowhere. If your husband is one who falls asleep within minutes of lying in bed, talk to him before going to bed or some other time of the day.

Generally speaking, men don't have the need for talking things out that women do, but wise is the woman who has the love and patience to gently dig for the things that are in his heart. It takes time, but you may discover you didn't know your husband as well as you thought you did. Ask how he feels about child training, finances, your housekeeping, what he would have you change, and more. Then listen and hear what he says. His answers might be painful at times, but defending yourself with a torrent of words will only slam the door down solidly on any more heart-to-heart talks in the future. On some subjects he must be absolutely sure you really care before he will open up. At the same time don't push and act like he must have an answer to your every question, because he just might not have an opinion on every subject you bring up. I know I don't have a very good, solid opinion about which tractor is the best one to buy!

It has been observed that a strong, outgoing, talkative woman is often married to a quiet, calm-natured husband. This can sometimes be a bit of a problem since the husband may not notice as quickly when things are amiss, such as children fighting or being disrespectful. Then the wife may be too quick to mete out punishment. Since the problem is resolved the husband might never even notice there was a problem. If he did notice, the wife took care of it anyway, so why should he? And so the cycle continues.

The other side of the picture is that soft-spoken, quiet women are often married to more aggressive leader-type men. Here the problem that sometimes surfaces is a temptation to side with the children when discipline is administered. Here the wife may tend to shield her children from justice and have a hard time getting the children to obey commands. This wife may be tempted to keep her hurt feelings to herself rather than expressing herself to her husband.

If the father is around when discipline is needed, as a general rule he should take care of the problem. When he is not around, problems should be dealt with as they arise, not wait until Dad comes home. Otherwise the children learn that Dad's homecoming is to be dreaded instead of being a joyful occasion. And do you think Dad feels like dealing with misdeeds a soon as he arrives home? However, if the misdeed was a lack in the child for which the father had given instructions, then he should probably deal with it unless he tells mother otherwise. Most important is communicating with your husband about how he wants discipline taken care of. If you've been married for some time and have fallen into a rut and things should change, a good talk between husband and wife can do wonders to clear the air. But it isn't all that easy to change something that is deeply ingrained. Satan isn't likely to leave alone a change for the better if he can help it!

There are numerous books out there that explore the workings of a proper marriage. Some of them are helpful and some are not! Be careful to take anything you read against the Word of God to

14 — Mops, Muffins, & Motherhood

discern whether what you read is safe to follow. Many books are a mix of good advice and advice that does not correspond to the Bible.

If you are in a marriage that has serious problems, get help! Confide in a friend, a trusted minister, or go for Christian counseling. There is a ditch on either side of the road of matrimony. The one is to never admit that you have problems, cover them at all costs, and suffer alone. The other is to tell everybody everything about how terrible your husband is and how badly he treats you. Neither one is helpful in working through the problems and will likely create even more problems with your children as they grow. It is imperative that the conflict be worked out as soon as possible, since most times relational problems will pass from one generation to the next. You need to face problems squarely with an open mind to seeing your own faults. Looking in the past at your own childhood and his can help you understand why things are the way they are, but blaming your parents for your problems will bring you to a standstill in problem solving. Besides, have you thought about what will happen when your children are old enough to blame you for their problems?? If your husband resists change of any sort, you must accept him as he is, no matter how hard it may be. The only one you have the power to change is yourself, with God's help. Prayer is the most powerful tool for healing relationships. Do not let yourself get too bogged down in past failures. Sometimes you may have to make a fresh start every few minutes when things are extra tense. Again, find someone trustworthy to unload to when the burden gets too heavy, and never forget to pray!

Marriage is hard work, but it also has so many rewards. Such as the flowing together as time goes on, adversity bringing you closer; and the comfort of having one who probably understands you better than you understand yourself. When the children are grown and gone, it will be your husband you end up living with, Lord willing. Don't neglect the relationship with him and end up feeling like you are living with a stranger. It might look so far in the future that you can hardly imagine that time will come, but build that marriage now, so when you are in the time of life that you can spend more time together, you will still want to!

✻ Listen to your husband when he advises about child training on certain issues. He is closest to the situation and can give good advice.

✻ Being married to a man who is laid back can have special challenges in the child discipline area. I struggled very much to know how I should respond when he is right there but hardly even notices there is behavior that needs correction. At times I would point it out to him, sometimes gently, sometimes not so nicely. His response might be a mild rebuke when it was obvious more should be done. Again and again we would discuss it and he agreed he should do better. His very nature and the many other responsibilities he had, made it very difficult for him to change. This brought much frustration and I knew I was not responding the right way, even sassing him in front of the children too many times. It is still a struggle, but I was helped greatly by the mother who told me that she has heard it is better to have children who are somewhat naughty; than for them to hear their mother scold their father and see the discord. They will lose respect for both of you. My mind rebelled at the thought of letting the children get away with bad manners and worse, but when I faced the issue squarely, I realized that my biggest problem was pride. What would others think of the way my children behaved?! Pride is something that every one of us must deal with in one form or another, and it comes directly from Satan himself.

❋ Make it a special night—comb your hair at bedtime. Try to look as attractive for him as you did before marriage. He will notice.

❋ Pick a bouquet of flowers for beside the bed (or get the children to); or in the winter burn a candle.

❋ We always sit on the couch a while and talk after the children are in bed.

❋ It is very important to be in tune with your husband, sharing goals and visions for your family. Share one on one with him; this builds trust. In turn, as a couple, the child training burden is shared. This is not your mom's, your sister's, or your friend's family. Be careful what you share with others.

❋ My husband appreciates his daily foot massage.

❋ Take time for each other as a married couple. Once a month take time to do something together. Go out to eat, go shopping, to the library, or even file taxes. Just do it together and make sure you communicate! It works well to trade babysitting with another family member or friend. When it's the most important is when your children are all small, and it's the hardest to get away.

❋ When Daddy has had a hard day at work, he doesn't like to be welcomed home by the sound of children fighting. Get the children to run to the door and say, "Hi Daddy!" It breaks up fights instantly.

❋ Take notice of your husband's masculinity. Comment about how strong he is when he is lifting something heavy, especially when he is doing something for you. Give him a little grin that lets him know you're impressed with him. Women greatly underestimate what this means to a man.

❋ Women tend to want to talk about feelings, but men talk about facts. Listen when he talks to you, even if you find what he's saying totally boring. If you don't understand what he's saying, let him know how impressed you are with how smart he is. And be genuine; make an effort. Think back to how you related to him when you were dating, and try it again. No, you're not the same as you were then and your love has deepened to something better, but it never hurts to relive some of those memories together. You might be surprised at how young you feel again!

❋ Here are some things I've learned: Husband has the final say. We as wives should be thrifty, but finances are the husband's responsibility. Have fun with your husband. He is special; treat him as if he is. Care about how you look. Don't talk about his faults to others. Be trustworthy and dependable.

❋ Make an extra effort to say at least one complimentary thing to him every day. If he gives you a funny look when you do it the first several times, you can know it was high time to do it! You may find it helpful to make a list and hide it away to look at every once in a while. Even the worst of husbands has some good points, so search them out!

❋ Greet your husband with a smile when he returns home, and encourage the children to greet him, but not tear him apart. Ask him later about his day and listen to what he says.

❋ If you want to talk to him, don't do it when he is engrossed in the paper or a book or magazine. Ask him when it suits to talk to you about important things. If he is one of those men that falls asleep almost as soon as his head hits the pillow, don't frustrate yourself by trying to get something meaningful out of him. Some farm wives talk while milking together or doing other chores.

❋ I like to tell my husband what I think and how I feel about things, but we don't agree on everything. Maybe it's best not to discuss those issues too much to avoid arguing. I feel that children should not hear their parents arguing.

✳ Beware of books! Romance books (even so-called Christian romance books) can cause much trouble. They are not realistic and have an unhealthy "and they lived happily ever after" slant. A man can't read a woman's mind; most men are so focused on making a living for their families, that they may have a problem realizing the needs of their wives. Books in which people seem to be perfect and suggest that if you are not, you aren't a Christian, can be a hindrance as well. Such books should be taken with a grain (or two) of salt. Strive to do better, but we never will be perfect as long as we are in this world. Reading books when we should be working or sleeping is another problem that can crop up. If you and/or your family are "bookworms", using self-control is vital; it is possible to be addicted to reading books. And finally, reading, even good, up-building books, should not take the place of devotions and Bible reading.

✳ Is there a reason the Bible tells the older women to teach the younger to love their husbands? It is a good, daily prayer that God will help me love my husband and children.

✳ Although it is good to spend time together, don't buy into the worldly idea that children are a bother and need to be "gotten away from". Simple family times together build a marriage, too. Snatch moments alone together after the children are in bed or are otherwise occupied.

✳ Marriage is a privilege not everyone has, and we should see it as such. Our attitude about the life we have affects every aspect of our lives. Those of us who are fortunate enough to still have our husbands should consider the widows among us and how our lives would change if this should ever be our lot. A conversation with a widow could be quite enlightening to some of us who take so much for granted. If ever you chance to have your husband gone for a night or two, you can feel a bit more how this would be. This is not something to worry about, but should be seriously considered; for some women it is reality.

✳ If your husband works away from home, send him out the door in the morning with a smile if possible. You never know how much he might need it till the day is over.

✳ Try to avoid going to bed or parting from each other when you are angry. Resolve to talk things over or forgive each other rather than stuff bad feelings away in your heart. Sometimes a little time and space is needed, especially if one or both of you is tired. There are times to bite your tongue and walk away, but learn to deal with the root of the problem, or it will come up again and again. Sometimes all we women need is a good night's sleep or a nap to set things right-side-up again. Wise is the woman who can figure out when to pursue a problem and when to let it go. Forgiving is a divine act and can only be done with help from God. Sometimes it is yourself that you must forgive, and that can be the hardest of all!

✳ Give of yourself, and when you are tired of giving, give some more! This is where true joy lies.

✳ Never be too "big" to apologize when you have said something hurtful. Even if you think it is true, your words need to be seasoned with love.

And Then There Were Two ——— 17

The *attitudes* of parents, guide the attitudes of their children.

Added Blessings

Lo, children are an heritage of the Lord: and the fruit of the womb is his reward. As arrows in the hand of a mighty man; so are children of the youth. Happy is the man that hath his quiver full of them: they shall not be ashamed. Psalm 127:3-5a

3. Added Blessings
Children

Can we count the ways children add joy and laughter to the home? The first tears of joy follow the miracle of birth and the relief that the labor is behind you. As they grow and develop, they charm you with their response to your smiles by cooing and smiling in return. As they start to master language, they say the funniest things at the funniest (and sometimes the most embarrassing) times. As they mature you can hold conversations with them, and by the time they are teens, the conversations develop to the level of other adults. Have you ever stopped to think about what a blessing normal development is? Ask the parents of a developmentally delayed or disabled child and you are sure to learn a lot!

Children add so much to a home. They have a binding effect, adding a closeness to a couple's relationship. This is especially noticeable in the bed that is meant to hold two people but can be stretched to accommodate many more on some nights. This brings new meaning to the word closeness! We really need to treasure this time of dependency, because when it is all over and the children are grown, we will likely remember with fondness those days of hectic busyness. At least, this is what I often hear from the older grandmothers around me. When the thought of getting through one day seems almost more than you can manage, then manage only one hour. If that is too long, manage the next minute. Inevitably, when we humans look back on life, it seems to have been short after all. Let your children teach you the joy of living; they know how naturally!

On the other hand, rearing children is hard work, too. It takes lots of time and effort to train children. Becoming a mother is a big change in life. You now have the responsibility of another soul to teach and train for God's kingdom. We have been taught the importance of parenting for as long as we can remember, but when we stop to really consider the far-reaching effects that stretch out into eternity, it can make us falter. The only way we can hope to have any lasting good influence on our children is to constantly seek God's will in our own lives. We will make mistakes, this is a fact. But God can take our mistakes and make good come from them. Children that live in a less-than-perfect household are many times better prepared for real life than those who grew up in a home that appeared "perfect", where problems were covered up and not acknowledged. Children have an uncanny way of reading a situation and will come to their own conclusions, right or wrong, even if their parents never said a word. If the relationship between you is open enough that they can ask you questions, you will have the opportunity to guide them in their conclusions. They will have a chance to see Christianity in action—that is, if you respond in a Christ-like manner. We teach children primarily by example, so we must consider that we are teaching them at all times, even when we are not aware of it. One time a mother got a phone call from a young friend who was on the youth committee. The young lady was asking if this mother would

20 — Mops, Muffins, & Motherhood

have time to bake a few pies and make some chicken noodle soup for a food stand at a sale the youth was operating to raise money for some worthy cause. This mother graciously assured the young lady she would gladly do it for her. After she hung up the phone, she grumpily told her husband, "Now I have to find time to do that yet!" After she had time to think about it, she realized to her shame that she was teaching her children by example to be two-faced and less-than-honest. Many times we never realize what impression we are leaving on our children when we show one face away from home around our friends and even strangers, but quite another with those we should care about the most. I have told my children more than once that I am thankful they know how to behave themselves away from home, but I wish they would use good manners and charm at home, too. Hmm…I wonder who their role model is.

Children need to learn to work and to be responsible. Teaching them to like to work is harder and more complex than making them do their jobs. A cheerful attitude makes the difference between work and play. If the children consider something to be fun, they will exert themselves much more than if you ask them to do what they consider to be work. Hearing Mother constantly complaining about all the work we have to do definitely sets the wrong tone for helping the children see that work is fun. If you use jobs they dislike for punishment, you might as well realize that they will likely never learn to care for that job, at least not until they are grown up.

Training and discipline are two words closely linked with child rearing. They mean very nearly the same thing and yet each has a slightly different connotation. Training is a gentle restraining again and again. Discipline involves punishing and controlling to acquire the desired behaviors and skills.

Training takes days, weeks, months, and years. Learning is done in increments; here a little, there a little. A child learns academics in little pieces, like building blocks. We don't expect a first grader to be able to do algebra. However, we expect a 12-year-old to have advanced beyond the basics. Some children find schoolwork more difficult than others. In the same way some children will find it easier to give in than others. Each child has a special place in this life. We must accept them as they are. An adult is the product of all the influences that have touched him in life and his responses to them. Parents are the most important, but not nearly the only influences, that shape and mold a life. Siblings, peers, teachers, ministers, and all those that have had any contact at all make impressions: some for good, some for bad. A bad experience can be turned for good if someone is there to point out how things should be. For example, if parents are made aware their child is along when mocking of someone else occurs, they need to explain why mocking is wrong and see that apologies are made, if necessary. On the other hand if a parent shrugs it off with the attitude that the person being mocked is odd anyway and probably deserved it, certainly that child will do it again. Two children, even siblings, can have the same experience, but respond quite differently because of their natures. As a mother we need to discern how each child needs to be handled.

Children need training and discipline. Training is a constant gentle tug or push in the right direction. When a grower wishes to have plants grow a certain way, he will use soft strips of cloth and gently bring the vine to the stake or wire he desires the plant to grow along. It is a constant gentle pressure to stay in the right place and the new growth must be kept after. One year we decided to string up our tomato plants using the "Florida weave". You pound stakes

Added Blessings —— 21

into the ground between every few tomato plants then start pretty low with baler twine and weave back and forth between the stakes carefully and gently catching the tomato plants between the twine. This way the plant grows out around the twine, but the main stem is supported. The weaving needs to be done periodically as the plants grow. Well, as is prone to happen at our place, it went several weeks and we just didn't get out in the field to tie those tomatoes up again. (We had done it once or twice.) The plants were growing out over the twine with no regard to boundaries. We gathered them up and tried to gently bring them where they should have been. Those poor plants were a sorry sight when we were done! Stems were bent in unnatural positions or broken off altogether. Leaves were stripped off and the stems were skinned where the twine had scraped them. We did get tomatoes off that row, but the yield was greatly reduced and although the plants eventually grew out, they certainly didn't look as nice as they would have, had we done our training bit by bit instead of in such an abrupt and cruel manner. I felt badly when I saw that row of tomatoes after we tied them up, but I saw a parallel to raising children. If we don't do our duty in gently correcting them as they grow, they will get their training in an abrupt and unkind manner from the world around them and their peers. Children will be scarred forever and struggle so much harder to produce Godly fruit if they are not taught the Christian virtues of always telling the truth, getting along with others, serving others, and the source of true joy, to name a few.

Discipline has a slightly different connotation. It is the consequences of wrong doing. If a small child touches a hot stove, the consequences are immediate and it is unlikely he will do so again if the pain was severe enough. His little brain tells him not to touch that thing again, causing him to avoid the stove even when it is cold. This is the way children learn what appropriate behavior is; do something undesirable, receive pain. The pain can be in the form of physical punishment, your disapproval, isolation, or any other result the child will avoid in the future.

One of the most important components of raising children is consistency. To me it also seems like one of the hardest parts. Some days it is just easier to be consistent than others. When you have a baby in your lap and the two year old deliberately cleans out the clothing drawer that he has been told not to, it is far easier to stay sitting and scold than to get up and do something about it. Especially if the baby is almost sleeping. Another scenario is when the child is half sick and you're not sure how hard to be on him. We have to take our own emotional health into consideration. Women are known to have fluctuating moods and that can cause us to be stricter sometimes than others. We need to seek a balance between too much leniency and too much rigid discipline. Although there are many situations where it is hard to know just what to do, one guideline is if the child has been given a clear command and ignores you or doesn't immediately follow through, it is disobedience and needs to be dealt with. It has been said that until the pain of staying the same exceeds the pain of changing, we will remain the same. This is true in so many areas of our lives as well as the lives of our children. Until you make the pain of dropping that coat on the floor in the middle of the room, greater than the pain of hanging it on the hook where it belongs, you will continue to trip over the coat! Until the embarrassment of getting caught with a very messy house is greater than the effort of keeping it at least halfway presentable, we will live in a pigsty. I once heard of a study that was done with mice that quickly learned if they pushed a certain button with their noses, they would get some food.

Then the men conducting the study made it so that it didn't deliver food every time; then eventually they didn't receive food at all. They wanted to see how long it would take to recondition the little mouse brains to give up and stop pushing this button. I no longer remember how many times the mice continued to do it, but as long as they got food sometimes, they kept on trying. After they no longer got any food, they still tried hundreds of times. What does this have to do with child training? Every time a child gets away with doing something he knows he isn't supposed to, you lengthen the time it will take to break him of his behavior. If the child receives the message, "I don't want to get caught the next time," he gets the wrong message! If he doesn't learn that what he did is wrong, and why, the discipline is ineffective. If we cannot explain the reason what he did was wrong, then maybe we need to consider why we punished. Was it out of frustration? What happens when we punish today, but tomorrow when we feel better or the day seems brighter, we ignore the same behavior?

A child needs to learn to obey us even if he doesn't understand the reason behind our correction or request. We are not obligated to answer every why they may have, but we should have a good reason behind what we instruct them to do rather than always saying "because I said so".

We hear more and more about abuse in our conservative circles. It can be difficult to define abuse in a society that considers physical punishment of any kind to be abuse. There is a fine line between abuse and discipline. Discipline is not abuse. Abuse is not discipline. To not discipline, is to abuse.

There are several kinds of abuse; physical, sexual, emotional, verbal, and spiritual. The Bible clearly supports physical punishment, but striking wildly in anger or frustration crosses over the line into abuse. As a child gets older and if the conscience has been properly developed, there should be less need for physical punishment. You can't use only the age of a child to determine when it is time to discontinue physical punishment, but need to take other factors into consideration as well, such as maturity and sensitivity. For most children the bulk of physical correction should be done by the age of 4-6 years old.

Sexual abuse is particularly devastating, and often requires counseling for the child. God has set certain laws in motion, and when these laws are violated, it must be dealt with at a deeper level. To brush off the wrong that has been done, is damaging to both the violated and the violator. God can bring healing to both, but the issue must be faced squarely. If authorities get wind of sexual (or physical) abuse, they may intervene and take the child out of the home, along with any other children. This problem among us is not to be taken lightly, but we need to work together to put an end to all abusive behaviors. If we as Christians are not willing to get involved and get help, the government will step in and attempt to fix the problem their way!

Verbal abuse and emotional abuse can go hand in hand and often end up as spiritual abuse. Verbal abuse is yelling and berating another when angry or frustrated. I have heard parents at stores yelling and swearing at their children, even saying they will kill them if they don't obey. This is quite shocking to us, but we need to realize that a little bit of yelling or raising our voices in anger in private is not okay either. Most, if not all, of us are not completely free of this problem. If we slip, we need to realize that we must apologize and try to do better. Constant verbal abuse takes an emotional toll on a child. Also in the class of emotional abuse is demeaning, mocking, and showing favoritism. An emotionally abused person has extremely low self-esteem, and may be a loud-mouthed show-off to cover the pain inside. He may

Added Blessings — 23

not even be fully aware that he has a problem. To him verbal abuse is just a way of life.

Spiritual abuse occurs when people try to control or threaten others with Biblical principles. One example is using the threat of going to hell to bring about desired behaviors. God is a God of love as well as a God of judgment. He means what He says, but He doesn't threaten people to manipulate them. Spiritually abused people have a difficult time viewing God as He really is, and have a warped view of Christianity in general.

We cannot give our children salvation and neither can we buy it for them, but we want to teach them what they need to know to make the right choice when they are old enough to understand what life is really all about. After the struggles you face together, what a joy it is to see the adult emerging and see them on the brink of their own life ahead; no longer dependent on you, but still a part of your extended family. And if you have the heartache of a child that has grown away and is not dealing well with adult life; yes, you must acknowledge you have made mistakes, but so have we all and it is only through God's mercy that any of us can have the satisfaction of seeing our children follow after God. You cannot see the future; your child may yet turn and serve God even more deeply because of what they have experienced. Those who have walked through these deep waters understand things in a way others never will. As long as there is life, there is hope. You can never tell what is happening in the heart of your child and how much good your unfailing love and prayers will yet do for him or her. The judgment of others is very painful, but you must remember it is the judgment of God we must all fear, and He is far more forgiving than many people are.

Like the subject of marriage, there are many good books available to help us understand all about rearing Godly children. Unfortunately they can't make us do the right things; we must apply ourselves. Also, we must take anything we read on the subject against the Bible to be sure it is based on the truth. Still, no one is perfect and in the end we must do the best we can, acknowledge we will make mistakes, and let the rest up to God.

✻ We found the third child to be the biggest adjustment (after the first one, of course). With two children there was a parent for each one, but when we had three, one of us had to handle two. By the time we had more than three, the oldest ones were getting to an age when they could take care of themselves and even help out in little ways.

✻ We find we can't expect anything from our children unless we, by example, are willing to do it ourselves.

✻ Some days you might feel like returning your baby to the hospital in exchange for another one!

✻ Satan is in the business of destroying homes, especially Christian homes.

✻ Stand together! The children can soon tell if Mom is soft on an issue that Dad is firm on. How rewarding it is when Mom insists on something and Dad stands right behind her or vice versa. It quells arguments from children really fast!

✻ We need to be careful not to let what other people say influence us too much. When we were expecting baby #4, several times right after each other someone mentioned how brave I was to have another baby because of how much work so many children make. I had to watch my attitude because after a while I started to believe them.

✻ Be firm and praise a lot!

✻ We like to have the children think things through for themselves, not just give them dos and don'ts.

✳ One thing a wife and mother should avoid as much as possible is to be too deeply involved in making money to support the family. It is a way of the world that is showing up more and more in our conservative circles. There are a few rare circumstances where it may be necessary, but generally the way for us to help with the finances is to stretch what is earned as far as possible by being thrifty and staying at home. Seek God in prayer before becoming involved in anything outside your home. In the end, though, you need to communicate with your husband and consider his wishes as long as they don't go against God's word. I've heard that it's not the high cost of living, but the cost of living high that causes our financial problems.

✳ A huge blessing for me was simply getting outside for a walk. It gave the children and me fresh air and new scenery. Sometimes I didn't feel like making the effort, especially in winter when we had to bundle up, but it is amazing what getting outside can do for a person. Sometimes the children would ride their bikes, and a lot of times we would walk with neighbors, which was another big blessing. My neighbor and I would walk together and talk about our children and share how our day and lives were going. It was heartwarming to be able to share frustrations and happenings from the day with someone who understood. We also live close enough that on rainy or extra cold days we called each other and took turns going to each other's homes for just an hour before naps. (Age 34)

✳ One thing we have found to help our family work together better is to inform the children ahead of time what is expected. When they are told the plans for the week, I have found out they gear up and work a lot better. Assign tasks to each child, and last but not least, work beside them as much as possible.

✳ If you catch yourself saying, "How many times must I tell you… ?" Stop! It is not the child's fault. He has learned you don't mean it the first time, or the second, or… do you really mean it at all? It makes him wonder how far he can go with you. He is not deliberately trying to irritate you; he is only following his human nature. Whenever I catch myself saying "How many times must I tell you?" I imagine God looking down at me saying, "How many times must I tell you to be kind, don't raise your voice, etc., etc." We all need God's grace. The perception our children have of God is strongly linked with the way their parents deal with them.

✳ For most of the first year of a child's life, restraining him is the best way of training. A light slap can stop a little one in his tracks and get the message across. When crying out of anger, a slight puff of air into the face each time he takes a new breath to let out another squall can stop him from screaming and you might then be able to distract him. Never blow in his face so that he can't get his breath; this will very likely cause him to panic and scream even louder, and you won't achieve your purpose.

✳ Sometimes a baby that just cries and cries will respond to being tightly swaddled with a blanket. Firmly wrap him in a soft blanket so that he can't flail his little arms and legs about, and rock and sing or walk around. This will not work for all babies.

✳ I was given a book about schedule feeding my babies that was very helpful. It has been such a controversial subject that I don't often share it, but I wish I had more courage to.

> Our 4-year-old son had this explanation, "One day Jesus put me in a box and put me in the mail. Mom went to fetch the mail and there was a box. She opened it and there I was. Mom had a big surprise!"

Added Blessings

✻ When a baby or toddler just seems fussy and uncomfortable, give them liquid Tylenol or Advil. They very likely hurt somewhere, but can't tell you where. I have gained a happier child many times by doing this. However, I will do this usually only once a day, and not many days in a row. If they persist in being grouchy, a visit to the doctor may be in order, especially if a fever is present. One exception to this rule is if you are pretty sure they are teething. If you remember when your 12-year molars came in, you might understand why they are grumpy!

✻ This, too, shall pass. During training sessions of toddlers, you know you will not be changing pampers on your 16 year old, neither will you be nursing/bottle feeding at 2 AM all your life (even if it sort of feels like it sometimes), a noisy toddler will learn to sit in church and not embarrass you every Sunday morning. (Although you might be surprised at just how many ways a child can embarrass you at church as they grow older). Various seasons of life seem to stretch out forever, especially when you are tired (as most mothers are). But remember eventually "this, too, shall pass." (Age 67)

✻ Try to teach the children to think of others first. That is the source of true happiness. Of course, they need a good example to follow!

✻ When giving my children the warning "If you don't…" I like to finish it with "…I'll need to punish." That way I can have more time to think about a punishment, if needed, that fits the disobedience.

✻ It works better to give a 5 minute warning when it is time to go to bed or end a game, to give them time to wind down and shift their focus. It can be difficult for us as adults to change directions and more so for some children.

✻ Slow obedience is no obedience!

✻ One thing that is so important to me is to spend time with and enjoy your children. Get their hearts when they are young and then you will have them as they get older. (Age 37)

✻ When you feel like you talk and talk, but nobody listens to your instructions, you need to stop and think about all the things your Mom and Dad said to you that you still remember (and very likely repeat to your children). "A new broom sweeps nice" (usually said in Pa. Dutch) in reference to new things being special but soon wearing off. "The one you throw the farthest away is the one you'll fetch first" was a warning when we made unkind remarks about one of the young fellows that was in the youth group with us. Many times we heard "Beauty is only skin deep" if our mother thought we were too concerned with the way we looked. And there is one my Dad said that I still hear in my head to this day when I hit a stick or stone or something else with the lawn mower, "A mower is not a land-leveling device!" So you think your children don't hear you? You might be surprised and chagrinned to find out what all they remember 20 or 30 years from now! So consider what you are saying.

✻ *But seek first His kingdom and His righteousness and all these things will be given to you as well.* Matt. 6:33 (NIV) Looking back from the perspective my age has given me, this is the verse the Spirit most often used to get me back on track after having run things off into the ditch. When you're young with all the youthful enthusiasm and energy that goes with that stage in life, one can so easily entertain the mindset (without really thinking about it), "I can do this myself." Actually this is a two-year-old mentality! Reading books on child rearing and organizational skills can be so helpful. However, if we don't put God first in our lives, we will find ourselves lacking. Someone has said, "Put God's will and His righteousness first in your life, and He will take care of everything else." (Age 71)

✻ When your children say amusing things, write

Mops, Muffins, & Motherhood

it in their baby book right away. If you don't write it down it gets forgotten. Reading them brings lots of memories back. A young mother has so little time to spare, but if you don't have time to write it in the baby book, jot it on a paper and slip it into the book to rewrite it later. My aunt once said she wishes she would have written more in the children's books.

✻ From an older woman- My memory isn't what I wish it was and the baby and infant stage seems so long ago. But at the same time, like everyone else, I will never regret the time and energy I invested in our children. When you're in the midst of it all, it seems life will always be this way — crazy, hectic, and sleep-deprived. But you need to try to enjoy life right where you are and not look too far ahead.

✻ A goal I have always tried to reach is to make a haven for my family; a place where my husband and children look forward to coming to at the end of the day. A place where they can be themselves, unload their troubles and be renewed. Maybe this seems to be more for older children, but I think it is catching at a very young age. Is it a special time when Daddy comes home? Everyone stops what they are doing and greet him at the door, sit down for a short time and catch up on their day. We have done this faithfully and now our teenage children say how much they look forward to coming in at the close of their day. I also enjoy preparing a nice meal to again share around the table most days. They really look forward to that time as well. Now, I realize toddlers would rather not sit and eat, but family mealtime together builds to what we are enjoying right now. (Age 44)

✻ Motherhood is a partnership with God, so our family must come first. Yes, it is mostly dirty work, one does not have to be educated and gifted to be a mother, but keep up your end of the partnership. Pleasing God will bring many blessings.

✻ Do your best. The children will be with you for only one childhood. These little things count, show your love by doing them willingly. This is a mother's role as chosen by God. Keep that lovely mansion with the crystal river as your goal in heaven. We'll be rewarded if we faint not.

✻ A piece of advice I appreciated was, "It won't always be like this." Or my mom would say, "It won't be like this when they go to school." This helped keep a balanced perspective when you were sure the tough days would go on FOREVER! A piece of advice I didn't really like hearing was, "Enjoy them while they're young… they grow up so fast." While I am realizing the truth of this now, back when people would say this to me, it would make me feel guilty because I was frustrated and I wasn't always enjoying them. It would be much better for people to identify with young mothers and recognize the challenges and frustrations. (Age 34)

✻ A grandmother told her daughter when she held her first grandchild, "When you take off his booties and later his shoes, always say a prayer to God for him."

✻ Clean children are easier to cuddle and they will sleep better. We adults can wait for food sometimes, but children will be happier when fed on time with healthy food choices.

✻ Naps taken in a cool room and a clean bed will give a child a good rest.

✻ When you get tired of shoes, boots, coats, lunch pails, and such like lying around where they don't belong, have a box handy to drop them into. Before the child may get them back out, he/she must do a job for you. This works well both in helping them remember to put their belongings away and also getting some of those jobs done.

✻ Coping when Daddy is gone at work all day can be quite difficult. It is best if you can have at least a little time during the day for a nap or a little quiet time. Some mothers have all the children have a rest period for a certain length of time in their rooms

Added Blessings — 27

after lunch. The older ones can quietly read or do some craft and the younger ones should rest.

❋ A piece of advice that my mom gave me is that when you take the time to sit and play with your preschoolers (read some books, play with toys, etc.) early in the day, it is amazing how nicely they will go and play on their own.

❋ Countless times when I am shopping, I meet older ladies who gaze longing at my little girls and say, "Enjoy this stage because it goes so fast!" If I don't have contentment in this stage, I probably won't have it in any other stage of my life. (Age 35)

❋ Enjoy your children and spend time with them while they are with you. They grow up so fast! (Age 39)

❋ A doctor once said that as long as the child needs a nap, the mother does, too.

❋ One time I told my husband that I could probably do better in discipline if we wouldn't have as many children as close together as we do. He corrected me by telling me I would probably be tempted to use that extra time selfishly, and in the end it would make no difference.

❋ Don't nag or try to bribe your child to obey. Be in control. Spare the rod and spoil the child. Note how often the Bible mentions the rod. It is necessary to always be consistent, so they know exactly what is expected of them. Make your no mean no; not maybe, later, or yes. Godly discipline builds respect.

❋ If we were going away in the evenings, I gave baths before afternoon naps, especially in the wintertime, when the children would stay indoors and not get dirty again. (Age 67)

❋ If you have a problem getting your child to lay still long enough to take a nap, it may work to set a timer for a certain length of time and tell him he may get up when it rings if he lays still. If he gets up or talks, the time starts over. This will usually tell you if he really is tired or not.

❋ Enjoy the stage where you are in life. It's gone way too fast!

❋ Keeping a schedule for evenings makes everyone sleep so much better. Our schedule (as much as possible between work and church) is: bath at 8:00, snack at 8:30, read books at 8:45, and prayers and in bed at 9:00.

❋ It is okay for M.O.M.s to occasionally take time out to do things they enjoy. It will help them to feel re-energized emotionally and mentally. (Age 39)

❋ Be consistent when disciplining so your children take you seriously.

❋ This too, shall pass. Enjoy every stage to the fullest! As the mom of a 15, 14, 11, 7, 5, and 1 year old… I can say that this is SO true, and I'm loving it! Right now is PRIME TIME, no matter what stage we're in, and believe me, we have many different stages at our house right now, from tantrums to hormones, from cute words repeated by baby to steps of faith in the older ones. (Age 37)

❋ I need to keep reminding myself to enjoy the moment! I know they grow up fast and this toddler stage will pass, but some days I'd like to fast forward my life by a couple of years. (Age 33)

❋ My mother used to quote, "What you don't have in your head, you must have in your feet." When I send a child for something and they forget, and come back without it, I do what my mother did, quote this saying! They need to use their feet to take extra steps to make up for what they forgot with their head.

❋ Don't let older children start complaining about jobs and it will be easier to train the younger ones. Consistency is the key.

❋ Chore charts and schedules can take some of the stress out of life by eliminating the need to figure out whose turn it is and who did it last.

❋ Children who are allowed to play outside and get dirty, run, and exercise, are happy children. (Age 60)

28 — Mops, Muffins, & Motherhood

✳ Try to keep a positive attitude towards work. It is rewarding; and be sure to point out to the children how much better something looks after you work at it. For example: weeding the garden or cleaning up the house. Also express your feeling of satisfaction at a job well done, and remind them how much better they feel if they did a job quickly and as well as they could.

✳ Don't forget to praise, but don't flatter. Constructive criticism is necessary, but constant negative criticism is down-heartening and a child (or adult for that matter) who feels he can never do it right, will stop trying. He will draw into a shell, and to others it may appear that he simply doesn't care and won't try no matter what you do to him. The only way to break the barrier is by reaffirming his worth with sincere praise. Everyone does something right. It may take a long time for him to believe you really do care, but it can be done. Some children seem much more sensitive to criticism, but it might surprise you if you knew what is going through the head of Mr. I Don't Care. He just might care far more than he wants you to know.

✳ Preteens and teenagers are working at becoming adults. And it really is work. One minute they can act like an adult and the next you are reminded more of a 2-year-old. Advice given at a teacher's meeting was that you should treat them like adults, but expect them to act like children. This helps avoid disappointment when they do act younger than you think they should.

✳ I've noticed that occupied or busy children are happy children and don't need as many punishments. Make sure they have things to do; even preschoolers don't need as much discipline if they are kept busy. Let them "help" when you are baking, washing, cleaning, and mine even like to sit beside me when I am sewing.

✳ No two children are exactly alike. Brothers or sisters with the same two parents, raised in the same environment can nevertheless turn out quite differently. What works for one may not work for the other. One might wilt with remorse from just a stern look. The next one seems to "bounce off" any scolding you may choose to deliver. One throws a temper fit, kicking and screaming. It is obvious he needs attention, and right now! But what about the one who learns early and young to keep his displeasure inside, and betrays it by only a muscle twitching at his jaw. Beware! Many a mother may have her children grow up only to discover that the one who seemed to be compliant is the one who still "twitches his jaw" when his will is crossed and does as he pleases anyway. And the one who so obviously needed correction has blossomed into a young person with strong convictions.

✳ I know this isn't new news, but I remember people telling me to enjoy the little ones, because they grow up so fast. At the time I wasn't so sure. Now I know first-hand how quickly that happens. When they are little they are very needy, but the needs are different than when they get older. They are all there safely tucked into their beds at night— no worries about where anyone is or when they will get home. There is lots of work when they are young, but we were all together all the time. It really is a sweet time of life and I would say make the most of each day. Read to your children and take time to listen. They are little people in progress, and this time will pass very quickly…I promise!

✳ You should never, ever say, "Why can't you be like your brother (or sister)?" God made each one just like He wanted them in personality, looks, and body shape and strength. It is up to us as parents to form and mold. Let us never be guilty of wounding an innocent soul by harsh words of condemnation for things out of the child's control. And if, like me, you realize you are guilty of this very thing, hasten

Added Blessings — 29

to make amends by apologizing immediately and reassure the child of your love.

✾ Many times it has been discussed in mother circles how the oldest child and the child(ren) most like us are the ones we struggle with the most. It has been said that the things that bother you the most about yourself are the things you dislike in others. It helps to analyze why one of the children in particular annoys you. It is quite likely you will discover it is because there is something in this child you struggle with yourself.

✾ Believe in your children, but don't always believe them. It seems that children have "slanted" memories. A child seldom tells an outright lie for the sake of lying. Either his immaturity causes him to interpret things in a wrong or slightly twisted way, or it may be pressure from fear of punishment or retaliation from others that causes him to reason things in a way that suits the event. He should be made to understand his error before meting out punishment.

✾ I had an aunt who left a deep impression on me when she offered this advice, "If you don't listen to your children when they are little, don't expect them to listen to you when they are big." She went on to give one example. They were having difficulties at school and she and her husband refused to listen to their boys' side of the story, only standing firm by telling them they must obey the teacher. Every time an issue came up, they took the teacher's side and told the boys they must do better, never hearing the boys out. Years later they discovered that the teacher was, in fact, a large part of the problem. Although children should learn to respect authority, they should also know you will give them a listening ear when they have problems. They should not be encouraged in any way to disrespect those in authority, but an older child especially can be encouraged to learn how to get along with people who do or think differently than themselves. This is a lesson that is vital all through life; along with learning how to respectfully approach and solve problems that arise between two or more people. This is far better than learning to handle differences by degrading or talking unkindly, gossiping, or having a "better-than-thou" attitude.

✾ Read stories to your children. Up-building, educational, or just plain interesting. Winter time is an excellent time, with the shorter daylight hours and the slower pace of life.

Family time

✾ Making family time can be difficult, especially during some seasons. Make it a goal to finish work early enough to spend a little time together before going to bed. These efforts pay big dividends when the children are older and know that family is important. If they feel all we can think about is how much work they can do for us, they will be anxious to get away and be with their friends. Family ties have kept many a teenager from trouble, and lack of them has been a contributing factor in the trouble many others got into, feeling there is no one who understands or really cares.

✾ I think once we're older grandmothers we might look back and say, "What were the special times?" Won't they be enjoying a new baby together, all sitting down at the supper table together, going to church together, and working together?

✾ We don't go away a lot, so to our children little things are special, such as summer evenings spent at the river, fishing or swimming, and maybe a stop at the Dairy Queen for ice cream occasionally. They also enjoy when Mom and Dad take the time to sit outside some evenings and watch as they trike and bike around. Deer spotting, spending time in the woods, and gardening together are all ways to build healthy family relationships.

In spite of our busy lives, we like to have Dad spend a little time alone with each child occasionally. Children really enjoy this! Doing this might mean that Mom has to give up something she wanted Dad to do for her. We moms need to decide what really is the most important.

✻ I enjoy reading a good book to my older school age (and beyond) children before family devotions in the evening. Usually the book is too advanced for the little ones so I try to read to them at naptime.

✻ My husband and I both appreciate birthday cards that each child signed and added a sentence of what they like or appreciate. It cultivates an attitude of respect.

Favorite family memory makers

✻ Eating popcorn and drinking hot chocolate by lamplight during the winter.

✻ Eating out at the picnic table. Using a dishpan or a large tray to cart the dishes and food around saves many steps.

✻ Singing together or romping around in the yard, catching fire flies on summer evenings.

✻ Taking bike rides together

✻ Hot dog roasts

✻ Going on hikes and sitting around campfires has made many good memories for our family.

✻ We have a spot on the basement walls where we mark the children's height each Christmas. The children love to see how much they've grown!

✻ Winter evenings when everyone's in the house is a great time to have your whole family sing together.

✻ Our family enjoyed a homemade waterslide made of a roll of tough plastic my husband got at a sale. We rolled it out downhill in our yard and set a concreted tire volleyball pole at the top end to keep it from sliding down the hill. A garden hose at the top set at a little more than a trickle, and liquid soap to make it more slippery, and you're ready to slide! Be ready to clean up a grassy mess, though!

✻ Special family times don't have to be big or expensive. Our children enjoy a picnic along the river.

✻ Campfires are memory makers. Roasting hot dogs and marshmallows and singing around the fire just fit together.

✻ Birthdays can be special. Maybe the birthday child can skip out on a chore. Use a special plate for the birthday child's meal. Or let them choose what they want for supper (within reason, of course!). Some families always have birthday cakes for the child.

One afternoon when I was doing my monthly grocery shopping, the cashier was ringing up my small mountain of groceries. I felt the need to simply state, "Well, this should supply our family of nine for a month." She stopped and looked at me, then said, "You mean you have seven children?!" I replied, "Yes, Ma'am, and we cherish each one dearly." She was very flustered but finally said, "How do you manage with such a brood?"

Added Blessings — 31

32 —— Mops, Muffins, & Motherhood

Time to Learn

A wise man will hear, and will increase learning; and a man of understanding shall attain unto wise counsels. The fear of the Lord is the beginning of knowledge; but fools despise wisdom and instruction.
Proverbs 1:5,7

4. Time to Learn
School/Homeschool

What is education? What is the purpose of education? How does education affect our Christian lives? The dictionary defines education as the imparting and acquiring of knowledge through teaching and learning. So really, education covers every facet of life. This section deals with the part of education known as readin', writin', and 'rithmetic by the old timers, or "book larnin" by the southerners. The purposes for education are many. It would be difficult to live a normal adult life without knowing how to read and have at least a good basic understanding of math. Other subjects, such as Health, improve the quality of our lives by understanding about how our bodies work; and Science explores the world God gave us. Social Studies and Geography help us to understand how people live in other cultures and climates. English and Language Arts help us with reading and comprehension, sentence structure, and teach rules of writing so we can be understood in written communication with each other. All together, a good basic education will enable us to have an intelligent conversation with other people. It quite amused us to hear that someone from Pennsylvania asked a person from Missouri if they felt the tremors from the California earthquakes. Or just ask a Canadian resident how many states there are in Canada, or who their president is. It is not so important to know everything about everything, but it is good to have a healthy interest about the world around us lest we become so narrow-minded that we think the way we do things is the only right way.

The most important aspect of education is how it impacts our Christian life. If no one could read the Bible, we would be very handicapped in understanding God's directions for Godly living. A well-rounded education helps us in more ways than we can imagine.

How to educate can be a matter of great debate and sometimes heated arguments. I don't want to address the pros and cons of the different ways, but feel each household has to make their own decision on which way is best. We have both homeschooled and sent to a private school. I have gone to and taught in a one room school. I have also attended a two room and a one-grade-per-room school. Some think bigger schools are better and some think smaller schools are better. I feel the best way is to make your decision with your husband and not judge others for their decision, nor be unduly concerned about what other people think about yours.

Slow learners are a hot topic. Again you will find as many and varied opinions as there are people discussing it. Some say these children are handicapped and can't help it. Some feel they are just not disciplined enough. Some think they eat too many unhealthy foods. Some are sure it is all in genetics; it runs in the family to be slow. Could it be that all of these things and more contribute to the problem? I have heard the question of why there are so many more slow learners than there used to be. I think it is a combination of the slow learner getting the attention he needs compared to years ago when they were pretty much ignored, made fun of, and/or pushed through until they were old enough to quit school. Another factor is that many of the conservative curricula being used these days may be more demanding than the old secular books. The books many of us use today cram what used to be almost 12 years of education in 8 years of schooling. This is fine for the average child, but leaves the slower child in the dust. He will get farther and farther behind his classmates unless he receives special help. This is also an extra strain on teachers of three or more grades, since many of these books assume the teacher will have time for oral drill and more individual time with any students that have difficulty grasping new concepts.

It cannot be stressed enough that a child needs a good first grade education since this is the foundation on which the information gleaned in future years rests. This may mean repeating the grade to gain that base. Another problem occurs when a child is sent to school too soon. Some children, particularly boys, are just not mature enough and their brains have simply not developed to the point that they can handle what they are expected to absorb. We experienced this with some of our boys. The first one was in first grade when we started to homeschool because of moving to a new community where there were no private schools. I had taught first grade previously and thought, "This is going to be so much fun!" It turned out to be anything but fun. He started okay, but it seemed he hit a wall when he had too many words to read. He always knew some words on the flashcards and never knew certain others no matter how many times I told him what they were. By the end of his first year, he could barely stumble through the first grade reading books. He didn't have much

trouble with math other than reading problems, but anything connected with reading was a challenge. He started second grade in a private school with a teacher that hardly paid any attention to him and his classmate, a boy with almost identical problems. They muddled their way through that year. By third grade, he seemed to suddenly snap out of it and by the end of the year he was reading encyclopedias for the fun of it! It was no special teaching style that made the difference. We are convinced that he just wasn't mature enough to fully grasp what was considered to be appropriate for his age. This was reinforced in our minds when we had similar experiences with the next boy and some more of our children. I'm afraid what happens to these children is that they learn to dislike school and feel like a failure before they are mature enough to perform what is required of them. I consider these children to be learning delayed rather than learning disabled. The teacher's biggest challenge for these children is to keep them from learning to hate school and feeling so inferior that they never learn they can do it and are not stupid. I have a nephew that just struggled and struggled to learn to read. Then the summer he turned ten, he picked up a book and became a reasonably fluent reader in a matter of a few weeks. Unfortunately, not all learning problems are overcome quite that easily.

Attention disorders are another whole area of debate. While there is a difference in how children are taught to apply themselves, there are very real disorders that need to be dealt with. It takes wise parents and teachers to discern whether training is lacking or whether the child has ADD or ADHD. Either way, much patience and love are required. Some children exhibit hyperactivity when they eat certain foods. Sugar and food colorings are common culprits. It is unreasonable to expect a child to control himself if it is beyond his ability to do so. Causes

Time to Learn — 35

should be ferreted out and dealt with. Consider how well you could sit still and concentrate on learning if you had a burr under your clothing that constantly poked you, and someone told you (getting louder and more frustrated with each statement), "Just ignore it and do what I'm telling you. You just aren't trying hard enough! Pay attention! What did I just tell you?!" It is cruel to parents (and their children) whose child has a learning problem, to be looked down on by other parents who "know they just didn't teach their children to obey" or other harsh judgments that are too commonly expressed. Being too lenient can be a problem, but it would be more prudent for us to consider our own child-rearing methods, than to pass judgment on those of our fellow parents. As in so many areas of our life, we never know how soon we may need to swallow our own words, and it is easier to do if we have not spread our critical attitudes to everyone else. Somehow it seems God has a way of showing us our self-righteousness by putting us in the very situation for which we criticized others. The moral here is to guard our thoughts and attitudes carefully, lest they be extremely bitter when we have to swallow them ourselves!

The fast learner presents another challenge entirely. He may get bored or consider himself to be superior to his classmates. Skipping grades might be an option if he can still fulfill the requirements of the laws in your state as far as age/years of schooling are concerned. When dealing with the laws in your state, never just take the word of someone else; check it out yourself. There have been cases where someone proclaimed to know what the law says and it was passed from person to person as fact until someone decided to actually check it out, only to discover it was never true. Maybe it came about from a misunderstanding from person to person, but be sure that the person who is informing you is actually knowledgeable.

✻ When our first child started school an older mother told me it won't be long until she's out of eighth grade. As hard as it was for me to believe at the time, I found it to be very true. Life flows along from one year to the next and it is our children's ages that remind us how old we are.

✻ We as parents don't appreciate too much homework. If a child brings home more than an hour's worth, we try to communicate with the teacher to find out if the child is goofing off or if the work load is too heavy. We don't feel like we send our children to school and pay tuition to end up homeschooling.

✻ It works best for us to have a set time in the afternoon/evening for doing homework. At the appointed time, make sure you know who has homework and see to it that they get at it promptly.

✻ After struggling with a son who had lots of homework and didn't know his math facts very well, the older ones got involved and started having flash card races with him. His teacher reported that things improved a lot. Inspired involvement on our part was a real benefit.

✻ I try to go through each school child's clothing several weeks before school starts, then go shopping if necessary. Of course, if you know you will need to do some sewing, it would be wise to start earlier.

✻ To keep school clothes looking nice longer, our children change into everyday clothing when they come home from school. They then wear the same clothes two days in a row unless they are too dirty. This cuts down on laundry. It is good to teach them to hang up their clothes to avoid wrinkles or having them serve as shoe rags.

✻ Tired of lunches, coats, gloves, boots, and school books and papers sitting where they landed when the children came in the door? If you consistently confiscate these items and require the child to do a job for you or pick up a certain number of things before they can have their belongings back, you will find that they can remember to put their things away.

✻ Assign one child to clean and wipe out the lunches and put them where they belong soon after coming home from school, all ready for the next day.

✻ After-school jobs for children can include washing the dishes that accumulated during the day to make less for after supper, peeling potatoes, baking or making something for school lunches, tidying up each room, and bringing in and folding clothes. It is nice to allow the children a bit of time to shift gears from school to home and a snack almost seems necessary for some!

✻ Some of the children that bring homework home can do better if they do it soon after arriving home, and others do better having a break and doing it after supper.

✻ If you have a child that has problems with his schoolwork, it may help to do some drill at home with flashcard games. It is much more beneficial if you can make it fun instead of drudgery. Try to help the child see how much easier math will be if he knows the answers to the number facts in a blink. Encouragement from home is sometimes more important than anything the teacher can do. Never allow the other children to make degrading remarks about the one that struggles.

My first grade son said he feels "trapped" when he's at school. I asked, "Do you feel claustrophobic?" "No, it's just that when I'm at school I wish I was at home!" was his reply.

Homeschooling

✻ If you are homeschooling, it is helpful to have lunch planned before you start with school.

✻ Bible memory can be included in family devotions by repeating a certain passage of scripture every morning and adding a verse or two to it each week. It is amazing what even very young children can retain.

✻ If you have a problem with a child who dawdles instead of getting school work done, try setting the timer for 10 minutes and have a set amount of work that must be done. Have a small reward if they get done and a punishment if they do not. The important thing is to be consistent with the rewards and punishments or else the child will soon know that it isn't anything to worry about if they don't get done. If you see that they really did try and you misjudged their ability, this is the time to use grace and tell them that you saw that they really did try, and this time they will get neither a reward nor a punishment.

✻ I keep a box of interesting, educational items for my little people. Then I pull it out when I have to do something focused that does not include preschoolers, primarily when schooling the older ones. This box should not come out just anytime, to keep it special. Also, if you are limited in space and love to collect good picture books, rotate them by putting half of them away, and then exchange them occasionally for "new books". (Age 32)

✻ It is important to have a schedule of some sort. Sure, it must be flexible, but if you don't have one, you will have an even harder time getting anything accomplished.

✻ If you are using a traditional curriculum, consider that the workbooks are designed to keep children in a schoolroom busy while the teacher is doing something else. It is not necessary for your child to do every problem unless he needs the drill.

✶ Charts are a good way to keep track of progress. There are many kinds available and many more can be made. If you have a problem with something that you would like to see improved, it often works best to reward first, then when they have shown they can do something, it is time to use negative reinforcement.

✶ Look for blank charts in Part 3 to use as your creativity dictates.

Lunches

✶ Slushies-pureed fruit frozen in small containers are just right to eat by lunchtime and keep the other items in the lunch cold. (Recipe in Part 2)

✶ Individually wrapped baked goods from the freezer, such as Whoopie pies, cookies, etc.

✶ Make up sandwiches ahead of time, using a whole loaf of bread. Put them back into the bread bag and stick in the freezer, or put into baggies first.

✶ If there is an oven at school, make extra sloppy joe or barbecued hamburger and put it on buns and wrap in foil. Then they can be heated at school. Many other foods can be done that way as well. Pizza or pizza bread (piece of homemade bread, sauce and cheese), and other favorite sandwiches for the oven include pork roll, leftover turkey, beef or chicken, or ham. Just add a piece of cheese and you have a delicious hot sandwich.

✶ A favorite for our children is a slice of pizza, heated in the microwave at school.

✶ We pack our lunches the night before and put them in the refrigerator.

✶ I buy large bags of chips, pretzels or other snacks and then either one of the children or I put them in individual size bags and put them into a large container with a tight lid and freeze to keep fresh.

✶ We require each child to pack their own lunch using this rule of thumb: sandwich or hot item, fruit, baked item, and snack. I do check occasionally to be sure they have healthy and balanced lunches.

✶ Have each child clean up their lunch and put it away when arriving home from school.

✶ Canned Danish dessert (Recipe in Part 2) makes a nice change from just fruit and it stretches the costly fruit farther.

✶ We bake every Saturday and wrap the items and freeze them in a separate container "for lunches only" for the following week.

✶ We sometimes make enough sandwiches for the week and stick them in the freezer. In the morning just pop them in the lunch. It helps keep it cold and the sandwiches seem fresher. If you like lettuce, just slip some into the baggy before you put it into the lunch.

✶ Our children like pizza bagels for the toaster oven at school. You can make them ahead and freeze.

✶ Our children pack the lunches, but sometimes I leave a note with ideas on the counter before I go out to the barn to make it easier for them. Sometimes we pack some things the evening before.

✶ A toaster oven at school gives you many options: leftovers, cheese toasts, chicken patties, hot dogs, soft pretzels and more.

✶ Some drink options are: chocolate milk, grape juice, cider, and tea. I don't like to put drink mix in because it seems like sugar water with artificial coloring.

✶ Pack the same food items in lunches every day. It's easier to know when you are out of lunchbox items this way. It's also faster packing the lunches because you know when you have everything. For example: I usually pack 5 items; a drink, sandwich, canned or fresh fruit, cookies, and chips.

✶ I use menus for lunch packing, making it easy for our 3rd grade girl to pack the 6 lunches we need every day. My menu consists of 5 things; a sandwich or something for the microwave, a salty snack, something baked, a cup of fruit, and a drink. Bigger children just get bigger servings. Sample menus: Monday - sandwich, pretzels, cupcake, applesauce, chocolate milk. Tuesday - soup, chips, cookies, yogurt, and grape juice.

❋ A quick, easy lunch food is pizza bread. Take a piece of bread, spread with pizza sauce or ketchup, and sprinkle with cheese. Heat in a toaster oven at school.

❋ Since the man of the house carries a lunch box, our noon meals are quite simple. Yogurt is our favorite with fruit or honey and waffles. During the summer, sandwiches are greatly enjoyed - onions, lettuce, radishes, tomatoes, etc. During the winter, hearty soups, cooked grains, etc. keep us warmed and filled. We are homeschoolers.

Our son found a container of moldy pears in his lunch at school. Apparently someone found them in the refrigerator and didn't throw them out right away, so he grabbed the wrong container to put in his lunch. Imagine my chagrin when his sister in the same classroom reported that he showed it to all the students in the room!

40 —— Mops, Muffins, & Motherhood

Ready for Company

And he said, come in, thou blessed of the Lord; wherefore standest thou without? For I have prepared the house, and room for the camels.
Genesis 24:31

5. Ready for Company
Housework/Housecleaning

Are you ready for company anytime? Or do you need several weeks' notice so you can get your house in order? Do you shrink with embarrassment or run around "like a chicken with its head chopped off" (as my mother used to say) when a vehicle drives in when you least expect it? I have good childhood memories of that "ready for company" feeling when guests were invited for Sunday dinner. The house was cleaned up and the table set with china and glassware. Delicious smells and pretty desserts enticed our senses of smell and sight. We knew better than to get out the toys and clutter up the house before the guests arrived. Now I wonder; were we trying to pretend we always looked like that? As a mother now, I realize that likely no one was fooled into believing an active household with 7 children was always cleaned up or that the children always behaved like they did when company was there. It seems good to invite company every now and then so we get some of the corners cleaned out that get neglected other times. But if getting ready for company sends us into such a tizzy that both our children and our husbands groan about all the work and the snappy, hard-to-please Mom, it's time to re-evaluate what we're doing.

If you know ahead of time that company is coming, start your preparations early to avoid the last minute crimp on time. If you are serving a meal, plan the menu by what you have on hand. If you don't have time, keep it simple. There is nothing wrong with simple foods served in a modest home by a relaxed and smiling hostess. There is nothing wrong with serving special food to show your guests how special they are either, if you have the gift of hospitality and the time to prepare. We all have our special talents and should not try to outdo each other or feel inferior to women who have a talent in the area of making people feel at home. However, it is good for us to get out of our comfort zone and invite guests in occasionally, even if we feel we are dreadful at being a hostess. The key is to make the guests feel appreciated and at home. Since most of us don't serve six-course meals to our family, or have our houses spotless during everyday living, there simply is no need to wait to invite people into our homes until we can achieve that. If the hostess isn't comfortable, no one will be.

If you get caught with a messy house by an unexpected visitor, it is okay to apologize once. Only once! I try to stick to this rule, but find it rather difficult sometimes, especially depending on who caught me. The Bible says we are not to be a respecter of persons and sometimes I need to remind myself of that. I am convinced that everyone has a messy house at one time or another. You might know some women about whom you are pretty sure that you could go into their homes and open any drawer or closet or cupboard door and you would find everything neatly in place instead of having to put your arm up to protect yourself from whatever might fall out and hurt you (as you would in my house). That might be so, but I'm pretty sure that even they

42 — Mops, Muffins, & Motherhood

have times when (if you could just catch them at it!) they have at least a messy room or two. This again, is an area where we have to finally accept ourselves as we are. Instead of moaning and getting depressed because you just aren't good enough, step back and evaluate what you might do differently.

One of the areas I think can make the biggest difference in the hassle of keeping a home looking presentable is to declutter! I don't think that is actually a word, but you know what I mean! In the first place, when you are at the store or a yard sale (big culprits-yard sales and thrift stores!), if you don't need it- don't buy it! It doesn't matter how cheap it is, or how cute, or how nice, or how much your children will like it; every item you buy must be evaluated with the thought of whether you really want to dust it/clean around it/try to fit it into already overflowing cupboards/pick it up (how many pieces, how many times?). Sometimes it is a good idea to stop just before going through the check-out counter to look at what all you have in your cart and decide if you really need it/can afford it/want it. I have put many things back after I held them or had them in my cart when I came to my senses about just how this would fit into my budget and house, and whether I really wanted the extra burden it would bring with it.

With the availability of cheap toys and games, comes the temptation to buy too much for our children. I think sometimes I'm tempted to buy something not so much because my children want it, but because I am intrigued by it. Games and toys with small pieces should be avoided or at least pretty heavily controlled. We have found that Legos and K'nex are good educational pastimes, especially for our boys. They learn to follow directions and learn about structures and building. But all those small pieces can be quite a trial, especially to a big sister. Rules about where and when they may play with them help keep it under control. Homes with babies in them complicate things further since all those tiny pieces present a choking hazard. Keeping control of the toys we own, throwing out what is broken and giving away what doesn't fit into our family, is a good idea before buying new ones. It works well to keep only some toys out at any given time, storing the rest in the attic or a closet to rotate so they have "new" toys periodically. This avoids much clutter from having too many toys around at once.

Teaching the children to put their things away when they are finished with them, is better than teaching them to help clean the house up when it is a mess later. This is a constant battle since it is human nature to drop things where they are and move on to the next thing. You as mother should set a good example in this, but Daddy gets the privilege of having others clean up after him. It is nice if he is neat, but it will cause friction in the marriage if you are constantly nagging him.

General

✻ For Saturday cleaning, make a list with all jobs included. Take turns choosing a job, crossing it off, doing it, then coming back to see the list dwindling.

✻ Clean that dirty soap dish, smudged wall, etc. right when you see it instead of waiting till cleaning day. Training yourself to keep after those little things can give you such a lift!

✻ Give little children a dust rag while dusting and assign them a corner.

✻ Keep a rag box handy for all those quick clean up jobs.

✻ As you move from room to room during your day, make it a habit to pick up things to put away in the room you are going into next. It takes some effort to remember at first, but after a while it is such a habit you will hardly be aware that you are even doing it.

❋ Each of our children ages 4-15 have an assigned room they must tidy up each day, usually after school. It rotates on a monthly basis, and I help the 4 year old.

❋ Accept it. Self-discipline is a big factor here and we're not all alike. Know what you and your family are comfortable with, especially your husband.

❋ I like to do my morning work. After breakfast it's time to clear table, wash the dishes, sweep the floor, maybe a general pickup of clutter, and making the beds. Then I'm ready to do other things.

❋ The upstairs gets done when Mom decides it is necessary, usually when you can't walk around up there without falling over something!

❋ I have found the fewer knick-knacks and other extras I have, the less I have to look at that is most likely dusty.

❋ It makes the weekly cleaning much easier if you simply tidy up the house each evening before going to bed. When you energize 7 people for a quick clean up, things can get done pretty fast.

❋ We have a small room for toys and I'll admit that it is a good place to put them and close the door in the evening. But on Saturdays we usually sort things into their containers and restore order and guess what? It's new to the little ones again.

❋ Years ago, as a young mother, I took an Emily Barnes Workshop. She shared something that day that impacted me and I still use it. When you have that certain closet, attic, room, or cupboard that is bothering you and you feel overwhelmed about cleaning it, set a timer for 15 minutes and then start cleaning. It isn't quite so overwhelming when you know you can stop after 15 minutes, but many times I had the lift I needed to finish the whole project, because the biggest obstacle was my mindset. However, if I did get interrupted after 15 minutes, that was okay too, because I had met my goal. (Age 44)

❋ Each of the children is expected to help clean up the bedroom they sleep in each week.

❋ Face it. Where there are children there are toys and clutter. We don't want to be too perfect, either. I remember having one or two children and feeling like everything has to be put away if company's coming. After having several more, I've learned it is fine to have things out. We have been doing something.

❋ After-meal chores at our house are done on a weekly rotating schedule. Each child (including the boys since we don't have many outside chores) takes a turn to wash dishes, dry dishes, clear the table, clean up the house, or sweep the kitchen floor. Four- and five-year-olds can work with an older sibling, then by the time they are 6 they go into "the system". When you have enough children, they get a week off.

❋ Unexpected company coming and the house is a mess? I have already filled a wash basket with dirty dishes and put them in a closet. If you keep after as a whole, you can make things presentable on short notice, but if you are sick or something... Well, this is how it is. You can tell them that sometimes it's even worse!

❋ John Deere Carpet Stain Remover spray can take almost any kind of stain out of a carpet. You need to buy it at a John Deere dealership or tractor supply store.

❋ Always clean up your main family/play room before you go to bed. Have your dishes done as well. Who wants to start the day with things that should have been done the day before? The biggest thing I had to learn was to get up before the children and get my day started. You get so much more done in the early morning hours. Then if you get your work done, and you're tired, lie down and rest and don't feel guilty about it. (Age 38)

❋ I do not allow toys in my kitchen unless they are being played with right at that moment. Usually all

44 — Mops, Muffins, & Motherhood

toys stay in the living room, bedroom, or basement. Cleanup is so much easier and I am not constantly tripping over toys.

✻ I'm a disorganized person who has learned to not lay things just anywhere. When you pick something up, put it where it belongs right away.

✻ Look at a messy room not as a whole, but in parts-one child picks up all the books, one picks up all the trash, one puts all the shoes away, etc. This brings a mountain down to a molehill!

✻ Keep the quantity of toys at a minimum; this results in less clean up and frustration. You can put half of them away and switch them every two weeks or so. (Age 64)

✻ We need to accept that not everything will get done - keep the children more important than the work!

✻ Assign a room to each child that they must clean every week. It is easier to teach them to do one room right than to teach every child how to do every room.

✻ Have the children pick up toys twice a day; before they eat lunch and before they go to bed.

✻ I am still working on the clutter part. Organization is not my strength. All I know is that I feel so much better and able to cope if my house is in order and not a mess. It helps you to be a better mom when you feel organized. (Age 37)

✻ As far as clutter, I am a cleaning person at heart, but I did and still do have what we call an "up the stairs basket". It is just a basket at the foot of the stairs where we put things that need to be upstairs. Then the next time you go up, you gather the things in the basket and take them along and put them away. This keeps things in place downstairs and cuts down on the clutter. (Age 44)

✻ When you just don't have time for weekly cleaning, try this to get things looking pretty good with a minimum of effort: run the sweeper in the kitchen and family room (the dirtiest places),

declutter the house a bit, and run a paper towel over your bathroom sink and over and around the toilet.

✻ Don't throw all the toys in one place. Use bins, totes, baskets and any other kind of organizing containers. This way even the littlest ones can put animals in the animal bin, etc. I put shoe boxes in their clothing drawers to keep the socks, underwear, and slips separated. (Hey, it sounds good on paper. This doesn't mean they always have neat and tidy drawers, though.) (Age 35)

✻ When your children are young, show them how to pick up toys and help them until they can do it by themselves. If you have room, put similar toys in separate plastic containers; matchbox cars, Legos, doll clothes, etc. If the children want to play with the Legos, they can get that container out without having to empty out the entire toy box just to find them all. (Age 38)

✻ Be careful what you buy. Is there a place to put/store it, or will it add to the cluttered feeling? When our children beg for something, I tell them we will write it down and think about it for Christmas or a birthday gift. In a matter of weeks they often no longer want that particular item. Who is setting the standard for how your home looks? Are you following friends or magazines? May your home be an inviting place where your children will want to bring their friends in the years to come.

✻ Allow children to be children and not little adults. Teach them to help with chores and that we all work together. For example, when the toys are picked up, we will go for a walk. If you will help me put away the socks, I will read you a book. We work together/play together/pray together.

✻ I like to have a plan for each day. Do laundry on Monday and Thursday, go grocery shopping Tuesday or Wednesday, and do the cleaning on Friday. That leaves Saturday with no big jobs, which leaves it free to tie up the loose ends that didn't get done earlier in

Ready for Company — 45

the week. I hopefully never end up too far behind on the really necessary things of the week. I feel free to do other things when the job of the day is completed.

❋ Write down everything that needs to be done. It keeps your mind freer and you don't forget to do things as easily. I keep a notebook in the kitchen, and at the beginning of the week, I write everything down that I can think of and then add to it as the week goes on. (Age 29)

❋ I have no advice. I still haven't figured it out. ☺

❋ Take a nap if needed, and work time will be much more productive! As you sink down onto the sofa, remember that, "He gently leads those that are with young", and know that He is cradling you, a tired, weary mother.

❋ Plan weekday meals 1 to 6 weeks in advance; although you can be flexible if you need to be. In the morning look what's for supper that night and you can be thinking about it/preparing it all day. This avoids that in-the-background-all-day nagging thought that finally comes to the forefront at the last minute, "Now what IS for supper?" (Age 37)

❋ Our penny pile was a very successful way to help cut down on clutter. On Saturday each girl was given a pile of ten pennies. Throughout the week if I found any of their belongings that had not been put away, I would remove a penny from the offender's pile. On Saturday, they could trade each penny that was left for a dime. Some have questioned the wisdom of paying to be good. However, how often in Scripture does God promise a reward for obedience?? (Age 71)

❋ One thing I have done for years is take the last half hour before Daddy comes home from work, and have chore time. There are certain things that get done every day at that time of day, such as; pick up toys, sweep the floor, set the table, empty the dishwasher, etc. Then when Daddy gets home, he appreciates everything cleaned up and nice for him.

It has become a great habit; my children just know what happens at 4:30. When they were all little, it sometimes felt like I didn't have much good help, but they were learning. Now they can go ahead and I can work on getting supper ready.

❋ Try never to go to bed with a messy house; it isn't pleasant to start the day in disarray.

❋ Lists are my favorite for getting my children to help with the work. Sometimes we take turns choosing jobs until they are all taken and then getting to work. Other times we do one job then come back and choose another one until they are all gone. We choose by putting our initials behind the job. Save some jobs for yourself but you might be busy with, "Mom, what shall I do with this?" and keeping the pokey one moving. The older children need to do more of the jobs than the younger ones.

❋ Clutter and being disorganized is a big thing to me right now. One of the small steps I'm taking is having all toys picked up before nap time, before bed time, and before daddy comes home for supper. Having scheduled jobs is something I am working on at our house. (Age 29)

❋ For every new toy or stuffed animal, give one away.

My standard answer to someone who says, "I only have two and they drive me crazy!" is, "You need half a dozen more!" They usually have to admit that it would have to change something.

46 — Mops, Muffins, & Motherhood

❋ My children like when I make a treasure hunt for our Saturday cleaning. I have a list of the chores that need to be done. Half the chores are written on paper, cut into pieces, then hidden, one at each of the other jobs. When they are doing the job they picked, they will find a slip of paper that tells them what to do next. Then they again choose a new job from the list until everything is done. It takes more time for Mom but cheerful helpers get work done faster!

❋ Stay at home as much as possible and do your work. If someone stops by on a "bad" day, don't apologize, everyone has those days. It helps keeps us humble.

❋ This challenge always worked with my children, "I can pick up faster than you can," or "I can pick up more than you can." Make a game out of cleaning up. (Age 34)

❋ Hide some pennies under the clutter. As they clean up, they may keep what they find. This really can make quick cleanup of a mess.

❋ Lists really help my children get their work done without much keeping after them. They like to cross the items off the list.

❋ I remember being told that you only have your children once; your work will be with you forever. Give your children the time they need when they are young. I've also heard it said that you should not do for your children what they can do for themselves. The sooner you teach your children to help you, the sooner life gets easier.

❋ Make lists of jobs for each child. That way each one knows exactly what they are expected to do. Sometimes I write the jobs on paper, cut them apart, and fold them, numbering them on the outside in the order I want them done. The child then picks them out and does them in the order they are numbered. Each child has their own pile. To make it more fun you can mix in some fun things like: Run around the house, do 10 jumping jacks, sing a song, read for 10 minutes, do flash cards for 10 minutes.

❋ Have a snack together when all the jobs are done.

❋ I loved the book *More Hours in my Day* by Emily Barnes. Being organized was very high on my list of things to improve, and this book helped me keep things more manageable. I was one to live by lists, charts, and plans, especially the 2 years I homeschooled. For me it worked, for others it won't. (Age 44)

❋ Don't have a lot of pretty stuff around that you have to constantly keep nagging your child not to touch.

❋ Teach them to clean up as they go. If you get the crayons out to color, put them away before you go on to the next project.

❋ At certain times, like when we had a new baby, I found that if the family had food to eat and clean clothes to wear, pretty much anything else was optional. My motto: "Cleaning and scrubbing can wait till tomorrow, but babies grow up, we have learned to our sorrow. So quiet down cobwebs; dust, go to sleep. I'm rocking my baby, and babies don't keep!" (Age 58)

❋ One lady said she always tried to keep at least one room clutter free, so she could feel sane in that room at least. I tried to do that and often it was the bathroom. I loved a neatly picked up bathroom-who feels good with hair on the floor or vanity, and towels and clothes dropped wherever? Sometimes I took a long "potty break" just to enjoy the neat room. And my bedroom was a must, too. Maybe it's just me, but I have a passion for keeping "our" room uncluttered and straightened up. It seemed more like a haven at the end of the day, and I think my husband liked it, too. It was "our space", BUT this doesn't mean I dusted it every week, just kept it free from clutter. Dusting happened about twice a month at our house and still does. (Age 42)

Ready for Company — 47

✻ I hate getting up to a messy house in the morning, so we start cleaning up about 7:00 PM, and then they read books to keep themselves occupied until bedtime.

✻ We don't have a big house, but each child that is old enough is in charge of one room for weekly cleaning.

✻ Our favorite quick-clean-up is to set the timer for 10 minutes, and see how many things we can set to rights before it beeps, or we have each child put away 25 things that are out of place. Even 2 and 3 year olds can help with a little guidance.

✻ I try to get the children to clean up the living room every evening before bedtime stories.

✻ We use what we call a Prison Box. If the children let their things where they don't belong, I pick them up and drop them in the box. Sometimes the rule is they must do a job or some type of work to get it back. Other times they must pay money.

✻ Print on paper everything that has to be done for a job and tape it in the room where it is not very noticeable. For example, to clean the living room: 1. Pick up all the toys 2. Pick up all the trash 3. Straighten up anything else. 4. Empty the trash can 5. Dust 6. Vacuum. The child is not finished with the job until he has done everything on the list.

✻ As for keeping your house tidy (some of us are not "natural-born" organizers), I heard someone give this piece of advice: Every day take 2-5 minutes per room to tidy up that room. Your children are more important than a house that is perfectly tidy all the time. Some day when your children are grown up, you may have a "perfectly" tidy house. (Unless you are blessed to have grandchildren nearby to take up where your children left off!) (Age 39)

✻ For young mothers, especially, it is important to remember that the children come first. They are more important than getting your housecleaning done regularly, so make sure all their needs are met first - physically, emotionally, and spiritually. I often just clean a corner where it is direly needed or a room some time when I have a little extra time or am inspired, or when it gets so bad it takes priority.

✻ Place relationships above work. This means spending more time with your child than scrubbing your kitchen floor. Children do not care about the dirt; it's the moms who do. I still remember when this first struck me. I visited a friend who was very busy with little people. Her house was nothing special, you could tell she didn't spend time decorating and she said she does not get much cleaning done. But posted on her wall was a framed paper that had "rules" for their home, and the one that stood out to me was to put people and relationships above work. I believe she really lived by that; she was more concerned about her children's character than a nice house. I often think about her as I clean my house. For me, it can also relate to fussing over clothes for my girls. Does it really matter as long as they are neat and modest? (Age 31)

✻ As I go through the living room (or any room), I like to keep my eyes open for objects that don't belong there and make it a point of putting them away, especially if they belong in the kitchen and I'm on my way there.

✻ Get the little ones to quickly put away their toys and books before nap time. If I'm in a hurry to have a mess cleaned up, I set the timer for 15 minutes and the children pick up and put away as many pieces as possible. Competition usually motivates them.

✻ The children enjoy if I write jobs on slips of paper, then they draw one slip at a time, finishing one job before picking the next one. For little ones who can't read yet, make simple sketches (i.e. squares for folding handkerchiefs or washcloths). Save the slips to use again another day.

✻ There's nothing more applicable to keeping a (relatively) neat house than the saying "A place for

48 —— Mops, Muffins, & Motherhood

everything and everything in its place". It's easier to put it away right away, even though it might mean a few more steps now, rather than cleaning up a big mess all at once, and maybe when I'm in a hurry.

✽ Although I don't enjoy getting up to dishes in the sink or a cluttered house, sometimes I'd still rather ignore the mess and go to bed for a good night's sleep. I usually feel energized and ready to tackle it in the morning. I know this isn't the "right" way to do things, but I don't fit into the perfect mold in other ways either!

✽ Don't always feel like you need to have everything together, and be humble enough to accept help if you need it.

✽ "Cleaning while the children are growing is like shoveling snow while it's still snowing"! But try to teach them not to put "snow" back on where you already "shoveled". Put misplaced items in a box and have them sweep the kitchen floor or some similar job before they can have it back.

✽ Laundry baskets are valuable tools in cleaning up a house quickly. Take one (and a trash can) with you as you go from room to room to throw things into that don't belong in that room. But don't forget to clean the laundry basket out later! This is a good job for children; they can take it from place to place and "deliver" things where they belong.

✽ Have children pick up 20 (or 40) things each. It's amazing how quickly a room can be cleaned up.

✽ Dishes- Here are the rules at this house. If the dishwasher (in this case it is usually Mom) catches up to the table clearers, they have to wash the dishes also. If the dish dryer is too slow, and the washer doesn't have room to put things on the drying rack, the dryer has to wash dishes also. If the dishwasher is too slow and the dryer catches up to him, he may go and the dishwasher has to dry if he needs more room on the dish rack. (Usually the one washing dishes doesn't call

the dryer until the rack is pretty well filled.) All this together makes a pretty fast job of the dishes (too fast sometimes), and it sure beats the dawdling around that takes place otherwise. If Mom is the dish washer it just doesn't take long to get the job done.

✽ If at all possible, try to do the dishes immediately after finishing eating. The longer it goes, the worse the job gets.

✽ If you have a shortage of time and help to get that dishwashing job done, have each child take his dishes to the sink where you have hot, soapy water all prepared. They shall each wash their own dishes and maybe those of a younger sibling or Dad's. Mom or an older child can put away the food and wash up what's left pretty quickly.

✽ Try assigning jobs by the week. This also avoids the constant "Whose turn is it?" syndrome. Or certain jobs are one person's duty until he grows out of it or the next one grows into it. At our home it is the same person's job to take out the garbage most every time (unless I specifically ask someone else to do it). The same person usually has to empty the dishwasher, etc.

✽ For Saturday morning cleaning try this: take a piece of paper and write down all the jobs that need to be done. If it is a big job, write it twice. Consider the age of your children when deciding what jobs to add. Now you can have each child pick a job, have them go and finish it, let them have the pleasure of crossing it off the list, then have them pick a new one and so on until the list is finished. You may want to offer a small reward when they are done. Or you can cut the list into strips with one job per strip, folding them so they can't be read and then have the children take turns picking the slips. If a child picks a job he is too young to handle, he just folds it back up and puts it back in then picks another one instead. When a child has finished all his jobs he is then free to do something else. We do allow them to trade jobs

Ready for Company — 49

if they wish. Each child must do first the jobs that would keep someone else from finishing theirs, such as the one who has to pick up toys must do it first so the one who has to vacuum can do his job.

✽ Dry erase boards or blackboards work well for keeping track of who is supposed to do what. Jot jobs down that need to be done when they come home from school, so you don't forget. How many times do you remember again the next day when they're in school again?

✽ One thing that helped me keep organized was my kitchen notebook. It was just a plain notebook and I would make a "to do" list in it for the day. It was great fun to cross things off the list. I would put very simple things on my list, such as; empty drainer, empty dishwasher, comb the girls' hair, comb my hair, etc. That way I could cross off at least some things! Because some days that is all you get done-the necessities. I also used this notebook to jot down birthday ideas, phone messages, or other things I needed a place for as I went through my day. It can help you keep focused on your tasks for that day and prevent you from getting sidetracked. (Age 34)

✽ I usually wash the dishes, but sometimes during extra busy times I will ask for a volunteer. After they have done it, they write their name on the calendar on that date. The next time one of the other children must take a turn, until they all have had a turn. This idea can be used for other jobs as well.

✽ My children don't clean their own rooms, but I have found that if they each have a wash basket and hooks in their rooms it helps to keep it neater. But remember if the clothes aren't on the hook, it's because the hook didn't catch it when it was tossed there!

✽ Doing weekly or biweekly dusting and sweeping helps to stay ahead of the dirt. Just staying at home as much as possible helps, too.

✽ Have the children take turns being "mother's helper", one per day. This is the person who does all those little running jobs; when you need something in the basement or freezer, dirty clothes to the hamper, a drink for a little one, get the mail, peel the potatoes, etc. You can write their names on a calendar to keep track of whose turn it is. Of course you have the right to ask any of the children to do anything at any time and they should respond.

✽ Although we don't pay our children for working on a regular basis, or even give them an allowance, we do occasionally pay for a big job well done. For instance, if we have a big corn freezing day, we might tell them if they have the corn husked by a certain time, they will each get a certain amount of money. Obviously, the one who doesn't help well will get his money reduced or lose it altogether. This encourages teamwork. No tattling should be allowed and the challenge can be for them to work together for a common goal. Another way to motivate them is to promise a picnic, a trip to the park, or something like that to be done at a later date.

✽ Have children pick up a certain number of things, according to the condition of the room(s) you want cleaned up and the ages of the children. Complaining or delaying can add to the number required for the complainer. Our oldest was smart enough to realize that if she got busy right away, she could pick up the easiest pieces. This worked like a charm, since the others soon caught on and dove right in and worked as fast as possible. Sometimes it is necessary to add to the number if the look of the room isn't as desired when they have picked up the allotted amount of things.

✽ If you don't have time to do much, just grab the broom and sweep the kitchen floor and clean it up.

✽ Clean off the table & stack dishes quickly if you can't wash dishes right now.

50 —— Mops, Muffins, & Motherhood

✳ Try to have the room that people enter when they come into your home, relatively clean; it can save a lot of embarrassment. Try to avoid having the toy box in this room if possible; it will get less messy that way.

✳ A quick cleaning tip we have used in our home is to have each child pick up ___ (you pick the number) toys, shoes, etc. and put them away. When the children are younger, they will need help with the counting, and it definitely helps their motivation to see you helping. When they are older, the children can work at it together without you. It is a fun method for the children most of the time; although sometimes it is necessary to make sure they put the things where they belong. (Age 33)

✳ I think sometimes that when I tell my children to clean up, they think that means to take things off the floor and put them "up" somewhere, anywhere, rather than putting them where they belong. I have found some things at some pretty odd places already.

✳ Rotate toys so some are "new" and there are fewer to pick up at any given time. Store the rest in the attic or closet where they aren't very accessible. Or trade toys with another family for a while.

✳ Wash windows when they are not in full sun, this will reduce streaking.

✳ Coming downstairs in the morning and seeing a cluttered house was just very discouraging to me.

My sister and her family came to visit for several days. As they were going out the door to go home, our 5-year-old son said, "Mom, are you glad they're leaving?"

Toys and all other clutter picked up before bedtime helped me start my day off in a much better frame of mind. (Age 67)

✳ Wipe counters, toilet etc. in the bathroom with the paper towel you use to clean the mirror. This will get the fine dirt and lint, and leave a shine.

✳ Use bicycle hooks for coats, with a shelf above and a small basket for each child for gloves, caps, and other small things.

✳ My favorite cleaner is Clorox Cleanup. It takes grape stains and others off the kitchen counters, and it cuts grease really well. I especially like it on and around the toilet in the bathroom, especially if you have boys with bad aim!

✳ It is a good idea to periodically tip the chairs and sofas towards the front to clean up all the things that have slipped under them. This will save extreme embarrassment if for some reason you have to do it when someone is there to see that you haven't done it in a while. It is quite amazing what all resurfaces under them, including food that had no business in the living room in the first place! (So that is where that peculiar smell came from.)

✳ Magic erasers are a sponge-type cleaning tool that can be bought in the cleaning section at the store and are an excellent way to get marks off walls and floors and other hard surfaces. There are off-brand ones available at less cost. These work really well at removing shoe marks on linoleum.

✳ A good vacuum cleaner is helpful in keeping carpets clean. A beater type head helps to fluff up carpets and does a better job of getting the dirt out.

✳ Remember this acronym-K.I.S.S. Keep It Simple, Sister. Less is more. The fewer unnecessary items that clutter your life, the better you can manage what is left. And the more time you will have for what is really important in life. The more "stuff" you have, the less likely you are to know what you have when you need it. There is a saying "What is the use of knowing all you know, if you don't know you know it, when you need to know it?" With a little modification, I think this also applies to household items and clothing, "What is the use of owning everything you own, if you don't know you own it, when you need it?"

✽ Here's another acronym to help you; "The OHIO Method"- Only Handle It Once. If you have something in your hand, put it where it belongs instead of putting it down wherever you happen to be.

Kitchen

✽ To make the job more manageable, I clean the refrigerator one shelf at a time. The first one when I do breakfast dishes, one at noon, and one with supper dishes.

✽ Try to clean all the counters off at least once a day to avoid buildup that looks overwhelming.

✽ We try to clean up every day with after-the-meal chores. We keep track with a monthly chart, that way everyone can remember better exactly what to do when the meal is over.

✽ When I don't have time to wash dishes before leaving the house, I try very hard to at least get the table completely cleared - it helps a lot for the looks of the kitchen.

✽ Keep two brooms in the kitchen for two children to sweep at once. This creates a goal by "who sweeps what part" by who starts first.

✽ After our meal is over, one child counts it a privilege to get out of doing dishes by cleaning up the floor of toys and miscellanea.

✽ We're dairy farmers and I almost always stack the supper dishes in the sink so I can read a bedtime story to the whole family. Then we talk. The next morning I do supper and breakfast dishes together. Do not just let them pile up!

✽ All those monotonous chores must be done daily; do the dishes and other work with your children.

✽ Dirty dishes on the counter are depressing!! Take a few minutes to wash them right away. The children can clear their own dishes when they leave the table. Works great! Yes, there are 20 things that should be done now….but it takes a lot longer to wash dishes after the food is dried on for hours.

✽ Mom is often in charge of the kitchen. I choose to remove as many "unnecessaries" as possible from my work area.

✽ To avoid the "not enough clean cups" scenario at mealtime, we purchased stainless steel cups with handles and personalized one for each child with an engraver, then hung them on their own hooks screwed into the bottom of the kitchen cabinet. Now whose fault is it if your cup is not around? This also seems to help halt the spread of sickness when it comes to our door.

✽ Cupboards - I keep most of my bulk foods in labeled glass jars, from pint to gallon size. It not only looks neater, but also saves time otherwise spent stirring through a disarray of plastic bags, etc. trying to find the one I need. This is my substitution for expensive Tupperware organizers. Spices in shakers are kept in a small low box so I can bring the whole box down to eye level and quickly find what I need. A rack for my various culinary herbs is helpful when cooking.

✽ A grain mill has been a helpful addition to our kitchen. We use a variety of grains.

✽ A big help in keeping the kitchen presentable is to clean off all the clutter from the counters every evening. It gives me a lift when I get up in the morning.

✽ It works best to discipline myself to clear away all the dishes right after a meal, sweep the kitchen floor and make sure the counters are all clear. Don't

52 — Mops, Muffins, & Motherhood

let dishes set from one meal to another; it's doubly discouraging to do it then! If I must do something else right away, I try to at least stack the dishes in the sink and run water over them so they don't get dried on. It's good to start the morning early enough that the school children have time to do the dishes before leaving for school.

✳ Plan a schedule for kitchen chores, don't go by who did it last; because they will forget (sometimes they all washed dishes last!) I assign certain days a week to always be theirs for specific jobs.

✳ It seems our kitchen trash can is always full and overflowing. It helps to keep a 33 gallon or larger trash can with a tight-fitting lid in a nearby room such as mudroom or laundry or a covered porch. Then put the larger pieces such as cardboard and plastic containers into it right away instead of filling up the kitchen trash can.

Housecleaning

✳ Why do we houseclean? It is just a good idea to deep clean each room once in a while. I well remember when it was almost mandatory to houseclean the entire house from attic to cellar twice a year. Certainly every good Mennonite and Amish woman did it or she would have been considered almost slothful! I'm sure many still do it that way, but many mothers have admitted that they no longer do it twice a year, or maybe not the whole house every time. Some do one job in several rooms at once, such as washing windows. Others do one whole room at a time.

✳ Years ago, housecleaning was done spring and fall. In the spring because coal/wood stoves left soot on ceilings, especially in kitchens. In the fall because windows didn't have screens and the fly dirt needed to be wiped off the ceilings and walls.

Those of us who don't have wood or coal stoves probably do not need to do housecleaning as frequently or thoroughly as those who do.

✳ I rarely tackle housecleaning the whole house at one time, but do it at different times throughout the year—one room at a time.

✳ The rooms in our house get housecleaned when Mom decides they are dirty enough! (Whenever she can't stand it anymore.) ☺

✳ Housecleaning at this house is done in the summertime when the woodstove is not being used and I have a "full crew" because of school being out for the summer. I start weeks ahead by eliminating unnecessary items, outgrown clothes, etc. Then tear the room apart, scrub walls, wash windows and floor and place the furniture where you want it.

✳ I houseclean when I can't stand my messy house anymore. Break it down into manageable pieces; maybe one room a week, or all the windows, or certain drawers.

✳ I do major housecleaning once a year, usually fall/winter. I do the windows before it gets too cold, but everything else can be cleaned in the winter. I don't wash off all the ceilings, just the laundry, kitchen, and living room where most of the fly dirt is. I use my kitchen table to stand on and can clean a large area at one time. I use a ladder in the laundry since it is small. I wipe off all walls, clean lights, and mottos and pictures. Clean out closets and drawers; then organize them. Finish up by cleaning the floor and putting furniture back in place. In the spring I'll go over things quickly; maybe lights and windows, clean out the kitchen cupboards again, wash up under the stove and refrigerator, etc. And when a mom is really busy… it doesn't matter if she skips housecleaning, does it? We can still be tidy. There's a big difference in people. Accept yourself, be cheerful and happy, or get a maid to help if possible.

Ready for Company — 53

❊ Each child has their own dresser with one drawer for "treasures". Housecleaning time is when they go through and eliminate "stuff" and organize their drawer. Otherwise I strive to keep rooms free of clutter. When 4 girls share a small bedroom and 3 boys likewise, there isn't room for extra clutter, or it makes me feel like pushing walls out for more room!

❊ If you have a cordless phone, it is possible to clean and organize cupboards while having a conversation.

❊ When planning to houseclean a room, wash the windows inside and out the day before. Or sweep down the walls and ceiling. You can do more rooms in less time if you do some of the work the day before.

❊ I do my housecleaning in the winter, when we aren't so busy with other things.

❊ I enjoy washing the curtains and cleaning the windows as I have time, and then do the rest of the room at another time. Closets and drawers wait for snowy days!

❊ I try to houseclean once a year, usually winter/spring. I do a couple rooms together such as curtains and windows one day, closets and cupboards another, and then clean the rest.

❊ Maybe when we find it too hard to accomplish our housecleaning, the problem is that we have too much "stuff". Trying to "keep up with the Joneses" can be the cause of emotional and financial stress, if our homes must be just so-so because we think everyone else's is.

Once, a shop customer came to the house while we were eating a meal. He looked at our family plus six cousins seated around our big kitchen table. He studied a bit then blurted out, "Are these all your children?!"

54 —— Mops, Muffins, & Motherhood

Flapping in the Breeze

And ye shall wash your clothes on the seventh day, and ye shall be clean... Numbers 31:24a

6. Flapping in the Breeze

Laundry

Laundry is one of those never-ending jobs that mothers must deal with. How you handle it will depend on the quantity of dirty clothing your family produces, what kind of washer you have, and where you live. Talking to mothers about the kind of washer they use brings some interesting observations. Wringer washers are not completely out of style. If you have a washhouse or somewhere else you can use one, you will find it is faster and some think it does a better job of getting the laundry clean, especially heavily soiled clothing. Although it is faster, you must stay with it and can't do much else while you are washing. It is a bit more difficult with a baby, too. The clothes aren't wrung out as well so it takes more time for them to dry. Some people put the clean, wet clothes through the spin cycle of their automatics to wring them out better. There are spinners available to do this job as well. Front load automatics are generally energy efficient. They take less water and soap. Less soap can be a savings, but less water isn't as important if you have your own well, although it does cost you something to heat your water. Most front load washers have a fairly long load cycle so it takes longer to run a load through, although many of them will hold bigger loads. Top loaders have been the standard for many years. They are available in regular, heavy-duty, suds saver, or energy efficient. After trying different kinds of washers, I am about convinced that for mothers in the country with lots of children, a heavy duty top loader or a wringer washer is the best. It just takes water and soap to get dirty clothing clean! Suds savers are getting harder to find, but some mothers really like theirs. When you go to buy a washer, be aware that the salesman is going to tell you what he's been told. Most of them don't understand the sheer volume of laundry some of us put through our washers. With six boys, we put 5-7 loads of jeans through per week. That is besides all the regular laundry, bedding, etc. Energy efficiency operates on less soap and water and they really push that, but you need to consider if that is really all that important to you. When they talk about the warranty and life expectancy of the washers, they are talking about the average American family of 1.5 children who hardly know what dirty clothes are!

Nothing beats the fresh smell of clothing dried on a wash line in the sun and breeze. However, the look on your face may be quite different if the neighbor (or your husband) chose laundry day to haul manure! A little smell of wood smoke is pleasant, but if it blows over the clean laundry all day, it can be overpowering. A dryer can be an important appliance if you are unable to hang laundry out to dry. Although it is a little hard to think of the extra money it takes to run a dryer, sometimes it is the best choice for your circumstances. We must not let what we think other peoples' opinions are get in the way of what works best for us. Sometimes it is presented as a virtue to pinch every penny by doing everything as cheaply as possible, when we actually end up cutting the family short because of what we think we must do to save

56 — Mops, Muffins, & Motherhood

money. Having said that, it is likely that most of us could be more saving in one area or another.

If you have space in the house, you can string clothesline to hang the wash up to dry. This works especially well if you have a basement or other little-used room. Run the lines parallel to each other and hang the laundry from one line to the next instead of along the line. Although this takes more pins, it saves on space. Setting a fan to blow up under the clothes speeds the drying process. If you have a wood stove or hot air heat, drying the laundry in the house in the winter helps put moisture into the air. Wooden drying racks are available in many sizes. Even small children can hang washcloths and other small pieces up to dry. Good shirts and dresses take less space and wrinkle less if put on hangers when they come out of the washer. Socks and other small pieces can be hung on "pin things" (look for an illustration on the next page), and hung indoors or out to dry.

A laundry chute is a useful addition to any home with bedrooms upstairs and laundry room on the main floor, or if the laundry is done in the basement. They can be built into the wall and save many steps. I pull the laundry out at the bottom of the chute and sort jeans, shirts and towels out as I put the rest into a wash basket. I have two washers and I start them both as soon as I have full loads for them. I can then move on to other morning chores before coming back and sorting the rest. I use baskets to sort clothing. Each basket holds about one load, so it keeps the laundry from being strewn all over the floor and getting mixed up while waiting for its turn in the washer. I will often wait until several loads are ready to be hung up before going out to do it, since there are usually many other jobs to do meanwhile. During the summer the children each have to help hang up a load or two. Hanging up laundry is a good job for children even if they don't think so. It takes a bit of supervision to get it done properly at first. It works best if you can accept the way things are hung up. With boys especially, it can sometimes be quite interesting to see how they place the clothes and pins on the line!

* Buy the same kind of boys' socks (of the same size) each time, that way when one wears out (or gets lost), the other one can be matched to a different one from the same pack. This also simplifies matching socks after washing them. Buy different kinds of socks for different sizes so you can see at a glance which ones belong together. For instance, buy grey-tipped socks for one size, all white ones for another, etc.

* If your boys are close enough to one age, they may be able to wear the same size socks and underwear.

* Use dots to tell one child's clothing from the next. I have 6 boys and the oldest one gets 1 dot, the second one 2 dots, etc. I use a Sharpie permanent marker and mark the jeans on the inside on the white part of the left pocket, shirts on the tag (if it's not too dark) or the back neckline. Be sure the marker doesn't bleed through. Socks can be marked at the toe. As one boy outgrows his clothes, just add a dot. It also makes it easier for others who might help you by folding your laundry. I assume this can also be used for girls' clothes, although I don't have girls close enough in age to need it.

* Use hampers or baskets (preferably stacking) for sorting wash. If you use colored hampers, children can be taught at a young age to sort wash. Whites in the white hamper, jeans in the blue one, nighties in the green one, etc.

* I have two washers which have greatly cut down on my laundry time. Look at sales for a good used washer. Front loaders generally have a bigger load capacity, get clothes cleaner and are

more economical to run since they use less water and soap than standard washers. We were told that washers are designed to last a maximum of 6 years, so sometimes used washers are a better bargain. If you buy new, look for the best warranty. Good soap is also important for clean laundry. The cheapest isn't always the least costly when you consider how much you have to use and whether it does a good job. Hard water will cause your clothes to look dingy and it might pay in soap savings to install a water softener.

❋ Clotheslines are the cheapest way to dry clothes. Pulley lines are nice if you can fasten the one end on the porch, but still out of the way. You need to be careful which direction you put them (north/south or east/west) because of wrapping clothes around the line, making it very difficult to bring in the laundry. Pulleys for washlines are available at many hardware and/or Amish or Mennonite owned stores.

❋ A clothespin apron can be made by first making a half apron then adding one extra-large pocket across the front into which to put the clothespins. Clothespin bags are also very handy, and can be as simple as a rectangular piece of cloth with an opening at the top and a hanger to hang it from the line, or as elaborate as one that looks like a baby dress with the bottom sewed shut.

❋ For drying socks, hankies, and other small items you can make or buy what we call a "pin thing". These can be made in various ways. One way is a wire clothes hanger with a triangular cloth covering it. When you sew the seam that will be at the bottom of the hanger, add little loops of fabric, ribbon, or anything narrow so they hang out the bottom after you turn the fabric over the hanger. Then fasten clothespins with string or keychain chain to these loops. These hangers can be hung out on the wash line or inside the house during inclement weather. A bigger version of the "pin thing" is a bicycle tire rim turned on its side and chains attached through holes drilled evenly spaced (either thirds or quarters) at the top of the rim. Bring the chains together with a heavy metal loop or hook of some sort for hanging it. Around the lower edge of the rim, drill evenly spaced holes (about 2-3" apart) and use either chain or string to hang the clothespins. You can either drill small holes in the ends of the clothespins or just put the string through the springs on the clothespins. Another option is to use 1" plastic PVC pipe, using pipe fittings to make it in the shape of a square. You can either use string strung from one side to the other or use T fittings and more pipe. Again drill holes for the string or chain to hold the clothespins. This one can be made any size, but the bigger they are, the sturdier a hook they require to hang. I have one of these bigger ones inside the house, and one outside on the porch. They are also great for drying mittens, gloves, etc. in the wintertime, especially if you have it beside a heat source.

❋ Laundry is folded and put on piles in a row according to age, and each child is responsible to put away his own pile. Piles of laundry that are not clothing and the clothing of those too young to put their own away, are put away by whomever is available. Or have an older child responsible for a younger child's clothes.

❋ Throw Sunday shirts into the dryer for 5 minutes to minimize and possibly eliminate the need to iron them.

58 —— Mops, Muffins, & Motherhood

✻ To remove that musty smell from dishcloths and washcloths, add a splash of Odo-Ban to the washer with the load of laundry. It is available at Sam's Club in gallon jugs and spray bottles. It also helps eliminate the pig or dairy barn smell on clothing. The spray bottle works well to use in vehicles, or on upholstered furniture, or where someone vomited or urinated on a couch or mattress.

✻ Five minute rule: If after 5 minutes of wearing the garment you can't tell if it was ironed — don't iron it!

✻ We wash every day, using a Maytag industrial washer. This washer is designed for heavy use, but it takes longer to do really dirty loads.

✻ We bought nice stacking baskets at Walmart, one for each person in the family. Their folded clothes go into them and up to their rooms. Each child that is old enough can take care of their own clothes and also can be assigned a younger sibling's to take care of.

✻ Get the younger children involved too! They can hang up washcloths, socks, and other small pieces if a wash line is hung low enough for them. They will feel important to have such a responsibility. Praise can do wonders for their egos! However this is a good time to train them that a job must be done, and done right even if they don't feel like it. It is best to not even ask them to help if you aren't going to enforce the job being done right.

✻ A little treat hidden under a pile of laundry that must be folded can get the job done fast if they know there's a surprise for them.

✻ I try to get the wash folded and put away the same day I wash. At least that's one thing that got finished that day!

✻ Most ironing can be eliminated by putting shirts in the dryer for 5 minutes, then hanging them on hangers immediately. How well this works depends on the fabric and also the washer.

✻ Using large capacity washers speeds up the washing.

✻ My heavy duty Speed Queen washer has given me good service for 20 years.

✻ We do a washer load or two of barn clothes every day. We have two sets of barn clothes per person. What is washed today is worn tomorrow. We don't fold our barn clothes. We then have our big wash days Monday and Friday.

✻ I save time by using my dryer instead of always taking the time to hang the wash outside. That way I do not have the uncertainties of the weather to deal with, either. (Age 64)

✻ Hanging dresses and good shirts on hangers when damp will avoid a lot of ironing. Beware of metal hangers, though, as they can leave rust stains. Avoid 100% cotton if possible. Poly/cotton is much better. Try the wrinkle test before you buy - scrunch up a handful of fabric in your hand and squeeze as tight as you can for a few seconds, then try to smooth it out. You can soon tell which fabric will wrinkle the most.

✻ Each child is assigned certain piles to put away. At a very young age, they love to put a few things away with supervision.

✻ I do laundry 3 days a week. On Wednesdays I only do 2 loads, usually towels or jeans and shirts. Monday and Friday I do all the laundry.

✻ I sort clean laundry into individual piles for each child as I fold it at the kitchen

When our 3-year-old daughter picked up a bird feather, her grandmother asked her what she has. She said, "It's a leaf from a bird."

Flapping in the Breeze — 59

table. Each child age 4 and up is expected to put their own pile of clothing away.

✱ If a child's drawer gets too messy, they will have to take time to clean them up to Mom's expectations.

✱ I use a wringer washer, and do my big wash on Tuesdays. On Monday before school, children sort wash. Keep piles simple for them, and make sure they know to turn clothes right side out and close zippers. Balled up socks just don't get very clean! I wash towels, Sunday clothes, and school wash on Monday. On Friday I wash bedding and other laundry.

✱ A small laundry cart all their own is a good incentive for children.

✱ With four boys, I hang their pants in age order, and then I fold them as I get them in. I always fold big items such as bedding and towels as I get them in. It saves so much time.

✱ Drying clothes in the winter can be a challenge if you try to avoid using a dryer or don't have one. Hang clothes that are on hangers on curtain rods (make sure they are sturdy enough or you'll pull them down). Wooden drying racks can be purchased at various Amish and Mennonite stores.

✱ To avoid wrinkles: hang your good clothes on a hook as soon as you take them off. Stop the washer before it is finished spinning. Shake out each piece and hang it on hangers. Or put items in dryer to avoid ironing.

✱ In the summertime, I wash every day. If you put up a low wash line, young children can hang up small pieces, then get them down and fold them.

✱ My goal is to always fold, iron, mend, and put away each day's laundry. I don't always achieve this, but we need fewer clothing if the laundry is taken care of promptly.

✱ On laundry day the children are responsible for throwing dirty wash down, then one child is responsible to get the dirty wash to the laundry and the other one is responsible for emptying the laundry basket of clean clothes for that bedroom.

✱ My pet peeve is inside-out socks, long sleeves, and pant legs. Socks usually get folded inside out. Sleeves and pant legs, I complain about, but turn them right side out. Usually till the long sleeve season is over they are starting to do pretty good! Hubbie's clothes I turn right side out as a "labor of love"!

✱ I like my Maytag washer. I wash about 3 days a week during the summer, and every day except Sundays, of course, during the winter. Washing clothes is another one of those monotonous chores a mother does, but just do it! Wash, dry, fold, put away; it's so simple and the children can help with every step.

✱ Our school children take the clean folded piles of laundry to the bedrooms. This avoids wash baskets setting around all week.

✱ I was frustrated looking for a safe, natural laundry soap that really gets the wash clean without bleach. Then I discovered that using hot water instead of warm makes a big difference. Also, I use Borax to soften the water and get the most out of the soap. Occasionally, I use 35% peroxide instead of bleach - 1 cup to a large washer load. We buy it in a 15 gallon drum.

✱ I do my regular wash 3 times a week, then do the diapers, baby wash, and bedding in between. That way there's not so much at one time.

✱ When I use my drying rack in the winter, I lay a box fan across the bottom rungs and blow air up through for faster drying. If you have hot air heat, set the rack over a vent. I try to fold and put the wash away the same day.

✱ We use the dot system for keeping the children's clothing from going in the wrong person's drawer. Use a permanent marker to put dots on clothing tags or some other inconspicuous place. The oldest boy's clothing get one dot, the second boy's get two… When

Mops, Muffins, & Motherhood

things are passed to the next child, it is quite simple to add another dot. Do this for the girls as well.

✳ We wash an average of 3 times a week, Monday, Wednesday, and Friday to avoid such huge wash piles. We use a wringer washer to wash the clothes, and then spin them in an automatic washer so it's not dripping wet. I like to soak socks, shirts, and such garments in plain water so they don't need to wash so long.

✳ I do laundry every day. Just keeping up with it all was a huge step for me, and now if for some reason I need to skip a day, I don't get swamped the following day. (Age 38)

✳ Preschoolers love to have a wash line down at their level, then they can pin up lots of small items. They can be made responsible for taking down and folding those things, too. During the summer our girls do most of the laundry.

✳ I do regular wash on Monday, Wednesday, and Friday; then bedding, diapers, etc. on the other days. Starting early helps. Sort clothes and throw a load into the washer before you go to the barn. Mostly I fold and put away the laundry the same day I wash it except in the winter when I use a drying rack. We don't keep a lot of clothes, so I have to wash more often.

✳ I like to put the clean clothing away myself so I can straighten drawers right away, but sometimes the children each take their own stack.

✳ We think a clothes pin hanger is a must for every large family. They are convenient for drying stockings, handkerchiefs, underwear, baby clothes, reused baggies, wet gloves in the winter, and so much more!

✳ We fold everything except school and Sunday dresses and shirts; they get hung on hangers. For us, it works best if Mom or one of the older girls puts the laundry away.

✳ Boys tend to plop the pile beside the dresser!

We like to get the wash in and folded the same day it was washed. If you have a good place to hang them to dry, it works well to hang school/Sunday clothes on hangers right away, maybe fluffing them in the dryer for 10-15 minutes first to eliminate some of the wrinkles. Hanging a pair of pants with each school shirt is a real orderly time saver.

✳ Instead of trying to stuff jeans into dresser drawers that aren't deep enough, we like shelves in a closet on which to stack them. Even though the boys might pull out the bottom pair and make a mess, at least it's not spilling out of a drawer and falling on the floor. This also avoids drawers with the bottoms breaking out from boys stuffing them too full.

Stain removal

✳ Shout works well to spray those grass stains on jeans' knees and more. Usually with any stain remover, the sooner you get the area saturated, the better.

✳ Soaking is the best for stain removal (if you remember it soon enough).

✳ I like to keep a bar of Hog Wash soap on hand to scrub stains on clothes before washing them.

✳ Blood stains: Shampoo and cold water will remove even old stains if they were not washed in warm water, dried in the dryer, or ironed first.

✳ Ironing scorch marks: Dab immediately with hydrogen peroxide to remove.

✳ Gum removal: Orange Miracle from Stanley Home Products works great on clothes. Try peanut butter to remove gum from hair or skin.

✳ Rubbing dirty areas with Lava bar soap really helps, but is time consuming.

✳ We have really learned to like Mean Green (check at Dollar General or Walmart stores) to spray on soiled spots or stains. It works better if it is given some time to work before washing the clothes.

Flapping in the Breeze

✻ Stain remover soak- ½ cup powdered dishwashing detergent, ½ cup Clorox bleach, 1 gallon hot water. The longer you soak a stain, the better.

✻ I use Amway SA8 laundry soap. The prewash stain remover spray they sell works great!

✻ Oxyclean is one of the best stain removers I've ever used.

Feeding the Hungry

She riseth also while it is yet night, and giveth meat to her household, and a portion to her maidens. Proverbs 31:15

7. Feeding the Hungry
Food Preparation & Serving

If there is an area of life that the Pennsylvania Dutch folks are well known for, it would have to be for our food. We have a heritage of growing and preparing delicious foods. Many of us take it for granted that a girl would know how to cook by the time she is of age, but this is not true in every culture. We do not want to put too much emphasis on making and serving many rich foods, but neither do we want to lose sight of the importance of families eating meals together, sharing the happenings of the day. In America, it is too uncommon to have families eating together. The breakdown of the family causes the breakdown of the church and the nation. All people need food and we do well to consider what we are feeding our families. Recently there has been much media attention on where our food comes from and what all is done to it before we ingest it. If we grow and process our own food, we know what we have put into it. Food allergies are more and more common and some of us find that we must know exactly what our families are eating.

A well-balanced diet includes foods of many different kinds. It is better to include fruits and vegetables and whole grain foods. Children especially need protein. Some people do need special diets, but most of us do well to eat all foods in moderation. If you have a problem with weight (too much of it, that is), the best thing you can do is write down every little bit you eat. See how it makes you feel to read that at the end of the day! Eat more fruits & vegetables and less starch & sugar; you will feel much better. Add a half-hour walk each day and you might be surprised at how much energy you have. Cutting out your favorite food altogether just makes you even hungrier for it and sets you up for failure, so allow yourself your favorites in moderation or keep them out of your house altogether. Try to avoid spending too much time thinking about food, but I know how hard that is when you have to cook three meals a day. Finding an understanding friend to support you in the struggle of trying to eat better can be one of the best ways to help you to success. If you feel weak and shaky, it is likely you need some protein. Eating sweets and starches (which turn into sugar) causes a spike in sugar in your blood, so the body responds by pumping out large quantities of insulin. This in turn causes the blood sugar to drop too quickly and you end up with low blood sugar. This is what causes that tired, worn-out feeling; protein will help level out the blood sugar content.

Now that we got the diet talk out of the way, let's move on to handling meal planning and preparation. Part 2 will give you some of our favorite recipes and tips on cooking. Planning and executing three meals a day can be a big burden to those mothers who don't enjoy cooking. Some of us tend to get in a rut of waiting until the last minute, scrambling to prepare anything we can think up, and haphazardly serving it. It is a good idea to stop and evaluate how we might simplify this important part of our lives. If your children are old enough, get them involved in planning and preparing meals, especially the girls.

64 — Mops, Muffins, & Motherhood

And you never know if your boys might someday have a sick wife (or no wife) and cooking skills will be greatly appreciated. Don't be too quick to say no to their suggestions even if you don't feel like doing up with the mess you know will likely ensue. Let them be creative but teach them to clean up their own mess. Most times you shouldn't let them make a mess and then run off in the middle of a project.

Sticking to the basics with food we can produce ourselves, simplifies food preparation and helps out on the budget as well. There are some items I like to buy in quantity and keep in my cupboard for our favorite quick meals. Meat and vegetables in the freezer and fruit and potatoes in the cellar-what more could we need? Elaborate and rich foods should be for special occasions, especially when we are pressed for time.

One very important thing to consider is how our husbands want us to cook. It is a woman's domain, but as women who want to serve our husbands, we need to defer to his wishes in this area as well as others. He may not understand the mechanics of food preparation, but he knows what his taste buds enjoy. If there is too much conflict in this area, you need to talk to him about his preferences and come to an understanding. It is interesting to see what happens when a couple gets married and two different ways of cooking must be merged. Like everything else, usually you end up with a little of one and a little of the other. I once read about a culture (Armenia) in which young girls were thoroughly taught the art of homemaking, with the exception of cooking. When a girl got married, she moved in with her new husband's family so his mother could teach her how to cook his food just the way he wanted it. I thought we could learn a lot from that practice. The drawback was that the woman in the story married a man who had moved to America and his mother lived in her native country. She had a very

hard time learning to cook because she didn't have even a basic knowledge of food preparation, which produced some funny stories. But no matter from which culture we come, all cooks make some mistakes and it is good to be able to laugh at yourself. When I was a newlywed young lady, my mother-in-law related how she was making cracker pudding soon after she was married. She said while she was making it, she thought this pudding is just too thin and kept adding crackers even though the recipe didn't ask for so many. By the time it had cooled and they wanted to eat it, it was so thick they could cut it with a knife. I remember how I had a hard time imagining her so inexperienced, since as long as I knew her, she was a good cook. Try not to be too sensitive to comments made by your husband about his mother's cooking. If you ever hear the words, "this is better than Mom's," treasure them and know you have been paid a high compliment. I was married a while before I realized that when my husband said, "this is half good," he meant he really liked it! If your husband sits down and eats what is put before him without comment, be thankful. There are women who may wish their husbands would do the same instead of criticizing the food. Teaching children to eat a little of everything is a good idea, but if Daddy doesn't support that, it is better to accept it that way than to cause conflict.

Try to avoid shopping for groceries more often than absolutely necessary. It is a fact that the more often you go shopping, the more you buy things you really don't need. A grocery store is set up in such a way that the perishable items are around the perimeter. If you make one trip around the outside edge of the store, you will find most of the items you need. Then only go down those aisles in which you need things. Browsing up and down every aisle is almost a guarantee that you will put things in your cart you really can do without.

Feeding the Hungry — 65

✽ I plan the meals but take suggestions from the family anytime!

✽ Boys or girls can learn to bake simple things even before going to school.

✽ Have the cookbook wherever mom is working, and the child can come ask what to put in next… It might make a bit of a mess, but the child is learning and it makes them feel needed, which is even more important.

✽ While you are cooking anyway, make double batches of casseroles and pizza. Take out the extra portion before serving, or you might find everyone eats more than usual and you are left with half a meal, which defeats your purpose.

✽ Double and triple batches of baked goods are good for freezing, too. Put frozen baked goods into lunches and they will be thawed by lunchtime.

✽ Old pillow cases make great dough covers, a place to cool cakes, cookies or bread, dry tea leaves on, or they work as a "fine" sieve for straining juices.

✽ Each of our children age 8 and up has one evening meal a week they either make or help to make. They often start baking cake mixes by age 8.

✽ When baking cookies, I use four cookie sheets. I put the first one on the top rack for half of the baking time, then put it on the bottom rack and add the second sheet. When the first one is done baking, I move the second sheet to the bottom and put the third one in the oven while I am filling the fourth one. By the time the first one needs to be filled again, I have it emptied and cooled a bit. By rotating them this way, the baked cookies have a little time to firm up before they need to be removed from the cookie sheet and because I rotate them through the oven, they tend to bake more evenly. It seems to make it less hectic, since you do one step at a time instead of filling 2 sheets at a time. I usually use a timer, since I can almost count on burning some if I don't!

✽ You may be able to buy a roll of butcher paper from a store or butcher shop if you ask. This works really good to roll out on a counter to put your baked goods on to cool. This is especially useful if you glaze donuts, dip chocolates, or do some other messy job. When you are finished, clean up is a snap: roll it up and throw it away!

✽ I use wooden dowel rods to hang donuts on when I glaze them. I got the rods at a hardware store, and cut them just long enough to lay the long way over big roast pans (commercial full-size steam table pans) that I have. Three rods with donuts fit in each pan. I fill one pan while the ones in the other pan are dripping off and getting hard.

✽ A calendar works well on which to write monthly menus. Monday night is breakfast night, Wednesday is soup night, Friday is casserole, and Tuesdays and Thursdays we have full-course meals. Saturday we have pizza, lasagna, or spaghetti type food. Make your grocery list according to your menu. Then you can do major grocery shopping once a month with fresh food stops every two weeks or as needed. You can also do 2 weeks at a time.

✽ Using cookie scoops helps me get cookies more uniform in size and keeps me from licking my finger with every cookie I put on the sheet. They look like miniature stainless steel ice cream scoops and are available in different sizes. Many bulk food stores or specialty kitchen stores sell them.

✽ Having casseroles and other foods in the freezer is very important to me. I watch for meat and other foods that are on special and freeze them. Make double portions of casseroles and other foods while you're making the mess anyway, and freeze one portion for later use.

✳ Children can help with the cooking at an early age. Our eleven-year-old son has been responsible for making breakfast on school mornings. I usually inform him what to make the evening before. One thing we like to do is mix up the dry ingredients for pancakes and keep it in a tight container we have just for this purpose. Then he only has to add the wet ingredients, mix, and fry.

✳ Planning supper right after breakfast was a way I organized my day. Peeling potatoes and letting them sit in cold water until time to boil them, and sticking meat into the oven after lunch eliminates the frustrated hurrying at supper prep time when baby is hungry and toddlers need attention, too. Waiting for Daddy to come home for supper was a great time to read to the children to pass the time peacefully. (Age 67)

✳ My weekly grocery day has been a blessing to me. I always go the same day of the week and around the same time. I sketch out a weekly menu so I know what I need, and keep a paper on my refrigerator on which I write the things I need as I go through the week. I try to look ahead at my calendar to see if I need to buy any different or special things. This helps me get my shopping done on one day and eliminates me having to make countless runs to the store. (Of course, there are weeks that it might still happen.) (Age 34)

✳ Never go grocery shopping when you are hungry!

✳ For us it was worth the money to invest in a commercial size mixer. I can mix two cakes or double-batches of cookies without flinging flour or batter over the sides.

✳ I like to keep some baked items in the freezer for emergencies.

✳ Keeping yeast in the freezer in a plastic container with a tight-fitting lid will keep it fresh much longer. When activating yeast in warm water, be sure the water is not too hot, since this will kill the yeast and your baked goods will not rise. If you have a problem with your bread not rising as high as you like, try adding 1 tsp. wheat gluten per loaf of bread. The gluten is what causes the bread dough to be elastic, holding the air bubbles in instead of popping and letting the dough go flat.

✳ I almost always make a double recipe when baking. It doesn't take much extra time to bake two cakes and then I have one for the freezer.

✳ Our children enjoy food traditions - pancakes on Saturday, popcorn Sunday evening, etc.

✳ Our 11-year-old daughter can manage recipes fairly well. She has been baking for about a year now. She usually uses the same recipes.

✳ I enjoy cooking most times, but I am not a plan-ahead cook. I cook what I'm hungry for, and guess what, I'm not slim!

✳ I am head cook, but even 2 and 5-year-olds help. Spend time in the kitchen; make good meals for your family. Study cookbooks and as the children get older, try new things. It's fun!

✳ This is your family, do your best for them. What a blessing to sit around the table, eating good food!

✳ Planning ahead will avoid last minute stress! I get meat out of the freezer the night before and put it in the refrigerator.

✳ Avoid making your kitchen even hotter on hot summer days by using a crockpot instead of the oven. Put the meat on high in the morning and then turn it to low later in the day. Six-quart roasters are also available. They can often be found at thrift stores and yard sales for a good price.

✳ Brown a few sticks of butter at one time, then store the extra in the refrigerator. Cut thin slices to top your vegetables, pasta, etc. and you will avoid making a pan dirty each time you need some browned butter.

✳ Break the spell of always meat and potatoes for supper. Make breakfast foods and add juice and a sweet treat such as baked oatmeal or French toast for dessert. This is super on a cold winter evening.

✱ Our 7 and 8-year-old girls enjoyed doing the cooking when our youngest was born. For them to be able to do this, our meals are very simple. Dessert is a rare occasion, usually reserved for birthdays or other special occasions, or cobbler when fresh fruit is in season. Fresh fruit is often used as a nutritious snack rather than with every meal.

✱ Our children start baking when they are old enough to read the recipes.

✱ Before a new baby joins the family, I like to put casseroles in the freezer. Line your casserole dish with foil, fill it, freeze it, and then pop the casserole out. This frees up your dish, and when you need the casserole, just plop it back in the baking dish, heat, and eat!

✱ My first step in meal planning is to get the meat out of the freezer the night before and thaw in the fridge, or get it out in the morning and thaw on the counter. Mom and daughters cook together with the daughters able to make meals alone around age 13. Baking alone is generally accomplished by age 10-12.

✱ We freeze meals only if we know in advance that we will have a need for them or if we have so many leftovers that we cannot eat them within a few days.

✱ Our girls make most of the meals (we have a large family with older girls). When the school girls get home they can expect jobs like peeling potatoes, making meatballs, mixing pizza dough, etc. Since our suppers usually consist of meat, potatoes, and a vegetable, we found it works well to sit down in the evenings and plan meals for the next day, then get out of the freezer the items needed so they can thaw.

✱ By the time they are eight years old our children can usually bake cakes and 9-10-year-olds can be responsible for cooking potatoes and such simple things. Of course this varies according to ability. School boys can bake, too, and have occasionally baked bread.

✱ We like to have one day each week that we stock up on baked goods. We make double batches and stash it in the freezer for a "rainy day".

✱ Keep your cookbook clean by slipping it into a clear plastic bag when using it, to avoid splatters that make the pages dirty. Clear acrylic cookbook holders work well, too.

✱ A scissors or kitchen shears is a handy thing to have in a cupboard drawer. It can be used to cut bacon into pieces before frying it, cut sausages, baby carrots or other food into small chunks, cut open bags that can hardly be torn open, and so much more.

✱ It's easier to plan meals when you are hungry. It also helps if you have a variety of meats in the freezer.

> One day when I was nursing my baby girl, her 4-year-old brother was talking on the toy phone telling a story about her. "She's not home right now," he said. "She's at the restaurant."

68 — Mops, Muffins, & Motherhood

Preserving the Bounty

Go to the ant, thou sluggard; consider her ways, and be wise;...She provideth her meat in the summer, and gathereth her food in the harvest. Proverbs 6:6,8

8. Preserving the Bounty
Freezing & Canning

The subject of canning and freezing food comes along with daily food preparation. If you want to start a controversial subject among women, ask them how they go about canning tomatoes. One carefully boils the jars, the lids, the tomato juice, and still cold packs them after they are in jars. The next one brings her tomato juice to a boil, pours it into clean jars and slaps the lids on them and tightens them with the rings. I have sometimes thought it appears that the harder you try, the more trouble you have with spoilage! After years of having trouble with spoiling tomato products, I have come to the conclusion that it doesn't have as much to do with the method of canning, as it does the hardness of your water, the acidity in the tomatoes, whether the season was sunny, dry, wet, or cool, and the environment of the storage area. After trying several times to can pizza sauce with little success, I decided one year to try again. This time I cold packed the jars after putting the sauce into them. I left them on the kitchen counter several days to make sure they were all sealed, and then had the children carry them into the basement. Several weeks later, I went into the basement for something and discovered some of the jars had unsealed and the sauce was spoiled. Over time I believe every jar unsealed, and I declared I was not going to can pizza sauce again! Several years and a move to another state later, I got the courage to try a recipe from my sister-in-law. I now can pizza sauce successfully every year and I can't tell you just what I do differently than I did then. You can find the recipe in Part 2.

Why put all the extra effort into preserving food in the first place? It is not always cheaper to can your own fruit if you have to pay too much for fresh fruit in your area. However, you have better control of what is going into the jars and you can be sure of the quality of the food you are serving your family. Many commercially processed foods have unhealthy additives and some of these can trigger allergies in certain people. There may come a day when we will be glad to know how to preserve our own food and not be dependent on commercially prepared foods.

If you live in an area where there is a produce auction, you may be able to get vegetables and fruits at a very reasonable price in quantity to can or freeze. In some cases it is easier to have one or two days of a big mess and get someone to help and have your corn (or other fruit or vegetable) all done in one day rather than drag it out all summer. This works better for some people than others and some mothers prefer to do it in smaller increments. There is a good feeling that comes from producing and preserving your own food for the winter. The knowledge has been passed down and added to from one generation to the next. It is a part of our heritage. However, it is not a shame if special circumstances in your home make it impossible or impractical to preserve your own food.

We have a free-standing stainless steel cooker that holds 32 one-quart jars. We use a two-burner, high

70 — Mops, Muffins, & Motherhood

BTU output outdoor burner for heat under it. Canners under which you can build a fire are also available.

When doing pizza sauce, we cut bushels of tomatoes, onions, and peppers into the cooker, cook everything until soft, and then put this mixture through a food mill that has been converted from hand crank to drill powered. If you want things to be done efficiently, get your husband involved. Mine usually doesn't do too much hand labor until he figures out a way to use a motor or something mechanical! He made up an adapter in the place of the handle on my food strainer that can have a cordless drill attached to it. (Husband Note: I took the food strainer shaft and threaded a connector nut onto the handle end. Then we use a corresponding socket adapter on the cordless drill. An electric drill can be used if you have a power source close by.) In our primarily boy family, it makes it easier to enlist help with canning projects when motors are utilized. One word of warning-no, two. First, keep small children away from the hot splashing juice that occurs when the boys (or girls) get too wild with the drill. Secondly, your food mill manufacturer probably won't stand behind the warranty if you modify it in this way, since they probably won't consider it "normal household use"! After everything has been pulverized, we pour it all back into the cooker, add spices and additional ingredients, and then bring it to a boil, stirring almost constantly with our large wooden paddle made for this purpose. After the proper cooking time, we use an 8-cup measuring cup with a nice spout and handle to dip into the sauce and pour it into the jars. After wiping the jar rims, attaching the lids (which were in hot water) and rings, we wash out the cooker a bit and fill it with enough hot water to cover the jars that have been returned to it. Boil for ten minutes, then remove the jars with a jar lifter and tighten the rings. This takes

place in our garage and it takes a good bit of table space to accomplish. All the mess is out there and it is a relatively easy matter to wash the mess down with a garden hose. We have a double laundry tub with hot and cold water to simplify washing up the dishes afterward, too.

At a sale somewhere we bought a small stainless steel table/cart on wheels that is a big help on canning/freezing days. Applesauce is done in a similar manner except we don't cold pack jars, since we prefer our applesauce frozen in containers (usually ice cream buckets!).

When we get corn ready for the freezer, we use a little different method. We often get a lot of corn in one day from a produce grower who has picked over the patch already and has only nubbins left. These ears are usually a little shorter, but still have plenty of corn on them. It takes so long to get the big cooker to boil water that we discovered it is much faster to use the two-burner outdoor stove and two large kettles. After we have husked the corn and taken off most of the silk, we fill the kettles and bring them to a full rolling boil. Then we take the corn cobs out of the boiling water and dump them into cold well water in the laundry tub for 5-10 minutes. From there we dump the cobs onto a plastic (or plastic covered) table to drain the water and cool them enough to be handled. One of the teenagers is in charge of cooking and transferring the cobs. Two others are using the creamers for creamed corn and I usually cut some off with a knife for whole-kernel corn for soups and casseroles. Creamers are much easier to use if you find a flat pan to firmly set the notch into, to keep it from sliding all over the place. The children using the creamers need to be old enough that they don't cut themselves, since most of us prefer our corn without skin and blood! Then if there is still a child available, he packs the cooled, cut corn into bags. I use the

Preserving the Bounty — 71

plastic bags that the local bulk food store uses to bag up their products. For quart bags I buy 4"x2"x12", and pints are 4"x2"x8". We set the bags into a tub and then carry them to the freezer. Doing things that go in the freezer in large quantities makes it a challenge to have enough freezer space to spread the new product out to allow it to freeze quickly enough. I well remember how my heart sank one year when I realized, too late, that the corn I had put in the freezer several days before was too tightly packed in and most of it had spoiled! I could have cried for all that hard work! It usually only takes one such experience to make us really careful in the future to spread things out and in different freezers until well frozen. Then they can be stacked together to save space. This all makes quite a mess, but we try to do all our corn in one or two days each summer. Again, it is fairly easy to wash everything in the garage down with the hose. Be sure to do this before the corn has dried on to everything. What a sigh of relief when this big job is done!

Green beans are a vegetable with which even small children can help. They can snap the ends off with their little fingers if you aren't too fussy about a bit of waste. They can also break them into smaller pieces if you don't mind if they aren't uniform. Before I grew Strike green beans, I used to french-cut the beans with a hand cranked frencher since this is how my husband liked them. Guess what, one day he helped me turn the crank and it wasn't long until he ran off and came back with the drill. He removed the handle from the frencher and attached the drill. That is how we frenched the beans after that. I was always a little worried about the beans pulling fingers along in and I didn't want to see what frenched fingers looked like, so I didn't allow the younger children to do that job.

Home butchering is not as common as it once was. Many of us send a beef or pig to the butcher and then pick it up, cut to order, neatly packaged, and frozen solid. We like to can some hamburger and beef chunks for quick, easy meals. I ask the butcher to save the meat and not freeze it. Pack it in clean quart jars, adding one teaspoon of salt at the top, wipe off the rims, and screw on a lid and ring. Do not add water to the jar. Put them in a canner and bring the water to a boil. Keep the water slowly boiling for 3 hours. Remove the jars and tighten the lids. (Note: Green beans can be canned this way, too, except fill the jars with water before ptting the lids on. They must cook for 3 hours also.) You must check occasionally while it is boiling, since it may be necessary to add more water. Canned hamburger and beef chunks make very good gravy, or use in casseroles. Using canned beef chunks is a fast and easy way to make beef noodle soup. Bring the meat and some water to a boil. Add a package of whole-kernel corn, and noodles, and then cook until soft. You can add beef base or bouillon cubes for extra flavor.

To wrap meats, cut a big square of freezer paper. Place the meat in the center and bring the straight edges (the ones you didn't cut) up with the shiny sides together and fold down twice, snugly against the meat. While holding the fold with one hand, take the top right corner and fold down, then the bottom right corner and fold up. Switch hands and do the other side. Now flip the whole package over and fold the cut ends to the back and firmly tape in place. This wrapping method helps avoid freezer burn and meat falling out of poorly-wrapped packages. It works well to use a

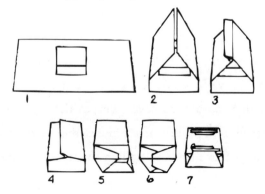

Sharpie marker to mark what is in the package and the year on the fold on the front of the package. Adding little sayings or notes on what is happening at the time can bring a smile when a package is taken out of the freezer to be used. It usually causes flashbacks in memory to the day you did the packaging.

Preserving your own food is rewarding and a good way to keep children occupied while they are learning an important life skill. Each of us has to find our own limit to what we can handle. If it becomes so stressful that we start to snap at the family or are too overburdened, it may be time to cut some things out and buy more. Following are some more ideas to help minimize the workload in the already busy summertime.

❋ Bring empty jars from the basement when you carry down the full ones. Wash them and turn them upside down on the counter and they are ready to go for the next canning day.

❋ We have a canning kitchen set up in the garage.

❋ We no longer cut both ends off the green beans. It is much faster just cutting off the stem end and the other end is quite edible.

❋ Chop strawberries with a chopper instead of slicing each berry. The chopper is a round metal ring with a handle. It resembles a donut cutter, but has a higher handle and no center. A donut cutter can also be used.

❋ It is generally best to eat pork within a year of freezing for best flavor.

❋ Our favorite sweet corn for freezing is Incredible; we plant Strike green beans and Early Frosty peas. Amish Paste tomatoes are a roma type that are good for making juice and sauces. They are much bigger than the regular romas.

❋ A calf bottle brush fastened to a battery or electric drill makes a quick job of de-silking corn. Fasten drill securely on its side and hold ear of corn against bottle brush as it spins.

❋ Corn de-silking machines are now available. Just feed the cob in one end, and presto! It comes out the other end nicely cleaned. These machines come with a hefty price tag, (approx. $550) but several families or a community can invest in one to share. Contact: Samuel and Lois Petre, 8306 Mapleville Road, Boonsboro, MD 21713, 301-791-9326

❋ I no longer bother with carefully de-silking corn. We try to get most of it off as we husk the corn, but the rest either cooks off or is easy to remove as you're cutting the corn off the cob.

❋ Keep as much of the mess outside as possible. We do our canning in the garage, but before that we did it outside at the picnic table. After you are finished, bring out the hose and squirt the mess away!

❋ We use a two-burner, high BTU output gas burner designed for outdoor cooking. Using two big kettles speeds up the process. You can buy these burners at a reasonable price at outdoor outfitters such as Cabelas or Bass Pro Shop. Those big turkey cookers with strainer baskets that often show up in stores around Thanksgiving work well, too.

❋ Use pillow cases for blanching. Just fill, dip into hot water, and pull it all out at once when finished blanching. Have the next one ready to drop in and you can save lots of time. Keep the mess outside and you can come back in to a clean kitchen. Providing you left it clean, of course!

✸ Pod peas and snap beans on a cement floor outside for easier clean up for all those little pieces that get spilled. I recommend sweeping before you get started unless you like dirt with your food.

✸ I like to keep a chart of all the foods I have canned and frozen for each year. By taking inventory and comparing one year to another I can better plan what is needed.

✸ I keep a tablet with garden information such as what kinds of peaches were canned or tomatoes that I planted. Also where I bought fruit, how much and what I paid, and what the quality was.

✸ If your family likes milk shakes, it works well to freeze fruits such as blueberries, peaches, or strawberries in single layer on cookie sheets. After they are frozen, store in ice cream pails and you can remove as much as needed rather than having one hard lump.

✸ I've helped several ladies with outdoor cookers on a big corn day. It is nice for some, but since my husband is not usually available to help all day, I do my freezing and canning in smaller amounts and more days. We may need to accept what works best for us even if it's not the easiest or fastest.

✸ My husband's family taught me to run the fan over the corn after it is blanched instead of cooling it in cold water. Use a big butcher knife to cut it off, preferably outside.

✸ If you want to can diced peaches or pears, set an apple corer/slicer upside down over your jar, and push the fruit halves through. The children will love the round pieces that come from the center. Diced fruit fits better into small lunchbox containers. Also more fruit fits into the jars, which in turn takes less sugar water.

✸ When canning pears, I get the children to help peel the pears with peelers. Then I quarter the pears to get the seeds out. They fit into the jars better than halves.

✸ A shortcut I take with canning fruit is putting the sugar (about ¼ cup per quart jar) directly into the jars on top of the fruit. I pour hot water over the sugar to fill the jar. I never see sugar at the bottom of the jar after it is canned and my fruit isn't overly sweet.

✸ Use a melon baller to get the seeds out of pears. It's a great job for children!

✸ You can avoid the mess cooking red beets make by adding ½ teaspoon vegetable oil.

✸ Do you enjoy crisp dill pickles? Slice raw cucumbers into a dish; pour hot syrup over them made from Mrs. Wages dill pickle mix as directed. These can be stored in the refrigerator for weeks. No canning needed and very delicious. Super on hamburgers!

✸ My husband likes to come up with easier ways to do things. He put a nut on my food strainer instead of the handle, then an adapter with a socket to fit the nut into a cordless drill. Now you're all set to 'crank' your applesauce or tomatoes through much faster. Set the drill on a low setting to avoid spattering everything in sight. Also make sure your batteries are charging so they are ready when you need them.

✸ We have learned when freezing sweet corn that the process is considerably shortened by omitting the de-silking step. Take the majority of the silk off when husking, and by the time it's cooked and cooled (in water) not much silk is left. Besides, corn silk is dried and sold in capsules as a supplement to aid in fighting urinary tract infections, so don't worry if a little remains!

✸ If you have only small children, it works best to get up early to get the produce picked before the baby is awake.

✸ Even small children can help snap beans, shell peas, and husk corn. Get them involved, it will make your life easier as they get older.

✸ Freeze hamburger in bags large enough that you can flatten them to about ½ inch thickness. This makes it very fast to thaw when it is needed.

74 —— Mops, Muffins, & Motherhood

✳ We package our meats and vegetables to be enough for a meal with maybe a little leftover for lunch the next day.

✳ We don't make syrup when canning fruit. It is much more efficient to fill the jar with fruit, then add the desired amount of sugar and pour hot water over it to fill the jar. We don't have a problem with sugar settling to the bottom of the jar.

✳ Make pea shelling and bean snapping times pleasant. Sing, tell original stories or ones that happened to you. Our children like to take turns saying, "I see something... (red)...The others guess what it is until they figure it out. This can cause fingers to go slower, so they need to be encouraged to keep at it while they are guessing.

Our 4-year-old son had this comment when tasting apple cider that was turning sour, "It feels like a cactus!"

Preserving the Bounty —— 75

76 —— Mops, Muffins, & Motherhood

The Great Outdoors

And the Lord God planted a garden eastward in Eden; and there he put the man whom he had formed. And out of the ground made the Lord God to grow every tree that is pleasant to the sight, and good for food...
Genesis 2:8-9a

9. The Great Outdoors
Garden, Yardwork, Flowerbeds & Chores

Gardening

Outdoor work is a good remedy for rowdy children. If possible, it is a good idea to grow at least some of your own food. Children can learn so much from helping in the garden: planting, tilling, mulching and pulling weeds. Make it exciting to plant, explaining what happens to the seeds and how they grow. We make comparisons to life about how much easier it is to pull weeds when they are small and how much easier it is to change bad habits when they are little instead of waiting until they are well established. If space is limited, you can be selective about what kind of vegetables you plant. Many viney plants are now available in more compact varieties such as bush cucumbers. Look for plants bred for container gardening. This is also another way people with limited space can grow more vegetables. Plastic barrels cut in half can produce an amazing amount of vegetables with minimal weeding, but they need to be fertilized and watered. Be sure to drill holes in the bottom of the container for drainage, in case it is a wet summer. This might work for some fresh vegetables when you have circumstances that don't allow for a regular garden. If you live close enough to a produce auction, you may want to try to make contact with someone who attends regularly, who can watch when things sell at a reasonable price. Almost every summer there is a glut at one time or another of every vegetable they sell. Another option is produce farmers who might leave their seconds in the field to rot. Many times they are glad to sell these seconds for very little or give them away.

Many produce farmers use black plastic to help with weed control. It is available on rolls in about a 4-foot width. After you have the soil worked nice and fine, you roll the plastic out where you want to plant your vegetables, shoveling dirt on the edges. Be sure to get every edge covered or the wind will come along and find that little open spot. It will get in there and blow until it pulls that plastic edge out from under the dirt and before you know what happened, you have a long piece of plastic merrily flapping in the wind. If you had already planted plants in it, they will look very sad from the beating they are getting. To plant the vegetables, use a trowel to make a hole through the plastic just big enough to be able to dig a hole in the ground. Gently work the soil around the roots of the seedlings, and then water each plant periodically until it is well established. Watering plants is a good job for children since they like to slop with water anyway. They may need some supervision at first to make sure that each plant gets what it needs, instead of it mostly ending up on the children! You can also purchase drip tape that can be rolled out under the plastic, for irrigation. You can use a garden hose to supply the water if you put the right adapter on the end of the drip tape.

78 — Mops, Muffins, & Motherhood

Seeds can also be planted under plastic by making short slits and planting in the ground directly below the slits. Most of the plants will come right up to the light; however, the more holes you have in the plastic, the more light there is for weed seeds to germinate. This plastic method is especially good for vining plants like cucumbers, cantaloupe, watermelon, pumpkins and squash. It also works great for tomatoes.

To grow huge sweet potatoes, try this: Work the soil pretty deep and fine. Make a ridge about 12-16" high. Run a drip tape slightly to the side of top center (don't put it in the center since it will be in the way when you want to make holes to plant) and cover with black plastic, making sure to cover the edges well with dirt. Use a hoe handle or similar tool and poke holes deep enough to get most of the sweet potato plant into it and gently press on the sides to get soil around the plant roots. Water as needed and for really big sweet potatoes, fertilize as well.

Many plants can be trained to grow up. Trellising and cages make picking an easier job, but they take time to get in place. Getting the fruit to grow off the ground often results in better produce, too. Peas are much easier to pick when chicken wire or similar trellising is staked by the row when the plants are small. At the end of the season, take it down, pull the dead plants off the wire, roll it up (stakes and all), and store it for the next year. This is an investment that we feel is worth the money.

Don't plant your seeds too thickly. This often results in a reduced yield and makes it harder to pick because of tangled plants and scrawny stems that can hardly support the plant. Really tiny seeds can be planted with a salt shaker. Of course, you have to make sure the seed is small enough to actually sprinkle out of the holes.

✻ Mulch the rows in the garden with grass trimmings, old hay, etc. to keep weeds down. Plant on plastic when and where it is feasible. A good, rear-tine rototiller is very helpful, especially if you have poor soil conditions. Stake tomatoes by using fence posts and baler twine.

✻ We save our empty cereal boxes and use them to mulch the tomato patch to keep the weeds down.

✻ Have one night a week that the whole family works in the garden. It can be lots of fun!

✻ Try weeding two rows each morning right after chores are done until you get over the whole garden.

✻ Placing a layer of cut grass between the rows in the garden helps me keep after the weeds.

✻ I try to have a garden every year, for fear it would be easy to not have one the next year, or the next…try having fewer varieties of vegetables or just less of each kind.

✻ Those that live in the areas where much produce is grown can often get seconds for little or no money. While this is an option for produce, we must consider the effects of the future if our children don't know even the basics of gardening.

✻ One year when I had a small baby, I chose not to have a garden and I didn't like it. A small garden is definitely better than none at all.

✻ When the garden needs weeding, I assign each child a row or two, or even half a row, depending on their age. With the assignment comes the warning that if they do a sloppy job or just pull the tops off the weeds, it will have to be done so much sooner again. If the child is too careless, he will need to do his row again in a few weeks.

✻ I try to keep one day a week for rototilling, pulling weeds in the garden, and going over the flowerbeds.

✻ As the family grows, the garden grows bigger, too, but the children can help more. We like to try some fun things like cantaloupe or watermelon. We use plastic under the vine crops for weed control.

✻ To keep up the interest in gardening, try something unusual. Some ideas are okra, Brussels sprouts, purple string beans, or just check out one of the many seed catalogues that come in the spring for ideas.

✻ Lay newspapers between your vegetable rows after you can't rototill between them.

✻ Put your biodegradable items on a compost pile to be worked into the soil after the produce has been harvested. One woman buried her garbage between the rows of peas to enrich the soil.

✻ Lay a three-sheet thickness of newspapers around your potatoes and then put grass clippings on it to hold it in place.

✻ If you have a big garden, having it perfectly weed-free is not realistic. Welcome to planet earth! Gardens can still be productive with some weeds. One year our boys planted pumpkins to sell. Every time I would nag them about pulling those big weeds out there, they would tell me that the pumpkins were using them to climb on, and they were providing shade from the hot sun. They had a decent crop and I don't believe they are convinced to this day that it would be worth the effort to pull the weeds. The pumpkins were planted on plastic, so they didn't feel the pressure from the weeds at first. Also, it was a wetter year than some, so they weren't competing for moisture as much.

✻ Anyone with children should try to have a garden. What better way to spend time with your children? Flowerbeds are more fun to have, but it's more work and the garden should be first.

✻ A good tiller has aided us in keeping ahead of weeds, but we try to do more mulching. We save paper grain bags and newspapers to put down first then cover with our choice of mulch. We use a lot of grass clippings and some mushroom mulch, but we still need to pull weeds.

✻ Grow your own herbs for seasoning. A good starter for us was chives and lovage. They are generally easy-to-grow perennials, and are good in many soups and casseroles. I grow a large variety of herbs, then dry and crush them with the larger portion being lovage and chives. Mix together and use a sprinkling in just about everything!

✻ I don't stay ahead of weeds, but I would feel lost without a garden, even if I don't keep after the weeds. If you have animals in pens, the used bedding is good, cheap mulch.

✻ Lightly hoe garden rows as soon as possible after the plants are up. Little white threads may be all you see in the lightly disturbed soil, but these are the roots that go down before the weeds pop up.

✻ Tilling the garden regularly is the #1 key to staying ahead of the weeds, with hoeing a close second.

✻ Plant potato rows close together to diminish space for weeds, and then lay newspaper between the rows before mulching with grass or shavings. Grass is excellent mulch for free, just be sure to cut it before it goes to seed.

✻ Everyone's help is needed in the garden; this can make pleasant family times in the evenings. It is necessary to realize that the garden can't always look tops if there are little ones to care for.

"The lightning bugs blink with a cordless drill," came from our son. I suppose it was obvious that the bugs weren't trailing a cord.

✱ The children ages 5-12 are good ones to send out to gather potato bugs. They need to be taught how to get them all so it won't need to be done so soon again. Cut one corner off the top of a gallon jug with a handle, have the children put the bugs in there, shaking down occasionally, and then pour boiling water into it when done.

✱ If you have poor soil, then you need to mulch, mulch, and mulch some more. No matter what type of soil you have, adding organic matter will make the soil nice and fertile over time.

✱ Seeding rye or another grain over the whole garden in the fall and then plowing down the new growth in the spring is a good way to add organic matter to the soil. Look for earthworms; the more you have the better.

✱ I learned something from my husband's grandpa. Till and hoe the garden before the weeds come. Do it after every rain when it is dry enough or once a week.

✱ Don't have a bigger garden than you can handle. If you have very little time, just have a small garden. You can buy good frozen peas and sacks of potatoes. As the children get older and can help more, enlarge the garden.

Yards/Flowerbeds

It is good to have a neat appearance outside our homes as well as inside, but that does not mean we need to have showplaces. When we have small children our flowerbeds should be pretty far down on our list of priorities. But a few nice flowers can help our children learn to appreciate the beauty God gave us in nature. Careful selection of a few prolific flowers can cover a large area in short order.

Use Preen and mulch in flowerbeds. Preen is a seed-germinating inhibitor, it doesn't allow new seeds to germinate. If you don't sprinkle it on right away when you work the flowerbeds, some seeds will germinate and the Preen won't stop them from growing. Preen is also not effective on root weeds, such as grasses or thistles.

If you plant perennials, you can minimize digging up new weed seeds. Just mulch the area well and it won't be necessary to dig it up every year. Whenever you disturb the ground, you expose more seeds to the light to germinate and produce a new crop of weeds!

If you choose not to plant a garden, you can plant tomatoes, peppers, or other vegetables in the flowerbeds.

Spraying Roundup at the fence rows and edges of walkways (and other places that generally grow up in weeds), makes a place look much better without as much effort as weed-eating and pulling weeds. We had a neighbor man that thought he had too many weeds in his lawn, so he sprayed it with Roundup. He had a hard time living down his brown lawn. On the bright side, it did kill his weeds (as well as his grass)! Roundup can be sprayed between garden rows, but extreme care must be taken to avoid the spray drifting on the vegetable plants. Large pieces of cardboard can be held by the children to shield the plants.

Pass mowing chores to your children, especially boys, as soon as they are old enough. How old that is, is certainly a matter of opinion and ability, and varies from child to child. The type of mower you own also has to be taken into consideration. We need to realize that a mower can be very dangerous and make sure the child using it is mature enough to handle emergency situations. Teaching other children to stay away from the area being mowed goes a long way in keeping our children safe. It is amazing how far a mower can fling a stone or other item its spinning blades may pick up. Taking little children and toddlers on a riding mower with an adult may be safer for the child at the time, but the

The Great Outdoors — 81

danger comes in the child running after the mower for a ride. They are too young to realize the danger if the driver doesn't see them.

✻ Perennials are a good choice for flowerbeds. They come up by themselves and you thin out what you don't want. Then if a puppy or a child wanders or rides through them they are usually hardy enough to take some abuse.

✻ Thistles in flowerbeds can be a big problem. Some kinds have a deep root system and just pop right back up within a few days of pulling them. About the only way to beat them completely is to very carefully put a touch of Roundup on the top of each thistle. Or dig up every plant that you want to save, and start over by first spraying the whole area with a weed killer. If you replant any of the perennials or shrubs you dug out, make very sure you have no thistle roots in the dirt clinging to the plant roots or you will start the cycle all over.

✻ Wave petunias (or a similar spreading type such as Proven Winner's brand - Supertunias) are a favorite of mine. They cover a big area densely enough to control some of the weeds and add lots of color to the flowerbeds. Although the cost per plant might be more, it takes fewer plants to better cover the same area.

✻ Dry weed preventer such as Preen really does work to keep the weeds down. You sprinkle it on the ground after you worked and planted the flowerbed then water it in. WARNING! This product works by preventing all seeds from sprouting. DO NOT use this product in any area you planted seeds that you want to grow. It will not stop weeds that spread through roots such as thistles or grasses.

✻ For an easy-to-keep-after flowerbed, put down landscape fabric, and then fill in the area with small rock. Add a few bushes and perennials and maybe a few larger rocks. Add an annual here and there for color all season.

✻ I sprinkle Preen on my flowerbeds in early spring, then mulch them in May. I have very few annuals.

✻ I use mulch in the flowerbeds each year. It does cost more, but really saves on weed pulling, but you also have to find time to put it on.

✻ Here's advice from my mom when I had little ones, "Remember your children are your flowers now, keep them growing nicely."

✻ For easy-to-maintain flowerbeds, plant shrubs and a few perennials.

✻ Wait to have a lot of flowerbeds until the children are old enough to help. A few clean ones are more beautiful than lots of weedy ones! Mulching helps to keep down the weeds.

Farm Chores

✻ Chores freshen your mind! Even 2- and 3-year-olds want chores to do. Housework goes better after being out of the house in the fresh air.

✻ Give the incentive to get chores done without dawdling so we can read, play that special game, or whatever appeals to you and them.

✻ If Mom is in the barn, it helps keep everything running smoothly and organized. Dad also appreciates Mom making it a family affair.

✻ Doing chores together is a wonderful time for visiting with each other and hearing about each other's day.

✻ We are dairy farmers and need to stay on schedule (including bedtime) as much as possible. Family and animals need to eat, so cleaning is closer to the bottom of the list, which means it might not get done.

✻ With two boys close one age, we needed to clarify who does what. The younger one works circles around his brother and Big Brother soon saw the work will get done even if he does goof off. So now they each have their own chores in the barn. And, yes, younger brother does work more but children do have different abilities.

* As a dairy farmer's wife, I know the cows must come first because they pay our bills. Taking turns choring with the children works well for us. Over the busy time everyone must pitch in. Put every effort into your occupation and work with the children as much as possible.

* The best place to raise a family is on the farm, but this is not possible for all of us. Next best is having a home business where the children can be with their father. This, also, is not feasible for all of us. For the sake of the children, it is good if they have chores or jobs of some kind to keep them occupied, and to use up some of their energy.

* Teachers can often tell if children are used to doing chores because they are more responsible. I'm not a farmer's wife, but help with finishing in our woodworking shop. It works best to have Mom or Dad involved with the children as they work, or at least checking on them regularly. Even a simple list helps them to know what jobs they are expected to do and keeps them oriented.

* I have to watch my tendency to snap and fuss at what the children didn't accomplish or do right when I check up on them. Do they know what tone of voice to expect when Mom steps in the door?

* Prompt obedience is a must, with discipline as consequences.

The Great Outdoors —— 83

Neighbors comment on the children lying in the yard and all the wash on the line. Nothing can replace simplicity; it is a beauty all its own.

What Shall We Wear

And why take ye thought for raiment? Consider the lilies of the field, how they grow... wherefore if God so clothe the grass of the field... shall He not much more clothe you? Matthew 6:28a, 30a,c

10. What Shall We Wear
Clothing, Sewing & Crafts

What is our main goal when we think of clothing for our families? First we think of modesty. There are many and varied opinions on what is modest and what is not. There are two things to consider when deciding what we and our children will wear: what our church standards are and what our convictions dictate. Most people would agree that the more skin that shows, the less modest we are. We need to be on guard against following society in general, which has become somewhat immune to scantily-dressed people. God doesn't follow styles! However, just having our bodies covered doesn't automatically make us modest. There are other factors to take into account as well. One of these is how thin the fabric is. If you are purchasing dress material, you should hold it up to the light if possible. There was a young mother who was modestly dressed in a dark colored dress with a long skirt. However, when she stepped in front of a window where the sun was shining in at an angle, the very shape of her legs was quite visible! Wearing a heavy slip or one with a shadow panel is very important with fabric that is a bit thinner. Another thing about slips is that they need to be nearly as long as the dress skirt or it defeats the purpose of wearing them.

Another area many of us have a problem with is how we just seem to get a bit bigger and rounder with every passing year. Unfortunately, our patterns don't grow with us! Tight dresses are not modest, even if they are made with a cape. It may be time to modify your pattern or get a new one. Along with thin and tight clothing comes the problem of panty lines (and those of other undergarments) showing. It is rather distasteful to stand behind a woman when you can tell exactly what she has on under her dress. Although men are responsible to keep their thoughts under control, a woman who flaunts her body will also be held accountable. It is a good idea to periodically take the time to stand in front of a full-length mirror and really look at what others see when they look at us. Be sure to use another mirror to see what you look like from the back and even walk away a few steps and bend over to get the full effect. You probably won't really like what you see, since not many of us enjoy examining ourselves in a mirror, but it can be quite enlightening as to where we should make some changes. Another way to do this is to ask a sister or a friend that you can trust to tell you the truth even if they know it will hurt a little. I once saw a chubby, middle-aged woman at church bend way down to retrieve something that had dropped on the floor and I never forgot the sight I saw! It made me very conscious of bending over when there are people around. In fact, it is much more modest to bend your knees and squat down because it doesn't pull your skirt up so far in the back. Making our skirts longer helps to keep us modest when we bend over.

Another factor to consider about clothing is cost. Many clothing can be bought at thrift stores and yard

86 — Mops, Muffins, & Motherhood

sales if you have the time and inclination to shop this way. The same warning applies to buying clothing as buying household things - if you don't need it, don't buy it! If you don't know for sure that you will need it soon, let it there. If you have too many clothes and can't keep them organized, you won't know what you have when you need it, and then what was the use of buying it in the first place? Sound confusing? Confusing and disorganized is just what you get if you don't control your buying urges. I should know; I have experience! I find it easier to keep control of the many clothing it takes for our family by hanging as much on hangers as possible. I like to have a closet or a rod in the attic where I hang up all clothing that can be hung up, that are not currently needed. I sort them into like kinds (shirts, dresses, nighties, etc.) and sizes from smallest to largest. It is so easy to get what you need because you don't have to sort through boxes and make a mess, and it helps eliminate not finding some things until the child has outgrown it. How frustrating!

I do store infant clothing in labeled boxes and also things like underclothes, socks, jeans and pants. It takes a lot of shirts in our family and I have a closet where I hang the out-of-season and not-the-right-size shirts. I have the long sleeve shirts hanging on one side and the short sleeve ones on the other. This way the boys can find one that fits when the seasons change. When I'm pretty sure the weather is going to stay in the new season, I hang the ones up from the prior season, which empties their drawers a bit again. Jeans are a challenge around here. Spring and fall I usually have each boy fit on every pair of pants in his drawer unless he can tell me for certain it doesn't fit him. I start with the oldest so that the next boy in age can fit on the ones that his older brother can no longer wear. I realize not everyone has 5 boys in row, which means you may know the next brother will not be wearing his older brother's

outgrown clothing right away, but the principle is the same. Store what doesn't fit in clearly marked boxes so you don't have to dig out the entire closet or attic to find what you need. Be careful what you store from one child to the next, especially if there is a pretty long age span. Stains get worse in storage, holes don't mend themselves and elastic breaks down and no longer functions after a certain length of time. For those of us with small homes with little storage, it is important to consider whether it is worth keeping clothing that can be replaced at yard sales and thrift stores. Passing everyday clothing on to those who can use them and then having someone share their outgrown clothing with you is an ideal way to control storing too many clothes. Somehow we also have to decide whether paying a higher price for better quality clothing is better than paying less for clothing that doesn't last as long, and even if the higher priced clothing actually lasts any longer. One thing to consider is how many children will need those particular clothes.

❋ Knee-length bloomers can be a help for modesty in little girls who are young enough to tumble around on the floor but have a hard time remembering to keep their dresses down.

❋ I have a clothing chart with a list for each child that I go over at the beginning of every new season with each child's clothes. I check off what each child has and then know what to buy to fill in whatever they still need. Sometimes a child's wardrobe will need replenishing during the season, especially if they hit a growth spurt.

❋ If you have things that were handed down from one child to the other and just never fit or for some other reason never gets worn, get rid of it! If it is in good shape, take it to a thrift store or donate it to Christian Aid Ministries or anther mission that takes used clothing. If it is partly worn out, cut it up for rags, give it to someone who needs chore clothes, or throw it out. It does no good to anyone if it sets in your drawers and clogs up the system.

✸ Beware of buying more clothing than needed just because you got them cheap! Also be careful when buying jeans. Be sure they are for boys and not for girls. It might work when they are younger, but they are cut differently the bigger the sizes are. I don't know too many boys that like pink or purple curlicues or flowers on their jeans! I have also noticed that the nicest button shirts are on the girls' racks or even on the boys' racks by accident. Some shirts look like they are boys shirts but button the "wrong" way. Again, it might work on smaller boys, but older ones just seem to have a mental block about this.

✸ We require our children to change clothes when they come home from school to keep the school clothing nice longer.

✸ Thrift shops and resale stores are a good source for reasonably priced clothing. Be careful not to buy more than needed or it becomes an organizational nightmare!

✸ It is easier to be efficient if there isn't a surplus of clothing.

Sewing/Mending

✸ I like to have all my mending completely caught up before I start any other sewing project.

✸ When I find a hole or a missing button at any time; that is the time to fix it! I probably won't have more time later.

✸ Cut several garments at once, but only if you're fairly sure you will get them sewed before pieces get lost.

✸ A good pair of scissors is worth the investment and so is a good sewing machine, if you sew a lot.

✸ I like to do chain sewing and iron each piece before putting everything together. For chain sewing, I pick each piece off the pile of cut pieces and sew darts, elastic casing, and such things one after the other without cutting the thread until I'm ready for the piece again. It's much easier to iron the pieces before they are sewed together. Avoid hand sewing as much as possible. Use blind hem stitch for hems.

✸ Use a good pattern that fits! If you need to alter your pattern, keep the old one the same and cut out a new one. If the new one doesn't work, throw it away to avoid confusion, and try again. If you need more space in your bodice (as it seems most of us do sooner or later), cut the pattern in half from top to bottom and in half again from left to right (quarters). Stretch it out a little bit both ways and cut a new one. Don't forget to widen the skirt to match.

✸ Put patterns in 6"x9" manila envelopes and put the size and description and a drawing (if you have the talent) at the top and store them in a filing cabinet or a box. Special boxes are available for patterns. They have a place on the front to write which patterns are in the box. Then you can easily find what you need by flipping through them, especially if you have them divided by sections: shirts, dresses, etc.

✸ Buy fabric when it is on sale, but only if you'll need it. Beware of stashing so much fabric that you no longer know what you have, or even where it is.

✸ Work at cutting out clothing one week and prepare extra food. Then you can spend the next week sewing.

✸ I keep patterns in clear plastic sleeves (paper protectors) and in notebooks. You can have patterns divided into sizes/kinds and mark the outside of the notebook to make it so much easier to find that pattern you need.

✸ Don't keep patterns that are missing pieces, unless you can improvise. One of the biggest battles in organization for us women can be the teaching we received on saving things. Because so much is available that is relatively inexpensive, we can easily overwhelm ourselves with "stuff". Clean out your sewing drawers and closets, and then resolve to think twice before buying anything, even if it is cheap. If you can easily live without it, you are better off leaving it there. It is better to have a few well-kept things than so many cheap, unnecessary items clogging drawers and cupboards.

❋ I don't enjoy sewing myself so it is frustrating trying to teach my daughter. Instead of trying to do it all in one day, I have her choose the fabric and pattern one day. The next day we tackle cutting it out. Day 3 - sew darts and maybe put bodice and cape together. Breaking it down this way makes it manageable for both teacher and student!

❋ I focus on spring sewing in February and March, school sewing in July, and winter sewing in October and November.

❋ I usually focus on the child with the biggest need first. I alter the pattern as needed, then cut the amount of dresses or shirts they need. Then I sew according to colors to avoid changing thread more often than necessary.

❋ Set the iron right beside you and iron the seams as you sew.

❋ Work at sewing while little ones nap. Sew for your family so it does not become a lost art. Remember that our great and great-great grandmothers had to make the cloth as well as sewing it. Why are we so busy?

❋ I keep my patterns in identical large envelopes, set up in a box, with a description at the top of what is inside them. It's easy to flip through to find what I need when they are kept together in categories - dresses together, starting with larger sizes to smaller, then shirts, pants, jackets, pajamas, etc.

❋ I buy fabric when it is on sale, then keep it in boxes that are labeled front and top: dress fabric, shirt fabric, flannel, etc.

❋ Since the little ones like to be wherever I am, I use one wing of my sewing machine cabinet for my things, and the little one gets the other wing to play with puzzles, little cars and tractors, etc.

❋ To speed up sewing, use simple patterns and avoid extra frills and doo-dads.

❋ Children do not need lots of clothes, nor do they need to be expensive ones. Have fewer clothes but keep them clean and neat.

❋ Use the blind hem stitch on the sewing machines for hems.

My favorite was a woman who met me when I was in another state without my children. When she found out I had eight children, she said, "You don't look older than twenty!" (Ok, she was in her sixties and her perception was a bit off... or maybe having children keeps us young looking?!)

Scrapbook Pages

❋ Use stencils or cookie cutters to cut shapes out of nice calendar pictures.

❋ We like using cute pictures for scrapbook pages, so I have several manila file folders labeled animals, children, farm, etc., and when we see a picture we like, we add it to the appropriate folder. You can buy folders with closed sides that prevent the pictures from falling out when using the file.

❋ Keep a notebook where you copy meaningful

and interesting poems and sayings to make scrapbook pages easier to do.

✽ If you have a computer, use it to store meaningful poems and sayings. I have lost papers and books, but I never lost my computer yet! Although I must say I have lost information in a computer crash, which is just as frustrating.

✽ Cut up a calendar picture into a design; then glue the pieces onto the scrapbook page allowing a little bit of the paper to show through where it has been cut. This can be as simple as diamonds and squares or as complex as puzzle pieces. A Bible verse or other saying can be written in these spaces.

✽ Keeping things in a safe place is good, but children must learn some things are not for them. When things are ruined by little ones, I remind the older ones that they are responsible to keep their things out of the little ones' reach.

✽ We store our magic markers and rubber stamping supplies in a Rubbermaid container on a shelf out of reach of toddlers.

✽ Invest in a few simple but nice stencils for scrapbook pages.

✽ One idea I've used is tracing the toddler's hand on a calendar page. Cut it out and glue it on your page. Beside their left hand calendar picture, trace their right hand and do the writing in there, Bible verse, poem, etc.

✽ For an 8 ½"x11" page, cut a calendar picture to approximately 7"x9 ½". Cut the picture from corner to corner both ways, forming 4 triangles. Glue the triangles against the edge of their respective sides. Use the space in between for a poem, verse, etc.

✽ For a very simple scrapbook page, cut a calendar picture the size of your page and write an appropriate verse on it with whiteout. Or glue on a typed verse. Remember, it is the thought behind it that counts!

✽ One very simple scrapbook page idea that even young children can do is to take a nice calendar picture and cut it into diamonds or squares. Spread it out slightly allowing just a little space between pieces. Lay it on the scrapbook page, then glue into place. Add a fitting verse or a poem.

✽ Children's art projects can be used for scrapbook pages.

✽ For a quick scrapbook page, use purchased decorated paper and type or print an appropriate poem on it. There are many pretty papers available to fit any occaision.

Crafts and Supplies

✽ Small, plastic, stacking drawers like you can buy at Walmart are nice for scrapbook supplies. You can buy larger ones for stamping supplies, and shallow ones for papers, markers, pens and stickers. These can quite easily be stashed on a closet shelf to keep them safe from little hands. Plastic boxes with hard-to-open lids are a good idea for markers (especially permanent ones) if there are little ones in your house that might enjoy decorating the walls or carpets.

✽ Store colored pencils and magic markers in gallon-size Ziploc bags. It keeps them together, but it's easy to find the one you're looking for.

✽ We enjoy knotting baby comforters for CAM on the kitchen table. The comforter can be two pieces of material put together with batting in between. No time consuming piecing needed. Bind the edges with the sewing machine. It's fast, easy, and gives the children a chance to help people who are less fortunate.

✸ I have very few markers and those are kept on a high shelf in a closed cupboard. Our children are not allowed to have markers without special permission.

✸ We have our craft items in drawers that are off-limits for little hands.

✸ Want to remember to send sympathy cards? I make a list on the side of the refrigerator as I think of folks to whom I want to send cards. Then I get them all ready at one time.

✸ Our daughter and her cousin were just little girls when we were all visiting at grandpa's house one day. They had recently installed new carpet in the living room of their retirement home. When we mothers realized they had been quiet a little too long and went to investigate, imagine our horror when we saw that those two naughty girls had found some magic markers and were happily adding their own touch to the carpet! Imagine also our relief to discover that the markers were the washable variety and the marks were easily removed with water!

I was working as a maid for my aunt and uncle when they had a new baby. The children's cousins who live near them also had a new sibling about a week later than theirs. One of the preschoolers exclaimed, "There must be something going around!"

92 —— Mops, Muffins, & Motherhood

Paying the Bills

Render therefore to all their dues; tribute to whom tribute is due... Owe no man anything, but to love one another: for he that loveth another hath fulfilled the law. Romans 13:7a,8

11. Paying the Bills
Bookwork

Whether Dad or Mom takes care of the finances, both should have a general idea what is going on. If something should happen unexpectedly to the one who normally pays the bills, it can be a real hardship for the other one who knows nothing.

In some households this job is done together at a certain time of the week or month. That way they both know what their financial situation is. When decisions must be made, it is best if it can be discussed and a mutual agreement reached. However, the husband should have the final say and the wife should support the decision as long as it doesn't go against God's commandments.

It is the opinion of some people that the finances should be totally handled by the husband. This is fine if that is the way the two of you want it. Some men prefer to have their wives do it with their supervision and that is okay, too. But when wives take over and start to tell their husbands how this is going to be done, it has become a problem. It is true that there may be a few marriages where for one reason or another, the husband is not able to take charge. This can be a very difficult situation and usually should involve other church brethren, and/or family, but it must be handled prayerfully and carefully since a husband can very quickly feel incompetent if his God-given authority is undermined.

It can be very beneficial to plan a budget, and then stick to it. There are many books available from Christian financial counselors that can guide you through setting one up. If your husband is a day-laborer it is easier to set a budget because the monthly income is more evenly distributed throughout the year. You need to put some money aside, if at all possible, for unexpected expenses such as illnesses or accidents, or suddenly needing to travel due to death.

It is important to set aside a certain amount of our income to support the church and those in need. We struggled with the idea that we are taking from our creditors to give to the church until one day the thought struck us that we are taking from God to give to our creditors. I am pretty sure that most of us have areas where we could reduce our spending to come up with the difference. Jesus made it very clear in the story of the rich men and the widow putting money into the treasury (offering), that giving what we don't need anyway doesn't bring the blessings that giving what we really feel we need does. Sometimes we hear the saying "Give till it hurts". When we think of sacrificial giving, we must give up our self-will in order for it to be sacrificial. This giving can be in many ways, not just money. It may be in giving up our husband's time at home for the work of the church, in the ministry, on committees, or helping those who are in need. It might also include being on the school board or lending an older daughter to help out an overwhelmed mother when you could use her help yourself. However, I don't believe it is a good practice to neglect your own family to help others all the time; this can create bitterness in your own children when they see that everyone else is more important than they are. We need to find a balance.

Have a drawer, a box, or some other specific place to put bills and other important papers when they arrive. As you look through the mail, immediately discard junk mail into the trash can. Children enjoy playing with junk mail, but be sure you know what you're giving them and have some way of keeping this separate from the important mail. For instance, only let them have it at their little table, desk, or someplace like that. Again, be sure to screen everything you give them.

Unless you have good place to store them, don't save magazines. If you come across an article you want to save, cut it out and keep a file into which to put them. One thing to do is take an honest look at whether you really will use this information again. If not, throw it out! Magazines with bright, colorful pictures are good for scrapbooks. They also keep grumpy children occupied if you allow them to cut and paste for a while. Old newspapers are good fire-starters for campfires and wood stoves.

✻ I learned that filing the bills as I go saves time when it's tax time. I write them in a regular tablet: one page for feed, one for vet, one for repairs, etc. Then at tax time, just add each page.

✻ Junk mail that has blank pages is saved for scrap paper for the children to practice spelling words, etc. Be sure to pay attention that what you save is fit for children to see, though.

✻ Use old newspapers and magazines along with cereal boxes for mulching the garden.

✻ Old magazines that you want to keep can be stored in cereal boxes. If you feel creative, you can cover and decorate the boxes and write the name of the magazine and the year on the outside for easy reference.

✻ As soon as the mail comes in the house, we like to separate the important mail from the rest; we go through other mail when we have time.

✻ Do bookkeeping together.

✻ Clean out magazines monthly and newspapers weekly.

✻ Use Velveeta boxes in whatnot drawers for organizing those small things that get jumbled together otherwise.

✻ We keep a mug of pens and pencils at three different work areas.

✻ The bills get paid by me. I mark the calendar when they need to be paid as soon as they arrive in the mail, and then they get put in a bill holder on the counter. I usually sort through everything in the bill holder at least once a month to make sure everything gets paid.

✻ All tax papers get held together at the same place until we go to the accountant.

✻ Daily newspapers get thrown out the following day.

✻ We keep an envelope in one of the desk drawers where we add a little money now and then. This has come in quite handy time and again. If you don't have cash on hand, squirrel a little away into the savings account.

✻ I have one morning a week that I do computer work, go over bills, evaluate what is needed for the month, and organize. Mail is gone through daily, magazines go into the magazine rack, and junk mail to "File 13" (trash can). A box in the garage holds newspapers until the box is full, and then we burn the surplus. We like to keep some on hand, but like to limit the amount.

✻ I have one day a week that I do bookwork. The rest of the week the bills get laid on a pile on the desk (or in a drawer).

✻ Mail accumulates until company is coming. Then it gets thrown out.

✱ Doing bookwork early in the morning while the children are still sleeping, works well for me.

✱ Have a certain time each week to do the bookwork. Keep things filed properly and don't let it pile up! We sort mail promptly. Important items like bills are placed on the desk for filing, junk mail is discarded, and reading material is placed in an end-table drawer. When we have time to read, we know right where to look.

✱ My husband is not organized with paperwork and it boggles his mind, so we work at it together. We keep files of paid bills, filed by business name and also have a miscellaneous one. We sort junk mail directly to the trash without even opening it. Be careful, though, because sometimes what looks like junk mail is something quite valuable.

✱ My husband does most of the bookwork, but I help as needed.

✱ Magazines on gardening, raising small animals, and woodworking are worthwhile.

✱ Throw advertising flyers and junk mail into the trash can right away before it gets scattered all over the house.

✱ Magazines and newspapers are read, only very noteworthy articles clipped and filed by subject, and the rest discarded. Copies of our family newsletters and *Keepers at Home* and other magazines we want to save are stored in marked boxes in order by month/year - except when the readers mix them up!

✱ I do the desk work and we have folders in the desk for paid bills sorted by category. We also have a folder for unpaid bills.

✱ Mom does most of the monthly bill paying. Bills are opened immediately when received and the mailing date is put on the front of the envelope. They are then arranged in order of mailing date and kept in a slot in our roll-top desk.

✱ Catalogs and monthly magazines are gone through several times a year. Magazines that are stored away at the end of the year have their own spot, too.

✱ Use cereal boxes for storing magazines that you want to keep. One year per box, and mark the outside of the boxes by year and name of magazine. These cereal boxes can then be stored in larger boxes, that are also marked, one or two kinds per box.

✱ We have a separate trash can for paper and cardboard. That way we don't have our trash pile out back full of burnable trash. These make good fire-starters or can be used in the garden for mulch, or burned to fine ash. If you pay for trash pickup, and have a no-burn ordinance where you live, it could be worthwhile to find friends that may burn trash on their property.

✱ My husband and I both do the bookwork, whoever has time or gets to it first. Every time a bill is paid or a check comes in, we write it in the book we have for this purpose, under the right heading. We then file the bill in a corresponding file with the same heading. At the end of the year we add each column and take the book to the accountant. We clean out the files and put them in a box with the year written on it and store it in the attic, and then we start the new year with a new book and empty file folders.

✱ I really like the Quickbooks program we use on our computer. Balancing checkbooks is a breeze-if you make a mistake or forget to put a check or deposit in, you just add it and the computer puts it where it belongs and does all the correcting math for you. No more scribbles! It does take a little time to learn to use, but it is worth it in time savings later. And preparing for the accountant at tax time is as simple as copying a disk or printing a report or two for him.

> Children aren't prepared to face life if they haven't learned submission and responsibility.

Let's Go on a Trip

And he said unto them, come ye yourselves apart into a desert place, and rest a while: for there were many coming and going, and they had no leisure so much as to eat. Mark 6:31

12. Let's Go on a Trip
Traveling & Packing

Traveling with children is usually more work than staying at home. Some families like traveling a lot more than others. It is also true that some children travel better than others in the same families. We were always pretty faithful about having our children strapped in their carseats. I came to the conclusion that if people always strapped their children in from the time they were infants, they wouldn't have such a battle getting their toddlers to stay sitting in carseats. I am sure it is true that if you don't enforce the seatbelt law with your children from the beginning, you will have more battles than you would have otherwise. But then we had a child that just didn't care for her carseat, no matter what. Once more I was reminded that I shouldn't make judgments based only on my own experiences. It is still the law to have everyone strapped in and is a poor witness to the world when Christians drive around with babies on their laps or with children standing on the seats. Never, ever strap a seatbelt around a baby sitting on someone's lap! Think what the seatbelt would do to the baby from the force of the bigger person's body if the driver had an accident.

Getting ready for a trip can be very exhausting for a M.O.M. Hopefully you have a little warning that you will be traveling, giving you time to prepare some things ahead of time. If you have any small electronic games, hiding them for a while ahead of time can make them special again.

Use a packing chart to help avoid forgotten items. Look in the chart section of this book for a sample. If you have something like that to guide you, it takes some of the stress out of packing clothes for many people. It doesn't guarantee that you won't forget something, though. If you think of something you need to take that isn't on the list, write it down right away.

Traveling at night works well with children if the drivers can stay awake. For some people this is not a good idea. The children usually sleep and the miles roll by smoothly. It can be a good opportunity for parents to have a sharing time, taking into consideration that little ears can be listening when you think they are sleeping.

For some people, taking a No-Doze pill or drinking coffee or a caffeinated drink works well to stay at peak alertness. Or try ice-cold water. Munching on crunchy foods such as chips, pretzels, crackers, or carrots and celery also help you stay awake. Moderation is the key, since the combination of too many snack foods and too much soda pop can cause a bit of a problem. As one man so aptly put it, "My stomach feels like a garbage dump!"

Finally, sometimes the wisest thing to do is pull over and take a nap. Is it really worth risking your life and the lives of others to arrive at your destination a bit earlier? During one 16 hour trip I fell asleep at the wheel during the early hours of the morning. I was rudely jerked awake by the vibration of the rumble strips imbedded at the side of the road, averting a certain accident with who-knows-what results. My husband's head popped up,

"Are you sleeping front there?" "Not anymore!" was my shaky reply. Yet a few miles down the road I was fighting sleep again. There comes a time when I can no longer force myself to stay awake. I knew it was time to hand the steering wheel over. One important strategy is to allow extra time, if at all possible, when traveling long distances. This allows a little leeway for unexpected delays.

Having a pleasant trip depends a lot on keeping the peace. Somehow that job seems to rest heavily on Mom. We find that it is not always the younger ones that cause the biggest problems. Teach the older ones to read maps and tell where we are, where we will be going next, how far to the next road, etc. This is a good idea even if you use a GPS unit. You can ask them for alternate routes and why you may or may not want to go that way. They should have a good idea where they will be in relation to other states or provinces. Traveling is a good opportunity for education.

✻ If the children are being naughty with their mouths, don't allow them to speak for a certain length of time. If they are being naughty with their hands (picking at others, etc.) they must sit on their hands.

✻ We really like to travel in a motor home. Watching traffic on your stomach or taking a nap on a bunk over the driver is fun. Having a bathroom on wheels sure helps to eliminate some of the "potty stops" associated with taking families on trips. Also, clothing and food can be packed right into the motor home and gotten out as needed, rather than rooting through suitcases.

✻ I try to have three of each clothing item (except shoes and coats) for each child.

✻ Traveling in a van that is larger than needed for the family allows you to take the back seat out and put a bed in its place. A piece of plywood makes a good bed, with 2"x4" legs long enough to stash all the necessary paraphernalia needed for the family under the bed. Add cushions, pillows and blankets and you have a comfortable place for a nap.

✻ We like to play the ABC game, watch for license plates from as many different states as possible, or sing as we drive.

✻ The front passenger seat is considered a place of honor and can be used as a reward for good behavior, or withheld for bad behavior.

✻ We use one duffle bag per child. We like them better than suitcases because they collapse as they are emptied and therefore take up less room. We usually use trash bags (we found the 13 gallon size to be about right) for the dirty laundry (or you can make your own from cloth). They also can be stuffed in where there's room.

✻ Our friends, a family of twelve, came visiting us pulling a trailer with everything organized: boxes were marked, a rod for hanging clothes, and hooks for hanging things. Everyone knows where to look for that "thing" for which they are looking.

✻ Use lists for packing; food - clothing - camping supplies - Sunday clothes, all on separate lists but on the same piece of paper so they don't get lost.

✻ Traveling with children - bring electronic games, light-up toys for nighttime, cheap glow sticks from Walmart or Dollar General, story tapes or CDs keep peace for a while. Check the local library for story CDs, but be careful to screen them. Some of them have inappropriate content.

✻ It helps if Mom sits back with the children. (Not too helpful if mom gets carsick!)

✻ Use one duffle bag for travel entertainment: books, games, etc.

✻ Take pillows along. Our children often sleep while driving.

Let's Go on a Trip — 99

✱ If you like to go camping, have a list of what you need in your recipe box. Give this list to your child or children and have them collect the items and cross them off the list.

✱ Several days before you plan to leave, fill gallon or half-gallon jugs with water and freeze them. Don't fill quite to the top to allow for expansion. Use them in the ice chest and you avoid having water in the bottom making a mess. And it supplies you with ice-cold drinking water - from home! We also keep one jug between the front seats from the start of the trip to drink right away as it thaws. Keep it in a basin or something to avoid condensation moisture making a mess on the floor.

✱ We like to freeze soup and spaghetti to heat on our gas stove when we go camping.

✱ Make a list for each person in your family, and then each child that is old enough can gather their own clothes. I always double-check the clothes they have gathered before putting them into their duffle. I have them put in a plastic grocery bag for their dirty laundry.

✱ Hands to yourself! This is a good rule for traveling and otherwise. We learned it from a tutor who had it as a classroom rule.

✱ We like playing the ABC game. Find the letters of the alphabet in order from A-Z outside the vehicle in which you are traveling. Mom can help the ones that are falling behind. Another fun game is "I'm thinking of someone". One person thinks of someone and the rest try to guess who it is by asking questions that can be answered with yes or no. The person that guesses right first, gets to think of the next person.

✱ Use 2-quart juice bottles with juice, tea, or water. Freeze them (don't make them quite full), and then use them for ice packs in the ice chest. As they melt you can drink them as you travel.

✱ I have found that when we're packing for a trip the children are more than eager to help. Give each of the school-age children a list of everything they should put into their suitcase, and how many of each item. When they are done, check over it to make sure it is satisfactory.

✱ Our older children like to read while traveling, or keeping track of how many different states' license plates they see. Sometimes I save an interesting book that none of them have read, to read aloud while we're driving.

✱ For the little ones, it is helpful to have non-crumbly snacks like cheese, carrots, dried or fresh fruit and water in moderation (to avoid too many potty stops).

✱ Allow yourself plenty of time to get to your destination. Try to laugh about it when you make three potty stops before you're ⅓ of the way there. (Getting cross doesn't help anyway!)

✱ Even very young children can look for simple things like trucks with more than one trailer.

✱ It really helps if I sit in the back and let one of the children sit in front beside Daddy occasionally.

✱ At times I have made an older child responsible for packing a younger one's suitcase, making sure it gets to the vehicle, etc., in addition to their own.

✱ I have fond memories of the special box my mom prepared when we were going on a trip. She filled it with things that we didn't get at other times and we could hardly wait until she deemed it time to get something out of the box. I realize now that the anticipation of just what might be in that box was often as special as what actually was in it. Some of the things I remember are the *Yes and Know* invisible ink books, twisty balloons to make shapes

> The younger children keep the older ones laughing. It works as a kind of drawstring, drawing the family together.

Mops, Muffins, & Motherhood

of animals, regular balloons and markers to draw faces, etc., candy and gum, activity coloring books and crayons, and more.

✻ Make a list of what clothing will be needed, thinking of each day you will be gone. Make a separate list of food items, medicines, and miscellaneous items needed. Don't forget a flashlight if you plan to drive when it's dark! Save your list for the next time you are preparing for a trip.

✻ Our small sons like taking Matchbox cars and tractors to drive on the seat. School-age children like to play Mancala. We take a supply of books, but don't take more than you need. It is very hard on books to be taken traveling unless you keep track of where they are and have a good place to keep them.

✻ An activity book is a good pastime for preschoolers. We made our own from fabric: the one page has a large ladybug with a zipper down her back. Inside are little ladybugs. Another page has shapes with one side of snaps. Then matching shapes with the other half of the snap on to match up. The same idea with balloons on another page, maybe matching colors this time. Small squares of Velcro can also be used. A football on one page is laced with a shoestring to tie. You can either use grommets or tiny buttonholes. One page has a little girl with yarn hair to braid… and so on.

✻ Sometimes we take songbooks along from which to sing or we sing by memory while we drive.

✻ Spanking might be an appropriate punishment, but should not be done where it is visible to the public. I heard the story of a family who was in a restaurant. One of the children was not behaving and the father took him outside and administered needed discipline. Someone saw it and called the police. As the policeman, the father, and the person who reported it were having a discussion, a small crowd began to gather. The father told the policeman that either I (the father) can discipline my son now, or you (the policeman) can do it when he is 16. The assembled people clapped their hands in agreement and the police left without any further action. There are still some people out there with common sense!

✻ We filled a peanut butter jar with slips of paper for the children to take turns picking and opening every 15 minutes or so. They said things like: Sing a song of Daddy's choice. Recite Psalm 23 together. Tell about something you look forward to on this trip. Ask Mom to tell a story from when she was a little girl. List the names of Daddy's siblings in the correct order… Use your imagination!

We had customers that weren't from our area and they took notice of a few of the children playing. One of them asked how many children we have. When my husband replied that we have eight, the one lady backed up, was quiet for a bit, then asked again "How many?!" She walked away a few steps, came back and said, "God bless you!" Then she came over and gave me a hug!

102 —— Mops, Muffins, & Motherhood

A New Home

Now the Lord had said unto Abram, get thee out of thy country, and from thy kindred, and from thy father's house, unto a land that I will shew thee.
Genesis 12:1

13. A New Home
Moving

Most families move from one home to another sometime in their lives. The longer you live at one place, the more belongings you will be likely to accumulate. Circumstances that dictate why you are moving, how far you are moving, and how much time you have to get ready all make a difference as to how organized you can be. I have experienced moving only a few miles several times and also across state lines twice. I have moved in a very organized manner and I have moved in utter chaos!

One of the first things to consider when you are planning to move is to discard, sell, or give away those things you really don't need. If time allows, you may want to plan a yard sale to get rid of excess "stuff". If you don't have enough of your own, you may want to get together with some others to make it worthwhile. Each person should price their own items and add their initials, or each person could have certain color stickers. Then as the items are sold, just remove the stickers from the items and stick them on a page in a notebook, one page per person selling items. This makes it simple to divide the money when the yard sale is over. If you have things that are not good enough to sell, try to find a family that can use them. This also is a good time to practice throwing things away that aren't good enough to keep but aren't quite worn out. It seems this is rather difficult for those of us that were raised to be thrifty, but it is not thrifty to move things that we will never use. One rule of thumb that I've heard already is if you didn't use it for a year, get rid of it. Of course, this doesn't include infant clothes and other things that most of us don't use every year. Thrift stores are another option for giving things away; the money from selling things goes for a good cause. Christian Aid Ministries will also take good, used clothing with no stains or holes. The cost for shipping clothing across the ocean to poor countries is so high that they are very particular what they send. It is also appreciated if you make a monetary donation to cover the cost of shipping.

If you have plenty of time, it is a good idea to start by packing seasonal clothing and items you won't need before you move. Using strong boxes of similar sizes works best, although we have to use what is available. Banana boxes are a possibility and can often be gotten at no cost from grocery or convenience stores. Meat boxes and apple boxes are other possibilities. Make sure the boxes are sturdy and won't fall apart after being jostled from here to there and back again. Mark each box with what is in it and if you know in which room you want it, include that information. I had rolls of large labels from a scale that no longer worked and I put one on each end of the box. Then I marked it with a Sharpie magic marker so we could tell what was in it no matter which end was turned out. If you are really organized, you can number the boxes and keep a file box with 2"x4" cards stating what exactly is in that box. Then if you need something, you can check in the file box to see what number box in which an item is. Find that number on a box and, presto! There it is. Some people use this method for storing things in their attics or closets.

If you have been to the house into which you are moving, try to get measurements and a floor plan of each room. Plan where the furniture will go and number each room. Then mark each piece of furniture and each box with the appropriate number. On moving day or the day before, put a large piece of paper on the doorframe of each room with the corresponding room number. This simplifies getting the right things in the right place with minimum effort from you on a day when you will already be pulled in many directions.

If you will be having lots of helpers to unload, let someone else plan and provide the meal. One time I made the mistake of saying I will supply the sandwiches. Lunchtime came… where are the sandwiches? Oh no! I forgot to get the bread out of the freezer. And where exactly was the freezer? It had a lot of things piled on top of it. And where was the microwave to thaw the bread quickly? The other supplies were in the refrigerator which was also hard to access. I learned my lesson - when someone offers, don't turn them down!

One evening our 3-year-old said she's hungry. When asked what she's hungry for, she replied, "I smell a cookie with sprinkles on it!"

✳ When packing, make sure you put all the bedding that will be needed right away at one spot.

✳ Have a night-light or two at an easy-to-find place so you can plug them in that first night at your new home.

✳ Heavy-duty contractor trash bags work well for packing blankets, towels and washcloths, shoes, coats, and rugs. These can be bought at Home Depot, Walmart, or a similar store. They are well worth the money, since they can be dragged across the floor and will not tear very easily.

✳ We just moved and I asked my husband what his suggestion would be. His instant response with a grin, was, "Hire somebody to do it!"

✳ A two-wheeled bag wagon or an appliance cart can save your back. Put it under one side of the dresser or other piece of furniture and flip it back and the wheels carry the brunt of the load. This doesn't work as well on stairs. Appliance carts can be rented from a rental place or some appliance stores might rent you one. If you use one for stoves, washers, or other appliances, be careful that you don't damage the appliance from the bottom.

✳ We left our clothing in the drawers of our dressers and shrink-wrapped the entire dresser. This kept the drawers from falling out and protected the dresser from scratches. We used a lot of shrinkwrap to protect the furniture from damage. Then we used a bag wagon to wheel these heavy pieces of furniture outside and up the ramp of the trailer.

✳ If jars of canned goods are packed tightly into boxes, they do not need to be individually wrapped. Make sure you use sturdy boxes with strong bottoms.

✳ Old blankets and rugs work well for packing around furniture for protection against scratching or gouging.

✻ Shrink wrap works well to wrap garden tools to keep them from damaging other things.

✻ Put screws, nuts, or bolts for a crib or bed or any other small piece off furniture into a Ziploc bag and tape it with wide clear tape to the frame so you can find them when you need to reassemble the furniture. Be careful to use the tape in a spot that won't be damaged when you remove it.

✻ The post office will give you a moving kit for free if you ask. This will help you with changing your address. After you move, any mail that comes with a yellow forwarding sticker on the front indicates that that person or business doesn't have your new address. Make sure you change the address with magazines that you want to receive, since they do not get forwarded automatically.

✻ Getting address labels with your new address on them and giving them to friends and family makes it easy for them to update their address books by sticking them over the old address.

✻ Ask around about doctors, dentists, hospitals, etc. in the area before you need them. That way if an emergency pops up, you have an idea of what your options are. For example, the local hospital may have a reputation for being high priced or providing poor care. Find out what your options are by talking to the people who have lived in the area for a long time. It may be better to go a little farther unless it is a dire emergency. If you are not satisfied with the doctor you first see, find another one. It is important to find a good doctor who will know your family and work with you.

Our goldfish were coming to the top of the barrel and gulping for air before we put them out in the fish pond. After his nap, our 4½-year-old wondered if the fish are still coughing.

Leftovers

Whatsoever thy hand findeth to do, do it with thy might; for there is no work... in the grave, wither thou goest. Ecclesiastes 9:10

14. Leftovers
Miscellaneous

✺ Keep a two-gallon thermos with ice water on the picnic table outside or on the porch during the hot summer weather to avoid the constant opening and closing of the refrigerator door, and the tracking in & out of the house. Freeze water in larger containers than ice cube trays so the ice doesn't melt as fast. Use containers with slightly tapered sides to avoid splitting out the bottom. Some kinds of ice cream buckets work well for this if your thermos has a wide top. Since they are not tapered they will split sometimes.

✺ Do you have a houseplant that you neglected to water? It is so dry the water just runs out of the bottom of the pot instead of soaking into the soil. Set the plant under the water faucet and let the water drip into the pot for an hour or until it is well soaked. Another way to rehydrate it is to set the entire pot in a bucket of water and then letting it drain after it is completely wet.

✺ If you see little unwanted insects clinging to your plants, just swish the foliage in your soapy dishwater after you are done washing dishes. This doesn't work so well if the soil is loose. You can mix a little dishwashing soap with water and use a spray bottle to apply it to the plants, making sure you cover every area of the plant.

✺ Hooks are easier than hangers for children's coats and jackets.

✺ When you have small children it is easier to park close to a cart return in the parking lot, so you don't have far to go after you unload groceries and children.

✺ When shopping, be very careful about children in the basket of the shopping cart. Once our 4-year-old child reached out for something when she was standing up and tipped the whole cart on its side, spilling her and her baby brother (who was in the front where he belonged) onto the concrete floor. This resulted in two howling children, an embarrassed and flustered mother, and an early morning trip to the ER with the baby to check for a concussion since he woke up crying and wouldn't stop. Another tipping danger is when they hang on the side of the carts.

✺ Don't procrastinate! (Sigh)

✺ Our children really enjoyed the tape "Raising a Family" by the Mountain Stream Melodies. Here are some of the words from one of the songs, "Toys on the floor like a carpet; smashed peas on the screen door, dirty, must be cleaned; soiled diapers, too; you're feeling blue. What can you do? Tears from your little daughter- cryin' cause her brother pushed her into the mud. What a dreadful sound! Her dress is brown - hem's falling down. Daddy's working hard to earn a living, asking God for strength to go through each day… Tapes or CDs are available from Kenneth Rutt, Lititz, PA 17543. 1-717-626-0428

✺ Fingernail polish remover will take magic marker off walls. Be sure to use a kind that does <u>not</u> have acetone in it.

✺ To remove smells from Tupperware or other plastic containers, crumple up some newspaper

108 — Mops, Muffins, & Motherhood

and seal it tightly for several days. Another method is to let it set in the sunshine and fresh air outside for a few days.

* Clean your dirty combs by throwing them into the washer with a load of dirty laundry.

Time management

* Beware of the telephone! Lengthy conversations can wreak havoc with your schedule quite quickly. Cordless phones can be a big help to continue with the work, but it seems the ringing of the phone is an automatic signal for the children to start into some mischief.

* Make lists! They help you stay on track and remember things that might otherwise go forgotten.

Health

* Burns on fingers feel better if kept in cold water for several hours. Little ones will let the burned area in the water as long as it hurts.

* The best burn treatment is B&W ointment and burdock leaves. There are people specially trained in this method in many of the Plain communities. It is a good idea to know how to contact a trained person before you have a need. This method is also being used in a few hospitals. The B&W ointment works on wounds, as well as burns.

* If you are allergic to most underarm deodorants, try the Naturally Fresh deodorant crystal available from Walmart as a roll-on.

* Stuffy noses in infants can be caused by more than just a cold. Dry air can cause irritated mucus membranes to swell. Use a humidifier to moisten the air in your home. If the dryness is being caused by a wood stove, keep an open kettle of water on the stove to steam all day.

* Another common cause of stuffy noses in infants is allergies. This can be harder to pin down since many times the symptoms are constant or only appear a few days after exposure to the offending allergen.

* If a child wakes up in the middle of the night with croup, take them into a small bathroom and turn the shower on hot water full force to fill the room with steam. Another thing that can help is to wrap them warmly and take them outside in the damp air.

* If you are suspicious your child may have appendicitis, have them stand up as straight as they can. Have them jump up in the air a little. This will cause a short burst of pain if the appendix is inflamed. Another way to check is to press firmly and deeply with your hand on the left side of the belly, and then suddenly release the pressure, or have them lie down and lift the right leg, then thump the bottom of the foot with your hand. Either way, this sends shock waves to where the appendix is and it will cause sharp pain. One thing that can happen with appendicitis is that it bursts and the pain goes away. The child will feel much better for a while, but the pain will usually return with fever. This can very quickly become an emergency as the poison spreads throughout the abdomen. Doctors will tell you that this is very rare, but it does happen sometimes. Another thing that is rare is that a few people have their insides reversed so that appendix pain will be on the left because that is where their appendix is! Appendicitis can be rather difficult to diagnose sometimes. With some people it moves quickly and presents classic symptoms, others just don't fit into the normal text book case.

* Meningitis can also be life-threatening. One way to check is to have the child put his head down until his chin touches his chest. Because of inflammation in the spinal cord, this will be very difficult, if not impossible. We had one of our infants to the doctor

Leftovers — 109

because of sickness, and he gently bent the baby's head to his chest to check for meningitis.

✱ Epiglottitis is not as common, but is a life-threatening emergency in a small child if it occurs. If you have a young child hanging his head with chin jutting forward, drooling and struggling to breathe, get help immediately! Epiglottitis causes the epiglottis (the little flapper at the bottom of your throat that keeps liquid out of your lungs) to swell and will cut off the airways.

✱ Stinky feet? When washing feet and putting on clean socks every day doesn't work for good-smelling feet, try Borax powder. Sprinkle a bit in your shoes daily. This helped us after we had tried different creams, etc. and got no help at all!

✱ Another cause of stinky feet can be the dye in the socks. Try using white socks. Some places sell black socks with white feet for this reason.

✱ Be sure you let your daughters know what to expect before you face this situation… While sorting laundry one day, I discovered I had failed to give my daughter some education she should have had about menstruation. This was an embarrassing situation and it's better to discuss these matters before something like this happens to you!

WHEN SOMEONE COMMENTS ON MY "WELL-BEHAVED CHILDREN" IN PUBLIC, I JUST SMILE AND SAY, "THANK YOU". THEY DON'T KNOW HOW HAPPY I AM TOO, THAT EVERYONE IS BEING NICE AND POLITE. IT ISN'T ALWAYS THAT WAY, ESPECIALLY AT HOME!

Part 2

·RECIPES·

Our Meal Ideas

...and other tips for food preparation and serving

Planning, preparing, and serving food takes up a large amount of a mother's time. There are menu planning books available to help with this aspect of life. However, many of us find ourselves winging it spur-of-the-moment a lot more often than planning meals in advance. And many times if we do plan, something comes up and we have to improvise anyway. We can avoid undue stress if we know we have some things on hand at all times that we can use to prepare a meal on short notice.

Some of the questions I asked the mothers who received the questionnaires I sent out are: What do you serve for meals on short notice? How do you cope with guests that show up suddenly that you hadn't planned to feed? What do you keep on hand for quick company meals? What do you make for supper when it is suppertime and you didn't plan ahead? Here are some of the responses I received:

Quick Meals

✻ Hot dogs and ice cream

✻ I can quickly make a thickened sauce with clear gel and add frozen peaches to cool it down fast. This is a good dessert served with Cool Whip.

✻ Hamburgers thawed a bit in the microwave then spread under the broiler in the oven is pretty quick for us.

✻ Ready-made pizzas are easy, but take a half-hour to bake.

✻ One of our spur-of-the-moment meals is hamburger gravy over boiled potatoes, with strawberry milkshakes for dessert.

✻ I like to keep canned sausage on hand for a quick-to-prepare meat.

✻ Frozen hash browns are easy to put in the oven to heat while I make scrambled eggs for an easy, but satisfying, breakfast.

✻ Our supper favorite for twenty years has been tomato soup with fried ground beef and onion. Adding 2 tablespoons brown sugar makes it extra special. Tip: Add a sprinkling of baking soda to the boiling tomato juice before adding milk to keep the soup from curdling.

✻ Try baking pumpkin pie filling in a 9"x13" cake pan without a crust for an easy dessert. We love it!

✻ Quick suppers for our family: Ramen noodles and hotdogs, pancakes, hamburgers, macaroni & cheese. For a veggie we might serve carrots & dip. A company meal might consist of Trio (instant) mashed potatoes, hamburger gravy, and peas, with instant pudding topped with mini marshmallows for dessert.

✻ I rely heavily on my canned foods such as soups.

✻ I try to keep frozen chicken breasts on hand. I arrange them in a pan and cover with cream of celery or chicken soup mixed with one can of milk. Bake until chicken is done.

112 — Mops, Muffins, & Motherhood

✽ One of our favorite meals is barbecue hamburger sandwiches and potato soup. Dice peeled potatoes into a kettle then add salt, pepper, onion, and a sprinkle of parsley flakes. Add water to cover and cook until soft and then add milk. Heat until hot, but not boiling. You can add diced hard-boiled eggs and browned butter.

✽ I was happy to learn that packaged hamburger meat thaws quickly when placed in warm water.

✽ Cake can be served without frosting, or one of the children quickly makes rice crispy squares.

✽ I like to can vegetable soup for such occasions.

✽ In the summertime when it is too warm to heat up the kitchen, I rely on my crockpot and grill.

✽ For a quick ham & bean soup, I dice and cook a few potatoes, then add a can of baked beans (we like the Bush brand). Add sliced hot dogs and a can (from the baked beans) of milk. Serve with crackers.

✽ Hamburgers on the grill are a quick meal for us. I like to serve them with lettuce, tomato, and onions for a more complete meal.

✽ Canned meat helps make quick meals and casseroles. I like canned sausage and chicken thighs. I can the chicken thighs with the bones, but take off the skin and extra fat first.

✽ Filled canning jars and stocked freezer to the rescue! Buy when things are on special and buy in bulk. Canned Danish dessert made last minute company dessert many times.

✽ Always keep macaroni or noodles on hand for a quick casserole, when you don't have time to peel potatoes.

✽ A call at 9:30 Saturday night from my teenager-can 5 boys come for Sunday dinner?? Thaw ground beef overnight, then make a casserole of any kind and serve with jelly bread, a vegetable, and pickles. No dessert made? Mix fruit for fruit salad or serve applesauce. It doesn't have to be the traditional seven sweets and seven sours. Make it simple, not stressful!

✽ Scrambled eggs are our fast-food. Sausage links are easy to thaw and cook quickly, and are our substitute for hot dogs. Peel a few carrots and cut into sticks to serve with dip, slice some cheese and open a jar of fruit.

✽ One of the easiest and quickest meals is boxed macaroni and cheese. Cook according to directions, and then add peas and sliced hot dogs. This is my son's favorite.

✽ Tomato or potato soup and sandwiches is what we serve for a quick meal.

✽ We eat barbecued "anything"-hot dogs, chipped ham, sliced pork roll, grilled burgers, etc. I make a barbecue sauce (page 126) then we add our choice of meat. Heat and eat with bread and a slice of American cheese or on a bun. This is a good and easy crowd pleaser if you put it in a crockpot or roaster, but can tend to stain clothing since it is rather messy.

✽ When I make pizza, I like to make extra crusts. Then I bake them for about 10 minutes, cool them, and put them in the freezer for later use. If I want to take a meal to friends or relatives, I like to take as many of the baked crusts as I think the family will need, add a jar or two of pizza sauce, some pepperoni and cheese. They can make and eat the pizzas right away or freeze them for later use.

✽ Mountain pies are a family favorite and are nice for quick Saturday evening suppers or campfire-with-company meals. Mom just has to set out the supplies and everyone makes their own. If you aren't familiar with mountain pies or hobo pies; here is an explanation. You need to buy (or borrow) the long handled contraptions with a metal square at the bottom. There are two sides, hinged at the bottom, and you place your sandwich between the squares, bring the handles together, and use them to place the sandwich into the fire to be toasted. Flip it from one side to the other until the contents of the sandwich are heated through. The irons

Our Meal Ideas — 113

are available in singles that make one sandwich at a time and doubles that make two. We like the doubles so an older child can make one for a younger child at the same time he makes his own. These irons can be purchased at many Mennonite or Amish stores, or hunting and fishing outfitters such as Bass Pro Shop or Cabelas. To make the sandwich, take two pieces of bread, and top with your choice of ingredients. Our classic is pizza sauce, cheese, mushrooms, peppers, onions, pepperoni, ham, sausage or hamburger (fried), or any combination thereof. Or you can make it as simple as ham and cheese. Spray the iron liberally with nonstick spray and place your sandwich on it. Toast and enjoy! Beware of putting too many toppings on the sandwich or it will be squishing out the sides and make a mess. You can make dessert pies by supplying pie fillings, mini marshmallows, chocolate chips, and peanut butter. Breakfast mountain pies can contain scrambled eggs, sausage or bacon (fried) hash browns, ham, salsa, cheese, and anything else that sounds good to you. After the initial investment in the irons, only your imagination limits what can be made in them. For us, this is a must-have when packing for camping trips. If enough of your family and friends own some irons, it is an easy way to host a meal. Have each family bring their irons, sauce for their family, and a topping or two to share with everyone. You can supply the bread, drink, and paper supplies.

✳ Pizza bread is a super quick food. Take as many slices of bread as needed for your family, butter one side, and place it on a cookie sheet. Top the bread with sauce, a slice of cheese, and any other toppings you have on hand. Bake in an oven or under the broiler.

✳ Cheese sandwiches and tomato soup... beef noodle soup, using canned beef... macaroni and cheese with fried ground beef and onion and canned green beans mixed together... hot dogs (of course)... barbecued hamburger and mac 'n cheese...

hamburgers on the grill... potato soup... boiled potatoes in their skins served with butter, salt, ground beef cooked with taco seasoning, cheese sauce (depending on time and ingredients).

Foods to keep on hand for quick meals

canned foods	frozen foods	other foods
soup	vegetables	instant potatoes
cream soups	hash browns	instant pudding
meats	grated cheese	Velveeta cheese
Danish dessert	hamburger	lunch meat
fruit	Cool Whip	graham crackers
pizza sauce	pepperoni	rice
spaghetti sauce		noodles
green beans		macaroni

Company Meals

Preparing food for company is one of my favorite things to do. (Now, if I could only figure out how to enjoy the cleaning up just as much!) We have so many options for food compared to most people in the world. What we choose to serve should reflect the purpose of the gathering and what is available. If you know ahead of time that company's coming, you can prepare and freeze some foods early in the week (or even before) to avoid the last minute pressure. Meals don't have to be multi-course, elaborate affairs. In fact, most people feel more comfortable with common foods served in a relaxed atmosphere. If I am invited to a home where everything is "just perfect", I hardly feel comfortable to invite them into our home where things tend to be more "relaxed". I try to keep this in mind to avoid intimidating anyone else. We all have different talents in the area of entertaining just like we do in other areas of life and we must accept ourselves as we are as we work to improve. It becomes easier to have company as

114 —— Mops, Muffins, & Motherhood

the children get older and can help more, especially if they take an interest in having company come. Our attitude will soon be reflected in the children.

Let's get back to preparation for company. Plan the menu, taking into consideration what you have on hand. Decide if it will be a meat, potatoes, and vegetable meal, or a one-dish casserole. Then decide on the side dishes. I have found that a casserole can be just as much work as a full-course meal, but you can have it prepared a day before and it cuts down on the last-minute details when the company is already there. If you plan to have bread or dinner rolls, have them baked and put in the freezer while they are still slightly warm for a fresh-baked taste.

One of our favorite company dinners is barbecued meatballs, cheesy potatoes, and corn. I thaw the hamburger earlier in the week and add the other ingredients, form the meatballs, and then freeze them in the pan I will bake them in later. Then I just mix the sauce, pour it over the meatballs and pop them in the oven to bake while we are at church. For the potatoes, I cook and grate them earlier in the week or use frozen, shredded hash browns (not the hash brown patties). Then I make the cheese sauce in the morning and pop them in the oven with the meatballs. The corn is thawed on the counter all morning and heated while we put the finishing touches on the rest of the meal. This same procedure can be used with the menu modified to your liking.

If you choose to do a one-dish meal, you can prepare the meat you will use i.e. fry the ground beef (which can be frozen again), gather the ingredients you will use and place them together in the cupboard, and thaw any vegetables you might need. If you will be using a roaster, you can purchase plastic roaster liners to minimize the cleanup afterward. Peeled, raw potatoes will stay fresh several days if covered with cold water and stored in the refrigerator.

My mother was known for serving chicken noodle soup to traveling guests. Travelers themselves, she knew what happens if you get served three large meals a day when you are getting little exercise. Many were the times we heard visitors express their appreciation for the light meal they were served. Although I enjoy cooking and entertaining company, I try to remember that we should not try to outdo each other. And when I think of the many hungry people in this world, some possibly not too far away, I question whether we are being as responsible with our bounty as God would have us be. On the other hand we need to be given to hospitality and our daughters will not learn to cook well if they aren't taught.

Following you will find many recipes to help you plan a menu for company or just one dish to compliment a meal. These are the recipes I use over and over and some that have been contributed by others. It is my belief that recipes are only a guideline and they are meant to be modified any way you wish. However, if a friend serves you a dish and you ask for the recipe, then don't blame her if it doesn't taste the same as hers did if you changed the recipe! I have found when compiling these recipes that I have many foods that I prepare with the "dump" method, and I can't even find the original recipe. For these I tried to take a good estimate. When I was newly-married, I couldn't fathom ever cooking the way my mother did, but experience and practice are the best teachers.

You may want to photocopy the following pages and slip them into plastic page protectors and keep them in a notebook.

Our Meal Ideas — 115

Once when we had about five children, I took them to a restaurant while my husband was deer hunting. The waitress told me someone had paid my bill and wouldn't tell me who.

The Recipes

AMERICA WAS A BETTER PLACE WHEN MEALS WERE OPENED WITH PRAYER INSTEAD OF A CAN OPENER!

Index

BREAKFAST
Baked Oatmeal....................120
Baking Powder Biscuits............121
Breakfast Casserole...............122
Breakfast Pizza...................122
Egg Sandwiches....................122
French Toast......................121
Granola...........................120
Homemade Cereal...................120
Man Made Pancakes.................120
Pancake Syrup.....................121
Quick Oatmeal.....................120
Sausage Gravy.....................121
Waffles...........................121

BREADS
100% Whole Wheat Bread............124
Cornmeal Rolls....................122
Crescent Rolls....................123
French Bread......................124
White Bread.......................123

MEATS
Barbecue Chicken Sauce............124
BBQ Hamburger.....................125
BBQ Hot Dogs......................126
BBQ Meatballs.....................125
Grandma's Pot Roast...............127
Ham Balls and Glaze...............125
Our Favorite Ground Beef..........127
Poor Man's Steak..................125
Porcupine Meatballs...............125
Sloppy Joes.......................127
Soft Pretzel Dogs.................126

SIDE DISHES, VEGETABLES & SALADS
Applesauce Salad..................130
Baked Potatoes (in a roaster).....127
Cheese Potatoes...................128
Coleslaw..........................129
Company Noodles...................128
Creamy Rice with Yogurt...........131
Delicious Macaroni Salad..........130
Easy Macaroni and Cheese..........131
Frying Pan Filling................129
Greens and Bacon Salad............130
Martin's Salad Dressing...........129
Our Scalloped Potatoes............131
Potato Filling....................128
Scalloped Corn....................129
Seven Layer Salad.................130
Stuffed Eggs......................131
Trio Mashed Potatoes..............128

CASSEROLES, SOUPS, & MAIN DISHES
4-Layer Dinner....................137
Beef & Potato Loaf................131
Beef Noodle Soup..................136
Beef Taco Skillet.................132
Cheddar Cheese Casserole..........135
Cheesy Enchiladas.................133
Chicken and Rice..................133
Chicken Corn Noodle Soup..........136
Chickenetti.......................134
Corn Chowder......................137
Cream of Mushroom Substitute......138
Dairy Casserole...................135
Hearty Chicken & Rice Soup........138

118 — Mops, Muffins, & Motherhood

Hearty Hamburger Soup 135

Meat-n-Tater Pie 137

Meat-Potato Quiche 137

No-Boil Lasagna 134

Pig Stomach 134

Pizza Hut Crust 132

Potato Filling with Meat 138

Potato Soup 136

Sausage Potato Bake 136

Six-Layer Supper 134

Slop 135

Tacos and Haystacks 136

Tator Tot Casserole 135

Yorkshire Pizza 133

MISCELLANEOUS

Chex Party Mix 139

Icy Holiday Punch 139

Jell-O Roll-up 139

Ladyfingers 140

Lime Slushy 139

Puffed Rice Balls 139

Soft Pretzels 140

Two-Layer Finger Jell-O 138

CANNING

Banana Pickles 141

Barbecued Green Beans 141

Canned Beef 142

Pepper Relish 141

Pickled Red Beets 140

Pizza Hut Pizza Sauce 141

Sweet Peppers 140

Tea concentrate 141

Tomato Soup 140

Vegetable Soup 142

DESSERTS

Creamy Fruit Salad 145

Danish Dessert 142

Dump Cake 145

Eclair Dessert 143

Fruit Dip 142

Fruit Slush 144

Grape Sponge 143

Homemade Ice Cream 144

Hot Fudge Sundae Cake 145

Ice Cream in a Bag 144

Layered Lemon Dessert 143

Maple Pudding 143

Old-Fashioned Apple Dumplings 144

Pick-a-Flavor Pudding 144

Pudding Topper 145

BAKED GOODS

1-2-3 Bars 151

Amish Vanilla Pie 150

Black Bottom Cupcakes 147

Cinnamon Roll Yeast Cookies 148

Cream Donuts 151

Double Crumble Bars 146

Energy Cookies 147

Fresh Strawberry Pie 150

Frosting (Non-Dairy) 149

Fudge brownies 146

Granola Bars 151

Our Favorite Chocolate Cake 147

Outrageous Chocolate Chip Cookies . . . 148

Peanut Butter
   Chocolate Chip Cookies 147

Peppermint Chocolate Cookies 148

Pie Crust 149

Pumpkin Chocolate Chip
   Whoopie Pies 149

Raw Apple Cake 146

Sour Cream Pear Pie 150

Strawberry Shortcake 149

Tandy Cakes 146

Two-Egg Cake 151

The Recipes — 119

Breakfast

Homemade Cereal

4 c. oatmeal (heaping)
8 c. cornflakes (crushed) (measure, then crush)
½ c. coconut
½ c. raisins (optional)
1 c. chocolate chips
½ c. honey
½ c. brown sugar
1 tsp. salt
6 Tbsp. butter
2 Tbsp. peanut butter (or more)

Mix honey, sugar, salt, butter, and peanut butter together and heat in microwave. Pour over cereal mixture. Bake at 225° for 45 minutes. Stir occasionally, breaking up chunks.

You can add other ingredients as your family likes it. I usually make the sauce 3x for a double batch of cereal. I add Rice Krispies and sunflower seeds.

Granola

6 c. oatmeal
¾ c. wheat germ
½ c. coconut
1 c. chopped nuts
⅔ c. honey or corn syrup
⅔ c. vegetable oil
2 Tbsp. water
1½ tsp. vanilla

In a large bowl combine dry ingredients. In another bowl combine wet ingredients, then add to first mixture. Stir to coat evenly. Bake at 300° for 25-30 minutes or until lightly toasted. Stir twice during baking.

Baked Oatmeal

2 eggs, beaten
1 c. milk
½ c. vegetable oil
1¼ c. brown sugar
2 tsp. baking powder
1 tsp. salt
¾ tsp. cinnamon (or more)
3 c. quick oats (oatmeal)
½ c. raisins (optional)

Mix everything together adding quick oats and raisins last. Bake in 8"x 12" (or 9"x 13" for 1½ batches) baking dish for 25 minutes at 350°. Yield: 6 to 8 servings.

This is a good one for Sunday morning or anytime you are pressed for time in the morning. Just mix it up the night before and refrigerate. Pop it in the oven in the morning and let it bake while you do other things.

Quick Oatmeal

For a quick breakfast for one or two, take 1 cup milk, ½ cup oatmeal, and ¼ cup brown sugar. Pop in the microwave or heat on the stove. Add fruit if desired. Multiply recipe for more people.

Man Made Pancakes

2 c. milk
2 c. flour
½ c. wheat germ
2 eggs
1 tsp. baking powder
½ tsp. salt
2 Tbsp. salad oil
2 Tbsp. sugar

Mix ingredients together and beat until well mixed. Let stand a few minutes before frying on a greased skillet at 400°.

Our family doesn't care for those fluffy "nothing-to-them" pancakes. I started to make these and they are our favorite. Wheat germ can be kept in the freezer to keep it from getting rancid.

Pancake Syrup

2 c. water
4 c. brown sugar
1 tsp. maple flavoring
2 Tbsp. butter (optional)

Stir together in medium saucepan and boil 1 minute. Store in refrigerator.

My family isn't too happy if I try to serve them bought pancake syrup. This recipe is easy and delicious. Sometimes I use more water to dilute all that sugar. Adjust to your family's taste. We use this syrup on pancakes, French toast, waffles, with biscuits and gravy, and on scrapple.

Waffles

2 c. flour
1 Tbsp. baking powder
1 tsp. salt
2 Tbsp. sugar
3 eggs, separated
1½ c. milk
½ c. vegetable oil

Combine first 4 ingredients. Beat egg yolks; add milk and oil. Stir in dry ingredients. Beat egg whites until stiff and fold into batter. Bake on hot waffle iron.

French Toast

3 eggs, beaten
1¼ c. milk
⅛ tsp. salt
½ tsp. vanilla
cinnamon (optional)

Dampen bread on both sides and fry until light brown. Homemade bread is best!

This is a good way to use up stale bread.

Baking Powder Biscuits

2 c. flour
3 tsp. baking powder
½ tsp. salt
½ tsp. sugar
4 Tbsp. shortening
¾ c. milk
1 egg, beaten

Sift dry ingredients together. Cut in shortening. Add milk and egg; knead. Roll out to ⅜ in. thick and cut with cutter. Bake on ungreased sheet at 450° for 12 minutes.

Sausage Gravy

1 lb. sausage
4 c. cold milk
2 Tbsp. butter
salt and pepper to taste
¼ c. flour

Brown the sausage and drain. Return to skillet and add butter and flour. Stir until the flour has coated the sausage. Turn heat to medium-low and slowly add cold milk, stirring constantly. Continue stirring until the gravy has thickened. Add salt and pepper and/or cayenne pepper. Use hot sausage for more spice.

Sausage gravy and biscuits is one of our favorites. The recipe for biscuits is easy and quick to make. I don't bother with rolling them out and cutting them. I just drop them by spoonfuls in a heap on the cookie sheets. I might flatten them slightly with my fingers but the children are going to tear them up before putting gravy on them anyway, so I don't worry about how they look. These biscuits can also be served as a bread to complement a soup meal. If you want to, you can buy the pop-and-bake biscuits at the store to make it really easy. For the gravy, I usually buy the peppered gravy mix and add fried sausage. I buy the mix at Wal-Mart.

Breakfast Casserole

1 lb. sausage, bacon, or turkey ham
6 slices bread
Velveeta cheese
9 eggs
3 c. milk
½ tsp. dry mustard

Place bread in buttered 9"x 13" pan. Top with meat (fry bacon or sausage first). Place cheese slices over meat. Combine eggs, milk and dry mustard and beat well. Pour over cheese, meat and bread. Cover and refrigerate overnight. Bake at 325° for 1 hour (or less).

This one can be frozen for a length of time. When you need it, put it in the oven (frozen) overnight on time bake. Wake up to a hot breakfast all ready for you!

Egg Sandwiches

Egg Sandwiches make a yummy and filling breakfast. Lightly fry buttered hamburger buns (or some other type of buns or bread), fry eggs, and place on buns. Top with a slice of cheese and add some meat if you wish, and the top of the bun. Pop in the oven or microwave briefly to melt the cheese. Meat options include bacon, pork roll, sausage patty, or ham. You can make these in quantity for larger gatherings or to freeze for a grab-heat-and eat sandwich. To simplify the egg portion of the sandwich, you can beat 18 eggs with ½ cup of milk, pour into a greased cookie sheet with sides and bake in a 350° oven for about 15 minutes or until the eggs are set. Let cool slightly, and then cut into squares to fit on the buns.

Breakfast Pizza

Breakfast pizza is another good, filling option. Use a baked pizza crust and top it with your choice of meat, scrambled eggs, cheese, sauce, hash browns, and vegetables such as onions, peppers, tomatoes, etc. Use your imagination and whatever is on hand!

Breads

Cornmeal Rolls

⅓ c. cornmeal
½ c. sugar
2 tsp. salt
½ c. shortening
2 c. milk
1 Tbsp. yeast
¼ c. warm water
2 eggs
4 c. flour (or as needed)

Cook cornmeal, sugar, salt, shortening and milk till thick like mush. Cool to lukewarm. Add yeast, dissolved in warm water and add eggs. Beat thoroughly and add flour till you have a soft dough. Knead well. Let rise till double. Punch down, roll out and cut. Brush with butter and sprinkle (dust) with cornmeal. Place on greased cookie sheet and let rise. Bake at 375° for 15 minutes.

My husband likes to tell people that we have six and one-half dozen children. (twelve)

Crescent Rolls

1 pkg. yeast (1 Tbsp.)
3 Tbsp. warm water
½ c. shortening
1 tsp. salt
1 c. hot water
2 eggs
½ c. sugar
4 c. flour
butter

Dissolve yeast in warm water; set aside. Place shortening and salt in hot water. Let set until lukewarm. Beat eggs and mix in sugar. Add shortening and yeast mixtures. Stir in 2 cups flour and beat well. Gradually add remaining flour, place in bowl, cover and refrigerate overnight. Two hours before serving, divide dough in half (or thirds). Roll out to ¼" thick. Spread with butter. Cut into 12 pie shaped wedges. Roll up each wedge, starting at the largest end. Place on greased baking sheets and let rise for 2 hours. Bake at 350° until lightly browned. One recipe makes 24 rolls.

I mixed them in the morning and rolled and baked them in the afternoon. Worked great.

White Bread

2 tsp. sugar
2 Tbsp. yeast
1 c. warm water
⅔ c. sugar
2 Tbsp. salt
4 c. warm water
6 Tbsp. vegetable oil (scant ½ cup)
14 c. bread flour

Mix together sugar, yeast and water. In a bowl, mix rest of ingredients. Add yeast mixture and mix well. Add 10 cups bread flour, and then 4 cups more as needed. To make a light wheat bread, use 4 cups wheat flour and 10 cups white. Cover with a cloth and let rise 2 hours. Punch down and let rise 1 hour. Form into 5 loaves and place in greased bread pans. Let rise 2 hours and then bake at 350° for 30 minutes.

For soft bread, dough should be slightly sticky. Kneading helps develop the elasticity needed to keep the bubbles from popping for light, fluffy bread. Adding a teaspoon or two of wheat gluten can help if you have a problem with flat loaves. I have a commercial mixer and I like to let it knead until the dough is firm and spongy, but not dry. As you add the last cups of flour, you have enough when the dough pulls away from the side of the bowl. Don't add too much flour or you will have dry crumbly bread. Store yeast in the freezer to keep it fresh. Make sure your water isn't too hot or it will kill the yeast and you will have flat bread.

The Recipes —— 123

French Bread

2 Tbsp. sugar
2 Tbsp. shortening
2 tsp. salt
2 Tbsp. yeast
1 Tbsp. sugar
6½ c. bread flour

Mix first 3 ingredients with 2 cups hot water. Cool to lukewarm. Dissolve 2 Tbsp. yeast and 1 Tbsp. sugar in ½ cup warm water. Add to liquid mixture. Stir in flour and let rise 10 minutes. Stir and let rise every 10 minutes at least 4-5 times. Dough should be slightly sticky. Divide dough in half and roll out to less than ½" thick. Roll up like jelly roll and place on a greased cookie sheet. Slash dough every 2" about ¼" deep. Bake at 400° for 20-30 min.

I like to use this recipe if I need bread to go with soup or spaghetti. You can make garlic bread by adding garlic salt or powder. It is best eaten warm.

100% Whole Wheat Bread
(Fresh-ground wheat)

5 c. water
1½ c. sugar or honey (sometimes I do half of each)
⅔ c. vegetable oil
4 eggs
5 tsp. dough enhancer (available at most bulk food stores)
9 c. fresh ground whole wheat flour
⅓ c. instant yeast
5 c. fresh ground flour
1 Tbsp. salt

Mix first five ingredients together, then add whole wheat flour and yeast. Mix for 5 minutes then let set 8-10 minutes. This is the first rise. Add 5 c. flour and salt. Let rise 30 minutes. Form into 5 loaves and place in greased bread pans and place immediately into a 350° oven and bake for 30 minutes. Or, if you prefer, let rise for 15 minutes before baking.

Meats

Barbecue Chicken Sauce

1 qt. vinegar
1 lb. butter
¼ c. salt

Second Part:
1¼ c. lemon juice
⅛ c. salt (less or eliminate)
2½ tsp. pepper (omit if using sprayer)
¼ c. brown sugar
½ bottle hot sauce (optional)
1¼ tsp. Worcestershire sauce
2½ c. ketchup
¾ lb. butter
1½ tsp. mustard

Heat first three ingredients till butter is melted. Spray on chicken while grilling.

Heat second part together until butter is melted. If spraying add 1 cup water. Stir well. Put on chicken when almost finished. (Approx. 50 leg and thighs.)

This recipe is for chicken made over a charcoal pit preferably using a rack that has the chicken between two wires and flips from one side to the other. The first part of this sauce is a tenderizer and helps keep the chicken moist. To apply the sauces, we use a 2-quart jar with a screw-on lid that has holes punched into it with a sharp knife. We shake the jar, splashing the sauce onto the chicken. Some people use a handheld sprayer, meant to be used to apply sprays on plants. They aren't real easy to clean and definitely buy a new one, not one you already used for spray materials! If you choose to spray it, do not add the pepper because it will clog the sprayer.

BBQ Hamburger

2 lb. hamburger
1 onion
½ c. ketchup
2 Tbsp. brown sugar
2 Tbsp. vinegar
2 tsp. mustard
1 tsp. Worcestershire sauce
1 tsp. salt

Fry onion and hamburger. Add rest of ingredients and simmer for 20 minutes. Serve on hamburger buns. This works well in a crockpot.

Porcupine Meatballs

1 lb. ground beef
¼ c. minced onion
½ c. uncooked rice
salt and pepper to taste

Mix together and form into balls. Place into greased casserole with tight-fitting cover. Combine in dish 1 can cream of celery soup and ½ cup water. Pour over meatballs. Cover and bake at 350° for 1¼ hours.

If your beef is too lean, add ½ cup water.

Ham Balls and Glaze

buy oven ready ham loaf
   ½ lb. per person is plenty

Ham Ball Glaze:
2 c. brown sugar
2 Tbsp. dry mustard
½ c. vinegar
¼ c. water

Form ham loaf into balls and put in pans. Pour glaze over ham balls. Cover with foil, shiny side down. Bake at 200° starting at 7:00. Turn up to 250° before leaving for church.

This is a good choice for company meals. If you don't have the time to form the balls, just make a loaf like meat loaf. If you don't have time or the ingredients for sauce, you can pour pineapple juice over the ham balls before you bake them.

BBQ Meatballs

3 lb. ground beef
1 (12 oz.) can evaporated milk or 1-1½ c. milk
1 c. oatmeal
1 c. cracker crumbs
2 eggs
½ c. chopped onion
½ tsp. garlic powder
2 tsp. salt
½ tsp. pepper
2 tsp. chili powder

Sauce:
2 c. ketchup
1 c. brown sugar
½ tsp. garlic powder (optional)
½ tsp. liquid smoke
¼ c. chopped onion

Mix together the first 10 ingredients and form into balls. Meatballs can be made ahead and frozen. Add sauce when ready to bake.

Sauce: Mix together stirring until sugar dissolves.

This is an all-time favorite with our family. You can make these meatballs ahead in large quantities, freeze them single layer on cookie sheets, then break them loose and keep them frozen in heavy-duty plastic bags or containers until you need them. Remove as many from the freezer as you need, put into a pan, and pour the sauce over them, bake and eat.

Poor Man's Steak

3 lb. ground beef
1 c. cracker crumbs
1 c. cold water
1 Tbsp. salt
¼ tsp. pepper
1 onion, chopped

Mix all ingredients; press out on cookie sheet to ½" thick. Refrigerate till cold. Cut in squares, roll in flour and brown in oil. Place in pan and pour 1 can mushroom soup and 1 can water over top. Bake at 325° for 1½ hours.

Here's another one that can be prepared early in the week and frozen until needed. A pizza cutter works real well for cutting them into squares.

The Recipes — 125

BBQ Hot Dogs

¾ c. chopped onion
3 Tbsp. butter or vegetable oil
½ c. chopped celery or
   ½ tsp. celery seed
1½ c. ketchup
¾ c. water
3 Tbsp. brown sugar
3 Tbsp. vinegar (optional)
1 Tbsp. Worcestershire sauce
1 Tbsp. yellow mustard

Sauté onion and celery in butter or oil until soft. Add rest of ingredients and bring to a boil. Add hot dogs and simmer until hot.

This sauce can be poured over the hot dogs (or other meat) and popped into the oven or a crockpot.

We use this sauce for more than just hot dogs. Chipped ham, pork roll slices and grilled burgers are also delicious. We have put this sauce into roasters and added grilled burgers to sell at food stands at sales.

Soft Pretzel Dogs

4 tsp. yeast dissolved in
   3 c. lukewarm water
Add:
¼ tsp. salt
2 Tbsp. brown sugar
8 c. Occident flour (or 1 c.
   whole wheat and 7 c. white)

Roll out dough and wrap around hot dogs or sausage links. First wrap a piece of cheese around each hot dog or link. Dip each dough wrapped dog in soda solution of: 1 cup water and 4 teaspoon soda. Put on a well-greased cookie sheet. Sprinkle with pretzel salt, and bake at 375° for 20-25 minutes or until golden brown. Brush with butter.

This is a Sunday supper special at our house. Usually Dad makes them with help from the children.

We use our gas grill quite a lot. We often keep hot dogs and preformed frozen hamburgers on hand. If you make your own burgers, it works better if you make sure to pack the meat as tightly as possible and then freezing them before putting them on the grill. Another specialty we sold at food stands that were a big hit was barbecued chicken breast sandwiches. Mix thawed chicken breasts, mayonnaise, and chicken seasoning and marinate them for several hours or days. They can also be frozen like this. Grill over medium heat until the center of the fattest part is no longer pink. Slather them with Sweet Baby Ray's barbecue sauce and grill just enough to make it stick. We sold them as sandwiches, but they are good just plain, too.

Another favorite for our grill is steak. Choose the better cuts such as T-bone, sirloin, or tenderloin. You can marinade them if desired. One of the easiest marinades is a bottle of Italian dressing. Let them soak in the marinade for at least several hours. Grilling in this family is done by Dad. He says fairly high heat and getting it done fast is the trick to tender steak. Before grilling, we pound them with a tenderizing hammer after sprinkling them with steak seasoning, usually Montreal Steak Seasoning. Do not salt or pierce them with a fork or they will be tough. We use a pinchers or long-handled flipper to turn them over.

Our 6-year-old daughter said, "We could have a baby tonight." To which her brother, 1½ years her senior, replied, "God could give us one every day."

Recipes from Others

Our Favorite Ground Beef

1 lb. ground beef
2 Tbsp. raw vinegar
¼ c. chopped onion
1½-2 c. yogurt
1 tsp. salt
½ tsp. herb mix or lovage, chives, sage, etc.

Pull beef apart slightly and sprinkle with vinegar. Toss together, cover and refrigerate 1-2 hours or overnight. Omit that step if pushed for time, but it does make it easier to digest, and improves flavor.

Brown ground beef with onion. When browned, remove from heat and add rest of ingredients.

Serve immediately. If you're like me and can't serve immediately, keep it hot, and only add yogurt when you're ready to serve. I serve this over cooked rice, or white or sweet potatoes with a vegetable.

Sloppy Joes

1½ lb. hamburger
½ c. onion
celery as desired
2 Tbsp. Worcestershire sauce
1 c. ketchup or tomato soup
1 Tbsp. mustard
2 Tbsp. brown sugar
2 Tbsp. vinegar
1 tsp. chili powder
1½ tsp. salt

Simmer hamburger, onion, and celery together until done. Add rest of ingredients. Simmer 5 minutes. Serve with warm buns.

Grandma's Pot Roast

1 (3-5 lb.) roast
1 pkg. onion soup mix
1 small onion
2 Tbsp. Worcestershire sauce
1 can cream of mushroom soup

Put in crockpot on low in the morning and have for supper. Turn roast every few hours if you are at home. Serve with mashed potatoes. 8 servings.

Side Dishes, Vegetables, & Salads

Baked Potatoes (in a roaster)

40-60 potatoes
melted butter
1-2 Tbsp. thyme
1-2 Tbsp. basil
1-2 Tbsp. oregano

(If you use large potatoes, cut them in half or quarters.) Mix together butter and seasonings and roll potatoes into this mixture. Place 3-4 cups water in bottom of roaster. Bake at 350° for 2 hours. Then turn very low for 1 hour.

These potatoes can also be baked in an oven at 350° until soft, about 1 hour, if they are put in a pan single-layered. You can make a whole meal around the potatoes by serving ground beef cooked with taco seasoning, cheese or cheese sauce, butter, salt, pepper, salsa, and assorted vegetables such as tomatoes, green peppers, lettuce, onions, or whatever is available that strikes your fancy. Other seasoning options are garlic salt and chives.

The Recipes — 127

Trio Mashed Potatoes

1 qt. milk
½ c. butter
6 oz. cream cheese
1 qt. water (hot from the tap)
2 c. potato powder
1 tsp. salt
1 tsp. onion salt or sour cream & onion powder
¼ tsp. pepper

Heat first 4 ingredients till almost boiling. Pour into mixer bowl and add rest of ingredients. Mix till combined and beat till fluffy.

This potato powder comes in a #10 can, and is sold under different brand names. It is not the instant potato flakes more commonly available.

This recipe is commonly used for weddings; just mix each batch separately until you have enough. One recipe fits into a Kitchen Aid mixer. Pour each batch into a roaster lined with a plastic roaster liner and keep hot until ready to be used. On a smaller scale, use a crockpot. These can be made on Sunday morning and will be ready to be served when you come home for lunch.

Company Noodles

2½ qt. water
3 tsp. salt
saffron
butter
1 lb. kluski noodles

Boil together water, salt, saffron and butter for 5 minutes. Add noodles. Turn off burner and let set for 2 hours or more. Delicious with brown butter.

This is another recipe that can be prepared on Sunday morning and be ready to serve when you get home from church. Be sure to use kluski, homemade, or another thick noodle, or you will have mush when you get home. I like to bring them back to a boil after arriving home to be sure they are hot when I serve them. I use a spaghetti server to dip them out of the water to avoid getting too much juice.

Cheese Potatoes

1½ qt. cooked potatoes, diced or shredded
2 c. milk
¼ c. butter
¼ lb. Velveeta cheese
¼ c. parsley flakes
1 Tbsp. flour
1 onion, chopped
8 oz. sour cream (optional)
1 c. cheddar cheese powder (optional)

Brown butter and add flour. Gradually add milk and cheese, then rest of items. Pour sauce over cooked potatoes to serve.

You can cook, peel, shred, and freeze the potatoes early in the week for a company meal, then make the cheese sauce on Sunday morning and pop into the oven or crockpot. Another option is to buy frozen shredded hash browns instead of cooking your own. You can also add cubed ham or another cooked meat and a vegetable and turn it into a casserole.

Potato Filling

½ c. butter, melted
1 c. chopped celery
1 med. onion, chopped
1 c. boiling water
saffron (optional)
4 qt. bread cubes
6 eggs
1 qt. milk
3 tsp. salt
1 tsp. pepper
1 qt. mashed potatoes

Combine first 5 ingredients together and cook for 15 minutes. Mix the rest of the ingredients together except bread crumbs. Gently mix everything together in baking dish. Bake at 350° for 45 minutes.

This is one of my family's favorites. Perfect with turkey and trimmings!

128 — Mops, Muffins, & Motherhood

Frying Pan Filling

Melt butter in a frying pan large enough to hold the amount of filling needed. Sauté onion and celery in butter until it is soft. If you don't have celery, use celery seed or celery salt. Add bread cut or torn into small pieces, and stir occasionally until lightly browned. In a bowl, mix eggs, milk, salt, and pepper. Pour over the bread and stir occasionally until the milk and egg mixture is cooked. I use bread crusts that I save in the freezer, since my family isn't fond of crusts. For my family, I use approximately one stick of butter, nine eggs, and six cups of milk for a large frying pan of bread cubes. I never measure anything anymore, so you may need to tweak the recipe to your own taste. How much liquid you want to add depends on whether your family likes their filling moist or dry.

Scalloped Corn

2 c. corn
1½ Tbsp. butter, melted
4 eggs
1 c. cracker crumbs (scant)
2 c. milk
¾ tsp. salt
pepper to taste

Beat eggs, add butter and mix with corn. Add seasoning. Add milk and mix well. Fill buttered baking dish half full and cover with half of crumbs. Add remaining corn mixture and rest of crumbs. Bake at 350°-375° for 30-40 minutes.

I usually just mix the cracker crumbs in last rather than making layers.

Coleslaw

1 lg. head of cabbage
¼ c. vinegar
¾ c. sugar
1 c. mayonnaise
½ c. half and half cream
¼ tsp. salt
grated carrots

Grate head of cabbage. Mix together vinegar, sugar, mayonnaise, half and half cream and salt; add cabbage and mix well. Add grated carrots for color.

Martin's Salad Dressing

1 c. mayonnaise
⅛ c. vinegar
¼ c. ketchup
1 Tbsp. mustard
1 c. sugar
½ tsp. paprika
¼ tsp. salt
3 tsp. water
¼ c. vegetable oil

Mix all together in blender. Our family likes this dressing better than any other bought or homemade salad dressing.

"I want to get some gushy bears." (Gummi bears)

Seven Layer Salad

1 head lettuce, shredded
1 c. diced celery
1 c. shredded carrots
4 hard-boiled eggs, chopped
2 c. slightly cooked peas (or frozen peas, thawed)
1 med. onion
8 slices bacon, fried and chopped
2 c. mayonnaise or Miracle Whip
2 Tbsp. sugar
4 oz. grated cheese
tomatoes (optional)

Place first 7 ingredients in layers in order given using a 9"x13" pan. Mix mayonnaise and sugar and spread on top. Top with cheese. Refrigerate 8 hours or overnight. Serve salad in layers or add tomatoes and toss when ready to serve. Variation: Carrots and peas can be omitted.

Greens and Bacon Salad

8 slices bacon
2 qt. broken salad greens
3 hard-boiled eggs
8 cherry tomatoes, halved
⅓ c. mayonnaise
2 Tbsp. sugar
2 Tbsp. vinegar
2 Tbsp. vegetable oil
2 tsp. dry mustard
1 tsp. paprika
½ tsp. salt
¼ tsp. garlic salt

Cut bacon into bite-size pieces and fry. Put greens in salad bowl; arrange eggs, bacon and tomatoes on top. Combine remaining ingredients and serve with salad.

Applesauce Salad

2 c. boiling water
⅔ c. bulk red Jell-O
½ c. red hots (cinnamon hearts)
1 Tbsp. unflavored gelatin
½ c. cold water
1 qt. applesauce

Melt candy in hot water. Add red gelatin and stir till dissolved. Dissolve unflavored gelatin in cold water and add to mixture. Add applesauce, stir well and chill until firm.

This is delicious served with cottage cheese. I like to make this in a ring Jell-O mold, and then serve it with cottage cheese in the center for a striking salad or dessert. You can also make it without the red hots for milder flavor.

Delicious Macaroni Salad

salt water
2 c. uncooked macaroni
2 c. salad dressing
2 tsp. mustard
1 c. sugar
salt to liking
2 hard-boiled eggs, chopped fine
4 stems celery, chopped
1 small onion, chopped

Add uncooked macaroni to boiling salt water. Cook 15 minutes. While this is cooking mix salad dressing, mustard, sugar and salt in a large bowl that you'll be using to refrigerate macaroni salad in. Then add rest of ingredients.

Add your hot, soft drained macaroni. Stir well. Refrigerate until cold, 8-12 hours.

Stuffed Eggs

6 hard-boiled eggs
1 tsp. mustard
1 tsp. vinegar
¾ tsp. salt
2 Tbsp. mayonnaise dressing

Cut eggs in half lengthwise. Remove yolks. Mash. Add mustard, salt, vinegar and mayonnaise. Mix thoroughly. Refill whites. Sprinkle with paprika.

Recipes from Others

Easy Macaroni and Cheese

3 Tbsp. butter
2½ c. raw macaroni
1 tsp. salt
¼ tsp. pepper
½ lb. cheese
1 qt. milk (I like to add extra)

Melt butter. Pour macaroni into melted butter and stir until coated. Add chopped or grated cheese, salt, pepper and cold milk to macaroni. Bake uncovered at 325° for 1½ hours. Do not stir while baking! Optional: Add ham or browned hamburger, vegetable, onions and/or potatoes and you have a main course for company on Sunday. When adding raw cubed potatoes, I like to turn heat high to get everything hot before leaving for church. Bake at 300° for 3 hours.

Our Scalloped Potatoes

Slice potatoes into a pan. Sprinkle with chopped onions, salt and pepper as desired. Mix in a small amount of flour. Dot with butter. Pour milk over top; don't cover potatoes with milk. Bake about 1 hour, unless you have a big amount, 1½ hours at 350° or 3 hours at 275°-300°, depending on amount of potatoes. Use your common sense!

Creamy Rice with Yogurt

1½ c. brown rice
½ tsp. salt
3 c. water
1 c. chopped carrots
¼ c. chopped onions
1½ c. yogurt
¼-½ tsp. herb mixture

Put first five ingredients in kettle and bring to a full rolling boil. Reduce heat and simmer approximately 45 minutes, (keep covered). When cooked, remove from heat and stir in yogurt and herb mixture.

Mix well, and serve with meat or add hot cooked meat before serving. If it boils after yogurt is added it will curdle, so if you have cold cooked meat, add it before the yogurt and heat well, then stir in yogurt.

Casseroles, Soups, & Main Dishes

Beef & Potato Loaf

4 c. sliced raw potatoes
1 Tbsp. onion
1 tsp. salt
⅛ tsp. pepper

1 lb. raw hamburger
¾ c. milk
½ c. cracker crumbs
¼ c. ketchup
¼ c. onion
1 tsp. salt
⅛ tsp. pepper

Mix first four ingredients together and spread in bottom of casserole. Mix together rest of ingredients and spread over potatoes. Top with ketchup or barbecue sauce. Bake at 350° for 1 hour.

Putting green beans on the bottom is good too. For church bake at 250°.

Beef Taco Skillet

1 lb. ground beef
1 (10¾ oz.) can tomato soup
1 c. chunky salsa
½ c. water
1 c. shredded cheddar cheese
8 (6") flour tortillas, cut into 1" pieces

Brown beef in large skillet or use a kettle. Add soup, salsa, water, tortillas and half the cheese. Cover and cook over low heat 5 minutes or until hot. Top with remaining cheese and serve. 4 servings.

Once when I was shopping with little children (maybe 4 or 5 of them) a lady said to me, "My, your hands are full." I replied, "Yes, but our hearts are full, too."

Pizza Hut Crust

Recipe x1:
1 Tbsp. yeast
1 tsp. sugar dissolved in
    ⅓ c. warm water
1 Tbsp. vegetable oil
1 Tbsp. sugar
1 c. cold water
½ tsp. salt
¼ tsp. oregano
⅛ tsp. garlic salt

Recipe x8:
½ c. yeast
8 tsp. sugar dissolved in
    2⅔ c. warm water
½ c. vegetable oil
½ c. sugar
8 c. cold water
4 tsp. salt
2 tsp. oregano
1 tsp. garlic salt

Recipe x12:
¾ c. yeast
¼ c. sugar dissolved in
    4 c. warm water
¾ c. vegetable oil
¾ c. sugar
12 c. cold water
6 tsp. salt
3 tsp. oregano
2 tsp. garlic salt

Mix yeast, sugar and warm water and let set for 5 minutes. Mix oil, sugar, cold water, salt and spices. Add yeast mixture and 3¼-3½ cups per recipe bread flour. Knead well. Let rise till double, punch down and roll out and put in greased pizza pan. Let rise 10 minutes. Top and bake.

I have no idea if this is actually the recipe that Pizza Hut uses, but this is the name that was given to me for this recipe. It is a family favorite and they say it is better than bought pizza if I use our own pizza sauce. I like to make a large recipe and then freeze the extras. This also makes excellent breadsticks. Roll out and cut into strips.

132 — Mops, Muffins, & Motherhood

Top with melted butter, garlic salt, and Parmesan cheese. Let rise and bake. Serve with melted butter mixed with garlic powder or salt, or with pizza sauce as a dip.

Yorkshire Pizza

½ c. butter
1 c. flour
2 eggs
1 c. milk
¼ tsp. salt

Melt butter in 8"x12" pan in 425° oven. Beat flour, eggs, milk and salt until smooth. Pour into hot pan. Bake 5 minutes. Top with pizza sauce, then other pizza toppings. (It will still be juicy when you add the toppings.) Bake at 400° until done.

This is a fast, easy substitute for regular pizza. A favorite for Saturday night supper. I usually put a double recipe in a 9"x13" cake pan, but don't double the butter.

Cheesy Enchiladas

Sauce:
½ c. butter
4 Tbsp. flour
3 c. milk
8 oz. Velveeta cheese
8 oz. sour cream
1 can nacho cheese soup (optional)
   (can substitute 2 Tbsp. cheddar cheese powder)
Heat until melted and thoroughly mixed.

Meat Mixture:
2 lb. hamburger
1 med. onion, chopped
2 Tbsp. flour
1 tsp. salt
1 c. pizza sauce or more
½ tsp. oregano
10-12 tortillas
2 c. grated cheese

Meat Mixture: Brown hamburger and onion, then add rest of ingredients ecept tortillas and cheese. Place 1 Tbsp. meat mixture into each tortilla and top with cheese. Roll up and place in greased pan. Pour cheese sauce over tortillas. Bake at 350° for 30 minutes.

Chicken and Rice

2-3 cans cream soup (mushroom, celery, etc.)
¼ c. butter, melted
1½ c. reg. rice
1⅓ c. milk
2-3 cans water (or more)

Mix all together. Lay chicken pieces on top and sprinkle with seasoned salt. Bake at 300° for 2 hours.

This will be very juicy, and chicken might sink into milk. This is a quick recipe to pop in the oven if you need to be gone just before supper

The Recipes — 133

Chickenetti

8 oz. spaghetti, cooked and drained
3-4 c. chicken, cooked and cut into pieces
1 c. chicken broth
¼ tsp. celery salt
¼ tsp. pepper
¾ lb. Velveeta cheese
2 cans cream soup
1 grated onion (optional)

Mix all ingredients, reserving 1 cup cheese to sprinkle on top. Bake at 350° for 1 hour. 8 servings.

I don't always put this into the oven, just cook it in a large kettle and serve.

Pig Stomach

1½ lb. ground sausage
1 qt. diced raw potatoes
1 onion, chopped
2 c. shredded cabbage
2 tsp. salt
1 tsp. pepper

Wash pig stomach well and soak in salt water. Mix rest of ingredients and stuff into stomach. Bake at 350° for 3 hours.

This is an old recipe. Some families grind up the stomach after baking to make it less chewy. If you don't do your own butchering, you might have a problem getting the whole cleaned stomach. This is a very ethnic dish. They say the Germans were so thrifty they used every part of the pig except the squeal! We like to make this without the stomach; just mix the ingredients and then bake in a roast pan. I have a six-quart roaster that is about right for my family.

Six-Layer Supper

1 thick layer raw potatoes
½ c. uncooked rice
1 thick layer onions, sliced
1 layer carrots, sliced
1 lb. ground beef
1 qt. tomatoes, canned
1 Tbsp. salt
1 Tbsp. brown sugar

Place all ingredients in a casserole in order given. Bake at 350° for 2½ hours.

Adjust the ingredients to suit your family's taste. Instead of tomatoes, I use tomato juice, pouring it over everything else.

No-Boil Lasagna

This is one of those recipes for which I can no longer find the original, so I will give you my version from memory. I generally fry 2 pounds of ground beef with some onion and 1-2 tsp. of salt in a large frying pan. I then add 1 quart of pizza sauce and 2 quarts of tomato juice and bring to a boil. We like the spicy flavor the pizza sauce adds, but you can use all tomato juice and add whatever spices you like, such as garlic salt, pepper, and oregano. I take a large baking pan and put a thin layer of the ground beef mixture on the bottom then a layer of dry lasagna noodles, a layer of meat, a layer of noodles, etc. Between the middle layers, I sprinkle some Parmesan cheese. If your family likes it, cottage cheese can also be added. After I have about 3-4 layers, I pour the remaining hamburger/juice mixture over the top of the noodles. The liquid should almost cover the top layer of noodles or you will have very dry lasagna. If you don't have enough liquid, just add water or more tomato juice. Top the whole thing with shredded cheese as thick as your family likes it. We like mozzarella or marble cheese, but others work, too. Cover with foil; bake 1 hour at 350°-375°, remove foil and bake 10 minutes more with oven turned off. It is easier to serve if you let it set 10 minutes longer.

Tator Tot Casserole

1½ lb. ground beef
1 onion, chopped
10 oz. can cream of mushroom
1 c. milk
8 oz. Velveeta cheese
3-4 c. frozen or canned green beans
tator tots

Brown beef and onion. Season to taste and add cream of mushroom soup and milk. In a 9"x13" pan layer beans, then pour meat mixture over beans. Add cheese slices and top with tator tots. Bake at 350° for 30 minutes or until hot throughout.

Dairy Casserole

8 oz. macaroni or noodles (cooked)
1 lb. ground beef, fried
2 c. corn
8 oz. cream cheese
1 can cream of mushroom or celery soup
1 c. milk
salt and pepper to taste
½ tsp. onion salt

Combine all ingredients. Bake at 350° for ½ hour.

Cheddar Cheese Casserole

2 c. macaroni
2 c. cheese
1 can cream of mushroom soup
½ c. tomato juice
½ c. milk
1 lb. hamburger
salt and pepper to taste

Fry hamburger. Cook macaroni in salt water. Mix everything together except ½ cup cheese to put on top. Bake at 375° for 30 minutes.

Slop

Fry hamburger with onion. In a kettle just right for your family, bring water and salt to a boil. Add pasta of your choice and cook until soft. Add hamburger and your choice of vegetable and/or cream soup, cheese, and seasonings. Heat thoroughly and serve. Another option is to use pizza or spaghetti sauce instead of cream soup and cheese.

As you can imagine, there is a story behind this name. Once when I was making this stovetop casserole, one of the children came by asking (like usual) what's for supper. I didn't know what to answer, since I was just dumping things together, so at the spur-of-the-moment, I blurted out, "slop". I got a funny look, but somehow it stuck, and now the children cheer when the answer to "What's for supper?" is "Slop"!

Hearty Hamburger Soup

½ c. chopped onion
1 lb. hamburger
½ c. chopped celery
1 c. diced potato
1 c. sliced carrots
1½ tsp. salt
⅛ tsp. pepper
1 tsp. seasoned salt
2 c. tomato juice (or more)
4 c. milk
⅓ c. flour

Brown the meat, add onions and cook until transparent. Stir in remaining ingredients except flour and milk. Cover and cook over low heat until tender. Combine flour with 1 cup milk. Stir into soup mixture; boil. Add remaining milk and heat, stirring frequently. Do not boil again. Makes a large kettle full.

Potato Soup

In a large kettle, bring to a boil several (depending on the size) peeled, cubed potatoes, onion, celery or celery seed. When it comes to a boil, add about one-half to one cup macaroni. Cook until soft. Use just enough water that you don't need to drain the vegetables when they are soft. Break two or three eggs into the vegetables and stir them in, then let them cook until firm. (This takes the place of hard-boiled eggs.) Add as much milk as desired, heat, but do not allow it to boil. Serve with crackers. Adjust the ingredients to suit your family.

Beef Noodle Soup

Bring a large kettle of salted water to a boil, to which has been added one quart of canned beef chunks and one quart of whole kernel corn. Add noodles and beef base to taste. How long you need to cook it depends on the thickness of the noodles. For a really quick soup, add fine noodles. I also make hamburger soup like this, substituting one pound ground beef, fried with chopped onion for the canned beef chunks.

Chicken Corn Noodle Soup

Cook chicken until soft, remove from broth. While chicken is cooling, add one quart whole kernel corn and 1-2 tablespoons chicken broth mix or chicken base to the broth; bring to a boil. Add noodles of your choice. Again, the thinner the noodles, the less cooking time that is required. We really like it with kluski noodles. Then I let it simmer until they are well cooked. Add the chicken cut into small pieces. Quantities of the ingredients depend on the size family you are feeding and how thick you like your soup.

Tacos and Haystacks

I like to keep bought tortillas on hand for tacos. This is usually our Saturday lunch. We fry hamburger and add taco seasoning. We heat the tortillas in the microwave and serve them with cheese, taco sauce, barbecue sauce, sour cream, lettuce, tomatoes, onions, and green peppers. I buy the tortillas at Aldi and keep them on hand in the refrigerator.

Haystacks are similar but are served on crushed corn chips instead of tortillas. Serve with taco meat, mashed potatoes or rice, toppings of your choice and cheese sauce poured over it all for the finishing touch. This is a popular meal for many people, served cafeteria-style. You can ask each family to bring an ingredient to share with everyone. The meat and cheese sauce can be made ahead and then kept hot in roasters or crockpots. Some baked goods and fruit make the meal complete without too much fuss.

Recipes from Others

Sausage Potato Bake

6 med. potatoes or
   a mixture of white and sweet potatoes
1 lb. rope sausage, cut in ¾" chunks or
   1 lb. ground beef seasoned with
   1 tsp. salt and ½ tsp. pepper
½ c. flour (I use rice flour, but others would work.)
¼ tsp. salt
   (I use about ¼-½ tsp. of my herb mixture.)

Scrub potatoes and slice in approximately ¼" slices. Mix together flour and salt. Sprinkle over potato slices in bowl and stir until evenly coated. Generously grease 9"x13" pan with butter, then put in potatoes. Bake at 375° for 25 minutes. Remove briefly. Stir and add sausage pieces. If using ground meat, just pull apart and layer over top. Return to oven, reduce heat to 350° and bake till potatoes are soft and meat is cooked, approximately 40-50 minutes more.

Meat-n-Tater Pie

¾ c. bread crumbs
½ tsp. salt
¼ tsp. pepper
1 Tbsp. mustard or 1 tsp. dry mustard (optional)
⅓ c. milk
1 lb. ground beef
2 eggs
2 c. mashed potatoes
¼ c. onion
1 tsp. parsley
2 Tbsp. butter
¼ c. bread crumbs

Combine first six ingredients. Press mixture into 9" pie pan or 8"x8" pan. Set aside. *I freeze a few homemade bread slices and whir in blender for a few minutes for bread crumbs.

Combine eggs, potatoes, onion and parsley. Spread over meat mixture. Bake at 350° for 35 minutes. Mix crumbs and butter. Remove from oven and sprinkle with crumbs. Return to oven approximately 10 minutes.

4-Layer Dinner

2 med. potatoes, sliced
2 med. carrots, sliced
2 sm. onions, sliced
1 lb. ground beef
1 c. water or tomato juice or milk

Layer in order given in 2 quart greased casserole, seasoning each layer with salt and pepper. Bake at 300° for 2½-3 hours.

Meat-Potato Quiche

4 Tbsp. olive oil
4 c. shredded raw potatoes
1 c. cooked meat of your choice
¼ c. chopped onion
1 c. grated cheese (optional)
1¼ c. milk
2 eggs
½ tsp. salt

Mix together olive oil and potatoes. Preheat oven to 375°. Press evenly in 8"x8" pan (up the sides as a crust) Bake at 375° for 20 minutes or until just beginning to brown. Remove from oven and layer on meat, onion and cheese. Beat together milk, eggs, and salt. Pour over other ingredients. Return to oven and bake about 40 minutes or until lightly browned and knife inserted 1" from edge comes out clean. Cool 5 minutes.

Corn Chowder

1 lb. ground beef or
  (sausage chunks cooked with potatoes)
¼ c. chopped onions
6 med. potatoes, cubed
1 qt. frozen crushed corn, thawed
½ tsp. herbs as desired
1-2 tsp. salt as desired

Brown ground beef with onions. Set aside. Cook potatoes. When soft, add meat mixture, corn, herbs and salt. Bring to a boil, and keep hot until ready to serve.

If you cook potatoes in about 2 cups water, do not drain, and that should be about right. Add water or broth if you like it juicier.

My standard answer to the question, "Are you having more?!" is, "Not today!" It usually brings an embarrassed laugh from the inquirer.

Potato Filling with Meat

½ c. chopped onion
½ c. chopped celery (optional)
¼ c. butter
*1 lb. ground beef
3 eggs
3 c. milk
1½ tsp. salt
½ tsp. pepper
2 c. cooked potatoes, mashed or diced
6-8 c. bread cubes
1 c. peas, fresh or frozen (optional)

Cook first four ingredients together till meat is no longer pink. If using cooked meat merely cook onion, celery and butter 15 minutes, *or 2 cups cooked chicken or other meat.

Stir together rest of ingredients. Add onion mixture and meat. Should be very moist. If not, add more milk. Place in greased casserole. Bake at 350° for 45 minutes. Can be frozen before baking. If you put in oven frozen, bake at 350° for 2 hours.

Hearty Chicken & Rice Soup

1½ c. chicken broth
3 c. cold water
½ c. uncooked rice
½ c. chopped celery
½ c. chopped carrots
½ c. cooked diced chicken
¾ lb. Velveeta cheese

Combine first 5 ingredients; cover and simmer 25 minutes. Add chicken and cheese. Adding bouillon cubes makes it tasty.

Cream of Mushroom Substitute

3 c. water
1 c. milk
4 chicken bouillon cubes

Heat milk and water. Add bouillon cubes. Thicken like gravy with cornstarch or flour. Optional: Melt cheese into it.

A crockpot meal we have tried is chicken thighs with rice and corn.

Our favorite easy meal is: the desired amount of cubed, raw potatoes, vegetable, cooked meat or browned hamburger and onions, with salt and pepper, and cheese as an option. Mix in cream of chicken or cream of mushroom soup, and milk. Bake at 250° for about three hours or make it on the stovetop if the potatoes are cooked a bit first.

Our favorite to put in the oven or crockpot on a Sunday morning is a roast or ham surrounded by potatoes, green beans, and carrots, and sprinkled with salt and pepper.

Miscellaneous

Two-Layer Finger Jell-O

3 Tbsp. unflavored gelatin
1 c. (or 3 pkg.) bulk gelatin (your choice of flavor)
3 c. boiling water
1 c. (½ pt.) heavy whipping cream
(do not beat the cream!)

Mix unflavored gelatin with flavored in a bowl. Add boiling water and stir until dissolved. Add whipping cream. Stir, pour into 9"x13" pan, and chill. Cream will rise to the top half. You can use cookie cutters to cut into shapes.

Chex Party Mix

3 c. Corn Chex
3 c. Rice Chex
3 c. Wheat Chex
1 c. mixed nuts
1 c. bite-size pretzels
1 c. garlic flavor bite-size or
    regular bagels broken into 1" pieces
6 Tbsp. butter or margarine
2 Tbsp. Worcestershire sauce
1½ tsp. seasoned salt
¾ tsp. garlic powder
½ tsp. onion powder

In a large microwave bowl mix cereal, nuts, pretzels and bagel chips, set aside. In small microwave bowl microwave butter uncovered on high about 40 seconds or until melted. Stir in seasonings. Pour over cereal mixture. Stir until evenly coated. Microwave uncovered on high 5-6 minutes thoroughly stirring every 2 minutes. Spread on paper towels to cool. Store in airtight container. Oven directions: Heat oven to 250°. In ungreased large roasting pan, melt butter in oven. Stir in seasonings. Gradually stir in remaining ingredients until evenly coated. Bake 1 hour, stirring every 15 minutes. Spread on paper towels to cool about 15 minutes. Store in airtight container.

Puffed Rice Balls

4 c. miniature marshmallows
6 c. puffed rice (or wheat)
½ c. butter

Microwave Instructions:
Melt butter and marshmallows on high for 2 minutes. Stir. Heat ½-2 minutes longer. Add puffed rice and mix well. Let set a few minutes, then form into balls.

If you try to form them into balls too soon, they will just fall apart. Wet hands while handling them to keep the marshmallows from sticking.

Jell-O Roll-up

1 c. hot water
1 c. Jell-O (or 3 sm. pkgs.)
3 c. mini marshmallows

Stir hot water and Jell-O till dissolved. Then add mini marshmallows, microwave 3 minutes. Stir. Microwave 1½ more minutes. Do not overcook. Spray 9"x13" pan with Pam. Pour in pan and cool. Roll long way and cut like a jelly roll.

Lime Slushy

1 (6 oz.) or ⅔ c. lime Jell-O
2 c. hot water
1 c. sugar, scant
1 (46 oz.) can pineapple juice
1 (12 oz.) can frozen orange juice
6 c. water
1 (2 liter) bottle ginger ale or 7-Up

Dissolve Jell-O in hot water. Add sugar, juices and water. Freeze. Thaw 2 hours before serving. Chop into slush with a spoon or other heavy utensil. Add ginger ale or 7-Up.

Icy Holiday Punch

1 (6 oz.) pkg. strawberry Jell-O (or scant ¾ cup)
¾ c. sugar
2 c. boiling water
6 c. cold water
1 (46 oz.) can pineapple juice
2 liter ginger ale

In a freezer proof container mix together Jell-O, sugar and boiling water. Stir in cold water and pineapple juice. Cover and freeze for several hours. Thaw 2 hours before serving. Chop into slush with a spoon or other heavy utensil. Add ginger ale and serve.

Note: You can modify this recipe by using different flavors Jell-O. Be sure gelatin is dissolved completely.

The Recipes —— 139

Soft Pretzels

1¼ c. lukewarm water
1 Tbsp. yeast, heaping
1 Tbsp. sugar
pinch of salt
3¼-4 c. flour

  Knead dough and shape into pretzels. Let rise for 10-15 minutes. Boil a solution of 4 teaspoons baking soda and 4 cups water. Drop pretzels into boiling solution. Boil for 1 minute. Put pretzels on greased cookie sheet and salt as you like. Bake at 450° to a golden brown.

Ladyfingers

  Take ½ of a graham cracker and break in half again. Between them spread a mixture consisting of equal parts white chocolate chips and peanut butter melted together. Dip in melted milk chocolate. Place on wax paper until set. A plastic fork works great for a dipping fork if you break out the two middle prongs. Be careful when melting chocolate in the microwave. Stir often to avoid burning it.

  If you are planning to serve punch or other drink in a punch bowl, freeze a portion of the drink in a Jell-O mold that is in a ring shape, and then let it float in the bowl as you serve the punch. This will avoid diluting the punch with ice and yet keep it cold. Tupperware sells a mold that works perfectly for this.

Canning

Tomato Soup

14 qt. tomatoes
7 med. onions
14 stems celery
14 sprays parsley
6 peppers

1 c. butter
1 c. sugar
½ c. salt
1 c. flour
pepper to taste

  Cook together tomatoes, onions, celery, parsley and peppers. Run through strainer. Put back in kettle and add rest of ingredients. Cook 20 minutes and can while at a rolling boil. Put lids on immediately and there should be no need to cold pack.

Sweet Peppers

4 c. water
2 c. vinegar
4 c. sugar
2 Tbsp. salt

  Boil together and pour into jars packed with sliced or cubed sweet peppers. Cold pack 10 minutes.

Pickled Red Beets

2 c. red beet juice
2 c. sugar
1 c. vinegar
1 Tbsp. salt

  Cook beets until soft. Peel and slice. Put in jars. Combine syrup ingredients and pour into jars. Cold pack 10 minutes.

Pizza Hut Pizza Sauce

2½ gal. tomato juice (or raw tomatoes)

4 green peppers

8-10 onions

1 pt. vegetable oil

2 Tbsp. basil

1 c. sugar

2 Tbsp. oregano

6 bay leaves, crushed (I put these in a spice ball)

2 Tbsp. red pepper, crushed (or less)

3 Tbsp. pizza seasoning

1 Tbsp. Italian seasoning

1 tsp. garlic powder

½ c. salt

Cook tomato juice, peppers, and onions and put through strainer. Add rest of ingredients. Cook together 1 hour, then add ½ gallon tomato paste (or thicken with clear jel). Process for 10 minutes.

I make this sauce in large quantities, since we use it for so many different things. It is the sauce I use for spaghetti. For more detailed instructions on how I do it, refer to Preserving the Bounty in Part 1.

Tea concentrate

6 qt. boiling water

6 c. loose tea (leaves and stems) packed tightly into measuring cup

Boil water, remove from heat, add tea leaves and let set for 15 minutes. Strain and add 10 cups sugar and dissolve. Put in quart jars and add 1 teaspoon lemon juice (optional) (keeps tea from getting dark) to each quart. Process in boiling water bath 20 minutes. One quart concentrate makes 1 gallon tea. Tastes just like fresh tea. Can also be frozen.

Barbecued Green Beans

3 qt. beans

1 onion

1 c. ketchup

1 c. brown sugar

6 slices bacon, cut in pieces

Mix together. Cold pack for 3 hours.

Pepper Relish

12 peppers (6 red, 6 green)

6 onions

1 c. vinegar

2 c. sugar

1 tsp. salt

2 tsp. mustard seed

Grind peppers and onions together. Cover with boiling water and let set for 15 minutes. Drain water. Add rest of ingredients. Cook over low heat. Simmer ½ hour. Put in jars and cold pack 10 minutes.

Banana Pickles

4 qt. cucumbers

3 c. sugar

2 c. vinegar

1 tsp. mustard seed

1 tsp. celery seed

1 tsp. turmeric

1 tsp. salt

1 c. water

Peel and cut cucumbers into slices from top to bottom like banana shapes. Big cucumbers are ideal. Pack into jars. Fill with syrup. Seal.

One day I saw our 5-year-old petting her dad's mounted deer. In a soft voice she was saying, "I like you. I don't know why Daddy shot you."

Vegetable Soup

	Single Recipe:	To Can:
corn	3 c.	3 qt.
peeled and cubed potatoes	2 c.	2 qt.
green beans	2 c.	2 qt.
finely diced carrots	2 c.	2 qt.
peas	2 c.	2 qt.
sliced celery	1 c.	1 qt.
salt	⅛ c.	½ c.
pepper	¾ tsp.	1 Tbsp.
minced onion	1½ tsp.	2 Tbsp.
chili powder	1½ tsp.	2 Tbsp.
parsley	1½ tsp.	2 Tbsp.
brown sugar	½ c.	2 c.
cooked ground beef	1½ lb.	5 lb.
ABC noodles	¾ c.	3 c.
beef broth	1½ qt.	6 qt.
tomato juice	1½ qt.	6 qt.

To eat immediately: Mix all ingredients together and cook until vegetables are soft. Add more liquid as desired. To can: Cook each vegetable just until starting to turn soft. Cook ABC noodles slightly. Mix all ingredients together, put into jars. Cold pack 3 hours for quarts or use pressure cooker.

Canned Beef

I can beef chunks and ground beef by stuffing quart or pint jars full of meat. Add 1 teaspoon salt and wipe off jar rims. Do not add liquid, but you may add ½ teaspoon of liquid smoke or experiment with other spices and seasonings. Screw lid and ring on just until snug, do not tighten them. Bring to a low rolling boil and cook for 3 hours for quarts or 2 hours for pints. DO NOT LET THE KETTLE BOIL DRY! The jars may explode. Remove jars and tighten rings. Green beans can also be canned this way, except for adding water in the jar up to the neck. This method is not recommended anymore by home-canning authorities since it may allow (rarely) botulisms to form that can be very dangerous if eaten. Thorough heating of the meat will destroy this botulism, so meat should never be eaten right from the jar. Pressure canning is the recommended method for meat and green beans.

Desserts

Fruit Dip

½ c. Cool Whip

½ c. cream cheese

4 oz. strawberry jelly (freezer)

Beat cream cheese and jelly together and add Cool Whip. Good with apples, grapes, bananas, etc.

A refreshing and attractive summer dessert, if you arrange the fruits on a tray. You can use a whole pineapple as a center focal point.

Danish Dessert

1 pkg. Kool-Aid (unsweetened)

7 c. water

1 c. sugar

¾ c. clear jel dissolved in
   1 c. cold water

½ c. gelatin (same flavor as Kool-Aid)

Add fruit as desired

Bring Kool-Aid, water and sugar to a boil. Thicken with clear jel mixed with water. Cook till thick. Take off heat and add gelatin and fruit.

You can use this recipe to can. Just cold pack for 10 minutes after adding fruit. Especially good for strawberries or peaches.

Maple Pudding

5 c. milk
3 eggs
2 c. brown sugar
1 c. flour
1 c. milk

2 tsp. vanilla
2 tsp. maple flavoring (or more)
butter size of an egg

Heat 5 cups milk. Beat together eggs, brown sugar, flour and 1 cup milk; add to hot milk, stirring constantly. Cook until thick, continuing to stir well. Remove from heat and add rest of ingredients.

Stir well and cool. Top with mini marshmallows or Cool Whip to serve, if desired.

Layered Lemon Dessert

1 c. cold butter or margarine
2 c. flour
1 c. finely chopped pecans

Layer 2:
2 (8 oz.) pkg. cream cheese
1 c. powdered sugar
1 cont. Cool Whip

Layer 3:
2 pkg. lemon pudding mix (cook)
4½ c. water, divided
1 c. sugar
4 egg yolks

In a bowl cut together butter and flour until mixture resembles coarse crumbs. Stir in pecans. Press into ungreased 9"x13" pan. Bake at 350° for 15 minutes. Cool.

Layer 2: Combine cream cheese and sugar. Fold in Cool Whip. Spread over crust.

Layer 3: Combine pudding mix, sugar, 1 cup water and egg yolks in saucepan till smooth. Add remaining water. Boil over medium heat. Cool. Spread over cream cheese layer. Top with Cool Whip.

Instead of the pudding mix, you can substitute one tube of lemon pie filling that can be purchased at most bulk food stores.

Grape Sponge

1 c. boiling water
⅓ c. grape gelatin
1 c. grape juice (prepared to drink)
1 (8 oz.) Cool Whip

Pour water over gelatin. Stir till dissolved. Add grape juice. Chill until cold, but preferably not completely set. Beat in Cool Whip. Refrigerate till firm.

Eclair Dessert

1 lb. whole graham crackers
2 pkg. instant vanilla pudding
31/2 c. pasteurized milk
8 oz. Cool Whip

Frosting:
6 Tbsp. cocoa
3 Tbsp. milk
2 tsp. vanilla
2 tsp. corn syrup (white)
3 Tbsp. margarine
1½ c. powdered sugar

Line bottom of 9"x13" pan with graham crackers. Mix pudding and milk. Beat at medium speed for 2 minutes. Blend in Cool Whip. Pour half of mixture over crackers. Place second layer of crackers on pudding mixture. Pour on remaining pudding mixture. Put on third layer of crackers and refrigerate for 2 hours. Beat frosting ingredients and put on top of pudding. Refrigerate 24 hours before serving.

This is a very easy and delicious dessert, but it takes a little thinking ahead since it must be refrigerated for 24 hours. One of our family favorites!

The Recipes — 143

Fruit Slush

6 oz. orange concentrate
3 c. water
2 c. sugar

Fruit:
peaches
bananas (makes it dark and strong)
mandarin oranges
crushed pineapples

Puree fruit and mix with syrup. Put in lunch size containers and freeze. These will be just right to eat by lunchtime.

Ice Cream in a Bag

1 gal. ziploc bag
   put in big scoop of ice or snow and
3 Tbsp. salt

1 qt. ziploc bag
   put in:
1 c. milk
1 Tbsp. sugar
1 tsp. vanilla

Mix together by squooshing bag then put into large bag with ice and squoosh, squash and squish until you get ice cream! About 5-10 minutes. Keep as much air out of bags as possible.

School children love it! Make sure they bring gloves to school. We like to do it when there is snow on the ground. You can add different flavors if you desire.

Homemade Ice Cream

We use the Junket tablets, following the recipe for ice cream on the pamphlet in the box. This recipe does not use raw eggs. It is a rich, creamy ice cream. You can add fruit or anything else you desire. One of our favorites is peppermint flavoring, green food coloring, and tiny semisweet chocolate chips.

Old-Fashioned Apple Dumplings

6 med. size baking apples
2 c. flour
2½ tsp. baking powder
½ tsp. salt
⅔ c. shortening
½ c. milk

Sauce:
2 c. brown sugar
2 c. water
½ c. butter
¼ tsp. cinnamon

Pare and core apples. (Do not slice.) To make pastry, sift flour, baking powder and salt together. Cut in shortening until particles are about the size of small peas. Sprinkle milk over mixture and press together lightly, working dough only enough to hold together. Roll dough as for pastry. Cut into 6 squares and place an apple on each. Fill cavity of apple with sugar and cinnamon. Pat dough around apple to cover it completely. Fasten edges securely on top of apple. Place dumplings 1" apart in a greased baking pan.

Sauce: Combine brown sugar, water and cinnamon. Cook for 5 minutes. Remove from heat and add butter. Pour over dumplings and bake at 350° for 45-50 minutes. Serve with milk or ice cream.

Pick-a-Flavor Pudding

Start with crushed graham crackers, or crushed chocolate, vanilla or peanut butter cookies. Add melted butter and press into the bottom of a 9"x13" pan or a decorative dish or two if you desire. Mix whichever flavor instant pudding you desire according to package directions and pour over crust. Top with Cool Whip, chocolate chips, mini marshmallows, shaved candy bars, or whatever else sounds good to you. Quick and easy; use what you have on hand.

Hot Fudge Sundae Cake

1 c. flour
¾ c. sugar
2 Tbsp. cocoa
2 tsp. baking powder
¼ tsp. salt
½ c. milk
2 Tbsp. salad oil
1 tsp. vanilla
1 c. chopped nuts (optional)

1 c. brown sugar
¼ c. cocoa
1¾ c. hottest tap water

Sift together flour, sugar, 2 tablespoons cocoa, baking powder and salt. Mix in milk, oil and vanilla with a fork until smooth. Stir in nuts. Spread in 9" square pan. Double recipe makes 9"x13" pan. Sprinkle with brown sugar and ¼ cup cocoa. Pour hot water over all. (This will form a sauce as it bakes.) Bake at 350° for 40 minutes. Let set for 15 minutes before serving. Delicious with vanilla ice cream.

This is a very rich dessert and one pan goes a long way.

Dump Cake

1 (1 lb. 6 oz.) can cherry pie filling
1 (1 lb. 4 oz.) can pineapple, crushed
1 pkg. yellow cake mix
1 c. melted butter
1 c. flaked coconut (optional)
1 c. chopped walnuts (optional)

Preheat oven to 350°. Spread pie filling over the bottom of a 9"x13" pan. Evenly arrange pineapples (with juice) over cherries. Sprinkle cake mix over fruit. Cover with melted butter, coconut and walnuts. Bake for 1 hour.

Recipes from others

Creamy Fruit Salad

instant vanilla pudding (I use sugar-free pudding.)
 Fruit:
apples
grapes
bananas

Mix instant vanilla pudding according to instructions on box, at meal time add the fruit.
Yummy refreshing dessert.

Pudding Topper

1 pkg. graham crackers
1 pkg. Ritz crackers
2 Tbsp. chocolate chips
1 Tbsp. peanut butter

Blend into crumbs in a blender or food processor. May alter amounts to your liking. Use as topping on pudding.

When our twelfth child was two, her teenage brother would say, "It's time we have another baby. What are we going to do when you get big and we don't have any little girls anymore?"

The Recipes — 145

Baked Goods

Fudge Brownies

1⅓ c. flour
2 c. sugar
¾ c. cocoa
1 tsp. baking powder
½ tsp. salt
½ c. nuts (optional)
⅔ c. vegetable oil
4 eggs, slightly beaten
2 tsp. vanilla

Combine flour, sugar, cocoa, baking powder, nuts and salt; set aside. Combine oil, eggs and vanilla. Then add to dry ingredients. Do not overmix. Spread into a 9"x13" cake pan. Bake at 350° for 20-25 minutes or until done. Delicious warm with milk! Makes 24 brownies.

Easy for short-notice baked goods. You can top with colorful sprinkles before baking or add ½ tsp. peppermint extract to change the flavor.

Double Crumble Bars

½ c. margarine
2 eggs
¾ c. sugar
¾ c. flour
2 Tbsp. cocoa
¼ tsp. baking powder
dash of salt
1 tsp. vanilla

Topping:
3 c. mini marshmallows
1 c. chocolate chips
1 c. peanut butter
1½ c. Rice Krispies

Mix and pour into a 9"x13" pan. Bake at 350° for 15 minutes. Sprinkle miniature marshmallows over top and return to oven till marshmallows are melted. Cool. Mix melted chocolate chips and peanut butter. Add Rice Krispies. Spread over cooled cake.

Tandy Cakes

4 eggs
2 c. sugar
1 c. milk
1 tsp. vanilla
2 c. flour
2 tsp. baking powder
1 pinch salt
1 c. peanut butter
1 c. chocolate chips

Mix the first 7 ingredients together well. Bake at 350° for 15-20 minutes. While hot spread peanut butter on top. Cool. Melt chocolate chips and spread over peanut butter.

Raw Apple Cake

Cake:
1½ c. vegetable oil
2 c. sugar
3 eggs
3 c. flour
1 tsp. salt
1 tsp. baking soda
3 lg. apples (chopped)
1 c. nuts or (1 Tbsp. black
   walnut flavoring) (optional)
2 tsp. vanilla

Glaze:
½ c. butter
4 Tbsp. milk
1 c. brown sugar
½ c. powdered sugar

Gradually add oil to sugar and eggs; mixing thoroughly. Combine with dry ingredients. Add apples, vanilla and nuts. Bake in a 9"x13" pan at 325° for 45 minutes.

Glaze: Combine butter, milk and brown sugar. Boil 5 minutes. Remove from heat and add powdered sugar. Glaze cake immediately after removing from oven.

146 — Mops, Muffins, & Motherhood

Our Favorite Chocolate Cake

2 c. flour
2 c. sugar
¾ c. cocoa
2 tsp. baking soda
1 tsp. baking powder
½ tsp. salt
2 eggs
1 c. vegetable oil
1 c. milk
1 c. coffee (prepared to drink)

Mix ingredients in order, adding coffee last. Beat until smooth and well mixed. Batter will be thin. Bake in a greased 9"x13" pan at 350° for 35-40 minutes.

This is a soft moist cake that freezes well.

Black Bottom Cupcakes

2 c. sugar
1 tsp. salt
2 tsp. baking soda
3 c. flour
½ c. cocoa
2 c. water
2 tsp. vinegar
⅔ c. vegetable oil
2 tsp. vanilla

Filling:
⅓ c. sugar
1 egg
8 oz. cream cheese
dash of salt
8 oz. chocolate chips

Mix sugar, salt, soda, flour and cocoa together; add water, vinegar, oil and vanilla. Set aside. *Filling:* Mix sugar, egg, cream cheese and salt. Add chocolate chips. Fill cupcake cup half full of batter, then drop 1 heaping teaspoon of filling to top of each cupcake. Bake at 350° for 20 minutes.

Peanut Butter Chocolate Chip Cookies

2 c. shortening
2 c. brown sugar
2 c. sugar
4 eggs
2 tsp. vanilla
2 c. peanut butter
½ c. milk

6 c. flour
4 tsp. baking soda
1 tsp. salt
4 c. chocolate chips

Cream together first 7 ingredients. Add rest of ingredients. Mix well. Stir in 4 cups chocolate chips. Bake at 350° for 12 minutes.

Energy Cookies

2¼ c. brown sugar
6 eggs
3 c. peanut butter
1 c. margarine
2 c. sugar
1½ tsp. vanilla
12 oz. chocolate chips
4 tsp. baking soda
9 c. oatmeal
1 lb. coconut

Mix first 6 ingredients. Cream until smooth. Add remaining ingredients. Bake at 300° for 10 minutes. Do not overbake.

Outrageous Chocolate Chip Cookies

1 c. margarine, softened
1 c. sugar
⅔ c. brown sugar
1 c. peanut butter
1 tsp. vanilla
2 eggs

½ tsp. salt
2 tsp. baking soda
2 c. flour
1 c. oatmeal
2 c. chocolate chips

Mix together first 6 ingredients. Beat till creamy. Stir in dry ingredients and add chocolate chips last. Bake at 350° for 10-12 minutes. Makes about 4 dozen.

Peppermint Chocolate Cookies

¾ c. margarine, softened
1½ c. brown sugar
2 c. chocolate chips, melted
2 eggs
2½ c. flour
1½ tsp. baking soda
1 tsp. salt
2 Tbsp. water

Icing:
⅛ tsp. peppermint extract
½ c. margarine, softened
3 c. powdered sugar
3 drops green food coloring
¼ c. milk (as desired)

Beat margarine and brown sugar. Add melted chocolate chips and eggs; beat. Add flour, soda, salt and water. Place on ungreased cookie sheet. Bake at 350° for 10 minutes. (If baked longer than 10 minutes cookies get too hard.) Let cool on cookie sheet a short while. Put frosting between 2 cookies, sandwich style.

Cinnamon Roll Yeast Cookies

1 pkg. yeast
¼ c. warm water
4 c. flour
1 tsp. salt
¼ c. sugar
1 c. margarine or shortening
1 c. milk
2 eggs, beaten
lemon extract (optional)
½ c. brown sugar
1 Tbsp. cinnamon

Frosting:
4 Tbsp. butter
1 tsp. vanilla
1½ powdered sugar

Add yeast to warm water; set aside. Mix flour, salt and sugar in a bowl. Cut in margarine. Scald milk and cool. Add beaten eggs to flour mixture and stir until blended. Add milk and yeast. Stir, but do not knead. Divide dough in half, and roll out to about ½" thick. Sprinkle with brown sugar and cinnamon. Roll the long way and slice ½" thick. Bake cookies at 350° for 10 minutes. Frost immediately. *Frosting:* Mix together butter, vanilla, powdered sugar and enough hot water to be spreadable. You can refrigerate dough overnight and bake in the morning.

A trucker who came to our shop regularly said, "I don't know how you do it with twelve children. My three are enough!"

Pumpkin Chocolate Chip Whoopie Pies

2 c. cooked pumpkin
2 tsp. vanilla
4 c. brown sugar
2 c. vegetable oil
4 eggs
6 c. flour
2 tsp. baking powder
4 tsp. cinnamon
1 tsp. salt
2 tsp. baking soda
3 c. chocolate chips
2 c. nuts (optional)

Combine pumpkin, vanilla, sugar, oil and eggs. Stir together dry ingredients. Add pumpkin mixture. Add chocolate chips and nuts. Bake at 350° for 10-12 minutes.

Frosting (Non-Dairy)

30 qt. bowl	10 qt. bowl	5 qt. bowl
12 lb. powdered sugar	4 lb.	2 lb.
9 lb. Alpine C shortening	3 lb.	1½ lb.
3 c. pie & pastry flour	1 c.	½ c.
1 Tbsp. salt	1 tsp.	½ tsp.
¼ c. vanilla	1⅓ Tbsp.-4 tsp.	2 tsp.
1 qt. water	1⅓ c.	⅔ c.

Mix for 10 minutes, then add an additional ½ qt. water for 30 qt., ⅔ c. for 10 qt., ⅓ c. for 5 qt. Mix 10 more minutes.

Makes a good filling for whoopie pies. Alpine C is a special frosting shortening and may be available from bulk food stores. Other kinds can also be used. Use clear vanilla for a very white frosting.

Strawberry Shortcake

2 eggs
1 c. sugar
1 c. milk
1 tsp. vanilla
2½ c. flour
2 tsp. baking powder
½ tsp. salt
2 Tbsp. melted butter
1 qt. sliced strawberries
1 c. cream (whipped) or
   2 c. whipped topping

Beat eggs. Add sugar, milk and vanilla. Stir in dry ingredients and add melted butter. Pour into 2 (8") cake pans. Bake at 375° for 25-30 minutes. Cool. Spread ½ of whipped cream on 1 cake. Add ½ of berries. Top with the other cake and remaining cream and berries. Variation: Eat hot with milk and strawberries and omit cream. Double recipe fills 12"x15" cake pan.

Pie Crust

4 c. flour
1¾ c. shortening
1 Tbsp. sugar
2 tsp. salt
1 Tbsp. vinegar
1 egg, beaten
½ c. water

Mix first 4 ingredients with pastry blender. Mix vinegar, egg and water together. Then add to flour mixture. Do not overmix. Refrigerate for one hour.

Sour Cream Pear Pie

2 c. peeled diced pears
½ c. sugar
1 egg
1 Tbsp. flour
1 c. sour cream
1 tsp. vanilla
dash salt
1 (9") unbaked pie crust

Topping:
½ c. sugar
¼ c. butter (not melted)
⅓ c. flour

Mix pie ingredients together, adding pears last. Pour into prepared pie shell. Bake at 350° for 25 minutes. Remove from oven and add topping. Bake for 30 minutes more. *Topping:* Mix ingredients together with a fork until it forms crumbs.

This is a pie we make only during fresh pear season, but I suppose canned pears could be used as well.

Fresh Strawberry Pie

1 c. sugar
1 c. water
1 Tbsp. light corn syrup
pinch of salt

3 Tbsp. clear jel
½ c. water

3 Tbsp. strawberry Jell-O
1 qt. chilled strawberries

Combine sugar, water, corn syrup, and salt. Bring to a boil and add clear jel dissolved in ½ cup cold water. Cook until clear. Turn off heat and add Jell-O. A few drops of red food coloring can also be added. Cool slightly. Add strawberries and pour into baked pie shell. Serve topped with whipped cream.

*Can also be used for peach pie, using peaches and apricot Jell-O.

Amish Vanilla Pie

½ c. brown sugar
1 Tbsp. flour
¼ c. dark corn syrup (or molasses)
1½ tsp. vanilla
1 egg, beaten
1 c. water
1 c. flour
½ c. brown sugar
½ tsp. cream of tartar
½ tsp. baking soda
⅛ tsp. salt
¼ c. butter

Combine ½ cup brown sugar, 1 tablespoon flour, corn syrup, vanilla and egg in 2 quart pan. Slowly stir in water. Cook over medium heat, stirring until mixture comes to a boil. Cool. Combine 1 cup flour, sugar, cream of tartar, soda, salt and butter. Mix until crumbly. Pour cooled mixture into unbaked pie shell. Top with crumbs. Bake at 350° for 40 minutes or until golden brown.

Cream Donuts

4 pkg. yeast
1 c. warm water
4 c. lukewarm milk
1 c. vegetable oil
1 c. sugar
4 tsp. salt
4 eggs, beaten
14 c. bread flour

Filling for Donuts:
8 Tbsp. flour
2 c. milk
3 c. Crisco
2 tsp. vanilla
2 c. powdered sugar

Sprinkle yeast on warm water. Mix milk, oil, sugar and salt together. Then add the rest after milk is cooled. Let rise 2 hours. Punch down. Let rise 30-45 minutes. Roll dough and cut. Let rise 15-30 minutes. Fry in 350° oil.

Filling: Cook flour and milk until thick. Cool slightly. Add rest of ingredients. Beat at high speed for 5 minutes.

These donuts are delicious if kept in the freezer until needed. Put them in immediately after filling or glazing them, while still slightly warm.

If you want to roll them in powdered sugar after filling them, use donut sugar. Regular powdered sugar will just dissolve and disappear.

Two-Egg Cake

½ c. shortening
1 c. sugar
2 eggs
1¾ c. flour
2 tsp. baking powder
¾ c. milk
½ tsp. vanilla
½ tsp. salt

Beat well. Pour into 9½"x13" cake pan. Bake at 350° for approximately 30 minutes.

This is a very simple, fast recipe. Delicious served with fruit.

Granola Bars

20 oz. mini marshmallows
¾ c. butter
¼ c. vegetable oil
¼ c. honey
¼ c. peanut butter
5 c. oatmeal
4½ c. Rice Krispies
1 pkg. graham crackers (crushed)
1 c. of any of the following:
   M&M's, chocolate chips, coconut,
   raisins, almonds and peanuts

Mix the first 5 ingredients until just melted; mix in remaining ingredients. Press into greased pan. Cut into bars when cooled.

Recipes from Others

1-2-3 Bars

2 c. brown sugar (or less)
2 c. Bisquick
3 eggs

Mix well. May add chocolate chips. Bake at 350° for 25 minutes.

The Recipes —— 151

Our little boy heard a cat howling one day. "That cat sounds grouchy," he observed. "She mustn't have had a nap today."

Part 3

·CHARTS AND LISTS·

Charts and Lists

Charts are useful for many areas of life. Here are a few ideas with suggestions for using them. You have permission to copy these as often as needed for personal use.

#1 Age-appropriate Chore Chart
#2 Pack List
#3 Camping List
#4 Grocery List (Aldi)
#5 Household List (Walmart)
#6 Courtesy Rules for Children
#7 Saturday Cleaning Job List
#8 Book List (recommended reading)
#9 Chore Chart
#10 Reward Chart - Game Style
#11 Pack Chart (for trips)
#12 Monthly Menu Chart
#13 Blank Charts

#1 Age-appropriate Chore Chart (Pg. 161-163)

This chart is only a guideline. The ages given are approximate, and you need to know the ability of each one of your children, keeping safety in mind. You may have more to add to the list; modify it as you need to for your family. I have found that I don't always think about just what one of my children might be capable of doing and a chart like this can be helpful in keeping us on track. It also includes many things that I may otherwise not even think about teaching them. Some things are obviously more for girls and some are more for boys, but it never hurts for either one to learn skills that belong primarily to the opposite gender. I also find it is easier to expect more of the older children and forget to train the younger ones at the same age as I did the older ones. It is a good idea to take the time to thoroughly teach each child how something is done, step-by-step, instead of expecting them just to "know" how. If you look at an item on the list for a certain age and say, "My child could never do that!"- don't worry. They probably are more skillful in another area. Again, these are just suggestions; make them fit into your family. Farm chores are not included.

#2 Pack List (for trips) (Pg. 164)

This is a sample of what you might include on the list that you don't want to forget to take along, but might not go into the duffle bag or suitcase. We usually take a hard sided case for personal care products for the whole family. That way we don't have to dig in duffle bags for these items. One exception is our daughter's seizure medication. She keeps it in her duffle which she keeps with her wherever she goes. Customize this list for your family, and keep a master list for subsequent trips.

154 — Mops, Muffins, & Motherhood

This will cut down on forgotten items. Don't forget to include a wedding gift if the trip includes a wedding!

#3 Camping List (Pg. 164)

If your family likes camping, having a master list like this greatly simplifies getting everything together. You can give the list to the children to gather the things together at a designated spot. Then you can check off each item on the list to make sure they got it. Always keep a master list at a safe place for future reference. That way you can write notes to yourself. You may want to make a separate list of all the food items you want to take along.

#4 Grocery List (Aldi) (Pg. 165)

This is a sample grocery list for the Aldi store. You will want to modify it to fit your favorite grocery store. Research shows that the customer <u>will</u> spend more if she goes up and down every aisle of the store. In other words, the more you browse, the more you will buy. Having a list of your usual purchases will help keep you on track and yet make it easier to remember what you need. This list is set up to match the local Aldi store as it is set up. As you come in the door, the chips and other snacks are the first thing to the right, followed by crackers and then flour and other baking supplies. As you go down the aisle, you should be able to get what you need without a lot of backtracking. Make your own master list, then before you leave home, check what you need and make your shopping list based on the order it is on the master list. If you need items that you don't usually buy, you can add them. Or you can make copies of the master list and

then just circle the items you need this time. Since stores are notorious for moving their product around, you may have to redo the master list periodically.

#5 Household List (Walmart) (Pg. 166)

This list is like the grocery list, but for a Walmart or similar store. Some of the items are repeated since I don't always get them at the same place. You can do price comparisons with these lists, too. If you buy your groceries and household goods at the same store, just make one master list for it all.

#6 Courtesy Rules for Children (Pg. 167)

#7 Saturday Cleaning Job List (Pg. 168)

This is a sample list of what the Saturday cleaning consists of when it is broken down into bite-size pieces. We use this list to pick jobs and then mark them off when they are done. Our favorite is cutting the list into strips, folding them in half, putting them in a bowl, and then taking turns picking jobs until they are all gone. If a child picks a job he is too small to do, he may put it back and pick another one. Some things are on the list twice because they are easier for two children to do them. If a child picks both of the slips, he may trade with another child for a different job, or he may choose to do it alone and do one less job.

#8 Book List (recommended reading)

(Pg. 169)

Books can do much to enrich our lives and broaden our horizons. It is imperative that we are careful what we feed our minds. We must be sure that what we read will pass the test of God's Word. There are many books available that present the truth mixed with worldly wisdom that sounds right and good at first, but when examined more closely they come short of the whole truth. This list is by no means a complete one, but includes some books you may find helpful in your quest for Godly living. However, we do not necessarily agree with everything that is written. Use your own prayerful judgment as you read.

#9 Chore Chart (Pg. 170)

You can put the child's name in the upper left hand box. This is a two week chart and can be used to keep track of many things besides chores. Write the jobs you would like this child to do (or habit you would like to teach him) in the boxes on the left-hand side of the chart. If a job only needs to be done on certain days of the week, you can put an X in the box (or color it in) under the days of the week it does not need to be done. When a child completes a job he may put an X in the box, or those small round stickers or small star stickers can be stuck in the box. You can add to the reward by allowing them a large sticker if they get all the jobs done well for that day. They could stick these around the edge of the chart to decorate it. Some parents pay a small amount of money for chores completed, others choose not to. Another way you can reward them is to give each job a certain amount of points. As a job is completed, write the number of points in the box. At the end of the day, those points can be added up and accumulated from day to day to work towards a bigger reward you may offer. This could be a desired toy, a trip to the park or anything that would give them the incentive needed to get the work done quickly and well. Each child could work for his own reward or all the children's points could be combined for a family reward. You may want to use the thermometer chart to keep track of points.

Sample Chore Chart

Judith	Monday	Tuesday	Wednesday	Thursday	Friday	Saturday	Sunday	Monday	Tuesday	Wednesday	Thursday	Friday	Saturday	Sunday
Comb Hair														
Brush Teeth														
Clean up Bedroom														
Make Bed														
Dishes (break.)	cl	w	d	cl	w	d	X	cl	w	d	cl	w	d	X
Hang up Laundry														
Bake														
Help Make Supper														
Clean up Living Room														
Sweep Kitchen Floor														
Supper Dishes	w	d	cl	w	d	cl			w	d	cl	w	d	cl	

cl=clear table   w=wash dishes   d=dry dishes

This chart could be laminated so it can be used for more than two weeks. Just use dry erase markers. Be sure that the charts are put somewhere that the marker isn't rubbed off by accident.

#10 Reward Chart (game style) (Pg. 171)

This is a fun chart for even very young children, and it can be used for almost anything that needs improvement in your household such as manners, chores, schoolwork, etc. You can have one chart per child or one for all of them, depending on what you want to accomplish. Set a few rules for moving forward a square, crossing them off as they go. Or glue it to a piece of cardboard and use different colored tacks for each child. White or clear tacks can be colored with magic markers. For added zest, fill a few of the squares with special incentives such as; go on a picnic, go to the library, no work day (except their own personal jobs), ice cream treat, mystery square (it's a good idea to have something in mind so you don't have to scramble when a child gets to it), candy or lollipop, small toy, etc. I bought a big sheet of foam board at Walmart and made my own big chart with more spaces on it. The children (ages 5-12) had a bad habit of either not doing a job right away when I told them to, doing it half-heartedly, or even not at all. They each had their own tack, but they all played on the same board. If they did a job well, and right away when they were told, they were allowed to go forward one square. If they didn't do it well, right away, or not at all, they had to move back one space. It was amazing how soon they heard what I said the first time and got up and did it right! It really is in the training. They were soon asking me if they could do this or that job. If I asked "Who wants to…" I usually got an immediate response. At the end of the path, hung a five dollar bill and enough ones for the rest, the first one there got the five, this kept the competition going to finish the game. I tried to have as many jobs for the younger ones as the older ones to keep it fair. However, it wasn't long after the rewards were past that the response started to regress. That is when it is time to use negative reinforcement, since they have proven that they can if they want to.

#11 Pack Chart (for trips) (Pg. 172)

Put each family member's name in the left-hand column. Put an X in each block under the items that that person does not need. For instance, next to Dad's name, put an X in the box under dresses. In the boxes under the things he does need, put the number of that item he will need. For example, on this trip he will need 3 pairs of pants, 3 shirts, etc. Since each family member needs one set of Sunday clothes, I put neither an X nor a number. As you pack each person's clothing, put an X over the number in the box or, if you have two pairs of pants and need one more, strike out the 3 and put a 1 there. Then when you have bought, washed or otherwise procured the other pair, make an X in the box. In the end, all the boxes should have an X in them. If the children pack their own clothes, they can look at the chart and see what is needed. After they have gathered everything, have them bring their duffle or suitcase, and you can check what they packed, crossing it off the list as you go. I usually

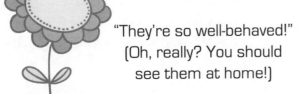

"They're so well-behaved!" (Oh, really? You should see them at home!)

	Sunday Clothes	Shirts	Pants	Dresses	Under-clothes	Socks & Belts	Jackets	Shoes & Boots	Swimwear
Dad		3	3	✗	3 sets				
Mom		✗	✗	4	3				
Jay		3	3	✗	3				
Nevin		3	3	✗	3				
Eric		3	3	✗	3				
Judith		✗	✗	4	3				
Tony		4	4	✗	4				
JuliAnna		✗	✗	4	4				

Sample Pack Chart

Note: Winter Trip - No swimwear needed

pack everyone's Sunday clothing together, so when Sunday comes, their clothing isn't all wrinkled from being balled up and rooted through. However, if children will be staying at a different place than you do, you will need to see to it that they get their clothing before Sunday morning. We have the boys roll their Sunday belt and stick it in one shoe and put their Sunday socks in the other one.

#12 Monthly Menu Chart (Pg. 173)

Using lists and charts can help keep our minds free from clutter. Planning menus in advance can help to keep our lives less stressful by taking the time to think of meals once, making sure we have the supplies on hand, then turning our thoughts to other things until it is time to make the meal. In the morning, you can see what will be for supper and make what preparations you can and then move on to other things the rest of the day. This avoids that annoying niggling in the back of your mind all day about what's for supper. You can leave some blank days on the chart to fill with the menu from other days when it didn't work out to have what was planned. Planning menus makes it easier to use a variety of meats and balanced meals instead of falling into the rut of the same foods over and over. One or two days a month can be delegated as "new recipe" night. You can use the same monthly menu from one month to the next, if you so desire.

Keeping a list of what foods are on your canning shelf and in your freezer is also helpful in meal planning.

#13 Blank Charts (Pg. 174-178)

The blank charts are for you to use your own creativity, but here are several examples. →

> Our son wanted to tell a story, "There was a bunny bear being bad." I said, "What else?" "I don't have any what else," he replied.

158 — Mops, Muffins, & Motherhood

clearing table = 15¢
washing dishes = 25¢
sweeping kitchen floor = 10¢

cleaning up toy room = 20¢
cleaning up living room = 20¢
making bed = 5¢

take garbage out = 10¢
hang up 1 load laundry = 25¢
fold towels = 10¢

														Total
Eric	10	5	5	25	10	25	15	10	25					
Judy	5	10	5	20	25	20	25	5						
Tony	5	5	10	10	25	20								
JuliAnna	5	5	10	20	15	15	25							
Eric														
Judy														
Tony														
JuliAnna														
Eric														
Judy														
Tony														
JuliAnna														

not obeying immediately – 10¢
not doing a job right – 10¢
talking back – 25¢

teasing or fighting – 10¢
not getting up first time you are called – 10¢
not staying sitting at the table – 5¢

Eric									
Judy									
Tony									
JuliAnna									

Dishes Schedule

	\multicolumn{4}{c	}{Breakfast}	\multicolumn{4}{c	}{Lunch}	\multicolumn{4}{c	}{Supper}
	Set Table	Clear Table	Wash Dishes	Dry Dishes/Clean off rack	Set Table	Clear Table	Wash Dishes	Dry Dishes/Clean off rack	Set Table	Clear Table	Wash Dishes	Dry Dishes/Clean off rack
Mon.	Eric	Judy	Tony	Juli	Eric	Judy	Tony	Juli	Eric	Judy	Mom	Tony
Tue.	Juli	Eric	Judy	Tony	Juli	Eric	Judy	Tony	Juli	Eric	Mom	Judy
Wed.	Tony	Juli	Eric	Judy	Tony	Juli	Eric	Judy	Tony	Juli	Mom	Eric
Thur.	Judy	Tony	Juli	Eric	Judy	Tony	Juli	Eric	Judy	Tony	Mom	Juli
Fri.	Eric	Judy	Tony	Juli	Eric	Judy	Tony	Juli	Eric	Judy	Mom	Tony
Sat.	Juli	Eric	Judy	Tony	Juli	Eric	Judy	Tony	Juli	Eric	Mom	Judy
Sun.	Tony	Juli	Eric	Judy	Tony	Juli	??	Eric	Judy	Tony	Mom	Juli

Sample Blank Chart

Use your creativity for the other blank charts. The one with larger squares can be used on which to put large stickers i.e. for every time your toddler goes to the bathroom. The thermometer can be used to keep track of many things. Just give each degree a name, such as points or dollars or cents.

• • • • • • • • • • • • • • • •

I was buying quite a few loaves of bread at the Aldi grocery store one day. One of the employees nearby saw me and I commented that it takes quite a few groceries for our family. She asked me how many there are and when I told her we have eight children, she acted rather flabbergasted and said, "Well, God bless you!" With a big smile I said, "He already has!" We laughed together and she said "Yes, you're right."

• • • • • • • • • • • • • • • •

160 — Mops, Muffins, & Motherhood

#1 Age-appropriate Chore Chart

Begin at age 2+
Pick up/put away toys
Hang pajamas up or put in hamper
Clear away his own dishes after eating
Wash hands and face
Take dirty clothes to wash hamper
No talking with food in mouth
Ask for food politely
Say please and thank you
Help clean up spills he created

Begin at age 3+
Dress himself
Stay sitting during meal
Set table
Help make beds
Fold washcloths and tea towels
Use dustpan
Use a napkin at the table
Dust furniture

Age 4
Put washed and dried silverware away
Shake out rugs
Hang small items on low clothesline to dry
Pick up trash outside
Dry dishes
Wipe down smudges on walls

Age 5
Memorize phone number and address
Make emergency calls. Teach about 911: how to call, what to say
Feed pets
Learn about coins and their value
Clean up a room
Help a younger sibling (if there is one)

Age 6
Wash dishes
Wipe down kitchen chairs
Take care of clothes when taking them off
Make a sandwich
Follow simple recipe directions
Measure ingredients correctly
Set oven timer
Sweep outside (porches/walks)
Clean up bathroom after using the tub or shower
Put his own clean laundry away and keep drawers neat
Fold medium size pieces of laundry and sort by owner

Age 7
Make juice
Proper way to answer the phone and how to take messages
Pack lunches
Cook canned soups

Our son was watching the birds at the feeder one rainy day. He observed a titmouse whose tuft was slicked down. "Maybe he used his legs to slick his hair down," was his comment.

Charts and Lists — 161

Read a recipe
Boil eggs
Make pancakes
Clear whole table
Sweep floors and use dustpan
Clean mirrors
Vacuum carpets
Change a pamper
Clean and trim fingernails
Wash hair
Clean out vehicle
Use hammer and nails, screwdriver and screws
How to use a toilet plunger

Age 8
Change sheets (with help)
Clean bathroom sink
Dress a baby
Feed baby
Make scrambled eggs
Mash potatoes
Make veggies
Make tossed salad
Help put groceries away
Sweep and clean up kitchen floor
Unload dishwasher/put dishes away
Hang clothes on clothesline
Polish shoes
Vacuum vehicle/clean interior
Water plants
Change a light bulb
Oil squeaky hinges
Reset a clock

Age 9
Load dishwasher and start it
Mop floor with a mop
Empty trashcan and replace trash bag

Care for a newborn
Change diapers
Fry hamburger
Set oven temperature
Sort dirty laundry (check pockets, turn clothes right side out)
How to use the washer and dryer (detergents and fabric softeners)
Fold clothes
Read a map
Count back change
Use fire extinguisher
Weed garden
Oil a bicycle
Check tire air pressure
Use a push mower

Age 10
Make simple meals
Use recipes/know how to double them, etc.
Bake cakes
Wash diapers
Mend straight seams
Sew on a button
Iron hankies and other simple pieces
Pick beans
Pick and arrange flowers
Empty vacuum cleaner/change bag
Clean toilet
Wash vehicles
Repair bicycle tire
Know first-aid procedures
Use a typewriter/keyboard

Age 11
Remove, wash, and replace curtains
Clean whole bathroom
Know when and how to use cleaners

162 — Mops, Muffins, & Motherhood

Clean lint trap in dryer
Reset breaker in breaker box
Sew simple items
Make a casserole
Bake cookies
Mow with riding mower

Age 12
Clean out refrigerator
Clean whole kitchen
Clean ceiling fans
Bathe an older baby
Dry flowers and use to make bookmarkers, etc.
Make rows in the garden and plant seeds
Buy simple items at the store/handle money
Sort laundry/start washer/use dryer
Wash windows (streak-free)

Age 13
Sew a quilt, matching corners neatly
Hang pictures/use stud finder
Use a level and chalk line
Paint outside
Lubricate squeaky doors, etc.
Wash/clean out/vacuum vehicles
Jumpstart a vehicle
Pump gas/diesel
Iron clothing
Turn off main water supply
Turn off main power supply/gas supply

Age 14
Defrost and clean out freezer
Pick peas
Unstop clogged drain with chemicals
Sew a dress alone
Clean light fixtures
Shampoo carpets

Do laundry alone
Check/refill oil in vehicle
Refill windshield washer fluid

Age 15
Be totally responsible for a newborn
Bake bread
Bathe an infant
Plan a week's menu
Strip and wax a vinyl floor
Paint a room
Make a bank deposit
Write a check/balance a checkbook
Plan and plant a flowerbed
Install a door knob
Change a sparkplug

Age 16
Do housecleaning without supervision
Prepare food for canning and freezing
Shop for groceries
Refinish furniture
Wax and buff a vehicle
Change furnace filter
Use power tools
Change tires
Change oil in vehicle

After reading Laura Ingalls' books, our 6-year-old said, "Mom, we should write books about our family. People would like to read about us."

#2 Pack List (for trips)

Money & credit cards

Books & small toys for entertainment

Toothpaste & Toothbrushes

Pills

Combs, brushes & hairspray

Barrettes & beads

Deodorants & perfume

Flashlight (if night travel)

Shaver

Trash bags for dirty clothes

Water thermos & cups

Snacks

Wet washcloth in a baggie or baby wipes

Purse & wallet

Bible

Hankies or Kleenex

Sunglasses

Dental floss

First Aid Supplies

GPS

#3 Camping List

Tent

Sleeping bags

Pillows & blankets

Rug

Broom

Lantern & flashlights

Clothesline & pins

Towels & washcloths

Jackets

Swimwear

Camera

Life jackets

Camp stove & fuel

Water hose

Drinking water thermos

Lighter fluid

Batteries

(Electric) Cords

Cups & plates

Utensils & silverware

Pots & pans

Mountain pie irons

Hot dog sticks

Food

Tablecloth

Paper towels

Dishcloths and tea towels

Dish soap

Lawn chairs

Folding table & chairs

Matches

Sand toys

First aid kit

Mosquito spray

Sunscreen

Personal items

Hammer

Campfire wood

Bibles & songbooks

#4 Grocery List (Aldi)

Chips

Popcorn

Nuts

Saltine crackers

Graham crackers

Flour

Sugar

Powdered sugar

Brown sugar

Instant pudding, chocolate or vanilla

Condensed milk

Chocolate chips

Marshmallows, regular or mini

Shortening

Oil

Velveeta cheese

Cooking spray

Honey

Salt

Pepper

Cake mix

Pancake mix

Pancake syrup

Salad dressings

Peanut butter

Mayonnaise

Ketchup

Mustard

Barbecue sauce

Vinegar

Cereal

Milk

Eggs

Yogurt

Sour cream

Cottage cheese

Sliced cheese

Shredded cheese

Butter

Coffee filters

Cream soups

Chili beans

Refried beans

Pasta- macaroni, noodles

Lasagna, spaghetti

Sauerkraut

Toilet paper

Kleenex

Paper towel

Plastic bags

Lettuce

Fruit

Tortillas

Carrots

Bread

Buns

Chunk cheese

Frozen meats

Popsicles

Juice concentrate

Ice cream

Cool Whip

Charts and Lists —— 165

#5 Household List (Walmart)

- Shampoo & conditioner
- Body wash
- Deodorant
- Hair spray
- Toothpaste
- Shaving cream & razors
- Female necessities
- Medications
- Batteries
- Hoses and outdoor needs
- Night light
- Light bulbs
- Hardware
- Craft and sewing supplies
- Scrapbooking supplies
- Paper, pens, & envelopes
- Tape
- Computer needs
- Printer ink
- Women's clothes
- Men's clothes
- Children's clothes
- Shoes
- Pet needs
- Laundry soap
- Fabric softener
- Cleaners
- Window spray
- Furniture polish
- Toilet bowl cleaner
- Dishwashing soap

- Pampers
- Baby wipes
- Pull-ups
- Baby food
- Milk
- Sour cream
- Sandwich meat
- Sliced cheese
- Chips
- Paper supplies
- Paper towels
- Toilet paper
- Trash bags
- Cereal
- Crackers & cookies
- Drink mixes
- Coffee
- Peppered gravy mix
- Ice cream
- Cool Whip
- Peanut butter
- Jelly
- Hamburgers
- Fresh chicken
- Barbecue sauce
- Breads
- Lettuce
- Fresh vegetables
- Bananas
- Fresh fruit

Courtesy Rules for Children

1. Look at others when you talk to them and speak clearly.

2. Say please and thank you when appropriate.

3. Four phrases to use as needed: Excuse me; I'm sorry; I was wrong; and I forgive you.

4. Never talk or laugh loudly, stare or point at people when in public.

5. Knock on closed doors before entering.

6. Offer your seat to adults if no other seat is available or if yours is more comfortable.

7. When at the table for a meal; sit and wait quietly, pass foods to the next person after serving yourself, chew with your mouth closed, and wait to be excused when you are done eating.

8. When answering the phone; answer clearly, if you need to take a message write it down and repeat it to the caller to make sure you got it right. Be sure to get the phone number. Give the message to the person as soon as you can.

9. When at church; be friendly and courteous to everyone, do not run, shout or play roughly in the building-this is God's house. Do not distract others during services and pay attention yourself.

10. When riding in a vehicle; wear your seatbelt, be considerate of other passengers, speak quietly, patiently wait for rest stops and meals, clean up any mess you make, do not throw anything out the windows.

11. If you must sneeze, cover your mouth with a hanky or the inside of your elbow. Make as little noise as you can.

12. Cover your mouth when you cough or yawn and say "Excuse me".

13. Never get into a car or go with people you don't know, unless your parents say it is all right. Do not talk to strangers unless your parents are there.

#8 Saturday Cleaning Job List

Pick up all the trash in all the rooms

Pick up all the toys in all the rooms

Put away all shoes

Clean out magazine rack

Gather Sunday shoes

Vacuum living room & toy room

Sweep down cobwebs

Take trash out/burn trash

Sweep porches & walks

Wash breakfast dishes

Take garbage out

Set table for lunch

Clear table after lunch

Wash kitchen floor

Wipe off kitchen chairs

Clean up toy room

Clean up toy room

Bake a cake

Clean laundry

Clean bathroom

Clean off porches

Sweep kitchen

Clean up yards

Clean up yards

Iron hankies

Shake rugs

Mow yards

Water flowers

Wash windows

Clean out van

Vacuum van

Wash van

Wash van

Dust

#9 Book List (recommended reading)

The Bible

A good study Bible

The Martyr's Mirror

Doctrines of the Bible *-by Daniel Kauffman*

More Hours in My Day *-by Emily Barnes*

Survival for Busy Women *-by Emily Barnes*

The 15 Minute Organizer *-by Emily Barnes*

Shepherding a Child's Heart *-by Ted Tripp*

A Heart for God *-by John Coblentz*

Christian Family Living *-by John Coblentz*

Getting Along with People God's Way *-by John Coblentz*

Prayers and Peanut Butter *-by Barbara Classen*

Lies Women Believe and the Truth That Sets Them Free *-by Nancy Leigh DeMoss*

Tea Leaves *-by Nancy Stutzman*

More Tea Leaves *-by Nancy Stutzman*

A Woman for God's Glory *-by Anna Mary Byler*

A Woman by God's Grace *-by Anna Mary Byler*

Managers of their Homes *-by Steven & Teri Maxwell*

Managers of their Chores *-by Steven & Teri Maxwell*

Living Life on Purpose *-by Kym Wright*

Love Your Husband, Love Yourself *-by Jennifer Flanders*

Large Family Logistics *-by Kim Brenneman*

Homeschooling with Joy *-by Frieda Thiessen*

Raising Great Kids *-by Dr. Henry Cloud and Dr. John Townsend*

The New Dare to Discipline *-by Dr. James Dobson*

What Shall the Redeemed Wear? *-by Simon Shrock*

One Anothering *-by Simon Shrock*

Slaying the Giant (on depression) *-by French O'Shields*

A good medical book such as one from Mayo Clinic

Charts and Lists — 169

Chore Chart

													Monday
													Tuesday
													Wednesday
													Thursday
													Friday
													Saturday
													Sunday
													Monday
													Tuesday
													Wednesday
													Thursday
													Friday
													Saturday
													Sunday

Mops, Muffins, & Motherhood

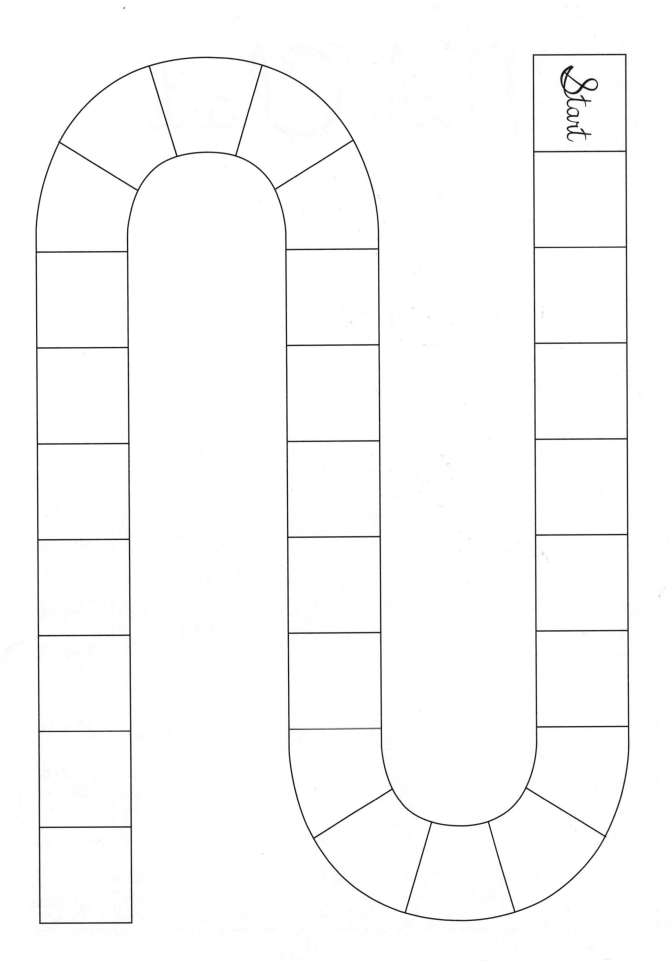

Charts and Lists — 171

Pack Chart

	Sunday Clothes
	Shirts
	Pants
	Dresses
	Under-clothes
	Socks & Belts
	Jackets
	Shoes & Boots
	Swimwear
	Nightwear

Mops, Muffins, & Motherhood

Month _____ Year _____

Sunday	Monday	Tuesday	Wednesday	Thursday	Friday	Saturday

Charts and Lists

Charts and Lists —— 175

176 —— Mops, Muffins, & Motherhood

Charts and Lists — 177

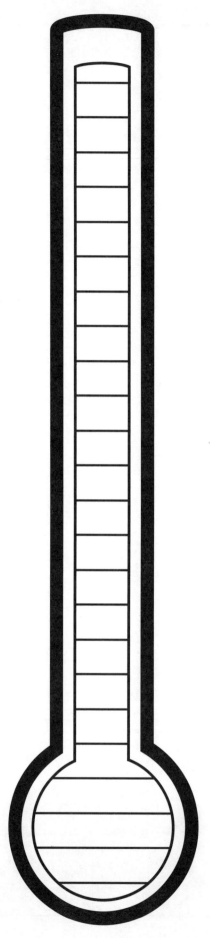

Contributors

Diane Burkholder (Harlan)	2 children	Baring, MO
Brenda High (Edwin)	6	Mt. Hope, WI
Edith High (Chester)	7	Fennimore, WI
Miriam Horning (Nevin)	8	Livingston, WI
Lorraine Hursh (Gerald)	7	Lititz, PA
Kimberly Hurst (Philip)	8	Seneca Falls, NY
Wilda Hurst (Paul)	11	Ephrata, PA
Lynette Leinbach (Curvin)	9	Bethel, PA
Alice Martin (Luke)	12	East Earl, PA
Edith Martin (Jerry)	4	Kutztown, PA
Louella Martin (Vernon)	4	Lititz, PA
Nancy Martin (Ivan)	9	Lancaster, MO
Rose Martin (Carl)	8	Narvon, PA
Susan Martin (Vernon)	3	Lititz, PA
Valerie Martin (Todd)	6	Claypool, IN
Vera Martin (Elvin)	5	Newmanstown, PA
Wilma Martin (Marlin)	2	Myerstown, PA
Ella Mae Nolt (Nathan)	8	Fennimore, WI
Janet Rissler (John)	9	Leola, PA
Karen Shaum (Dorvin)	5	Nappanee, IN
Michele Stauffer (Willie)	3	Denver, PA
Wanda Weaver (James)	7	Ephrata, PA
Darlene Wenger (Clair)	8	Bernville, PA
Darlene Wise (Kevin)	5	Newmanstown, PA
Elaine Zimmerman (Harlan)	4	Akron, IN
Fern Nolt (Harlan)	8	Richland, PA

Notes

Notes

Charts and Lists — 181

Notes

Notes

Charts and Lists — 183

Notes